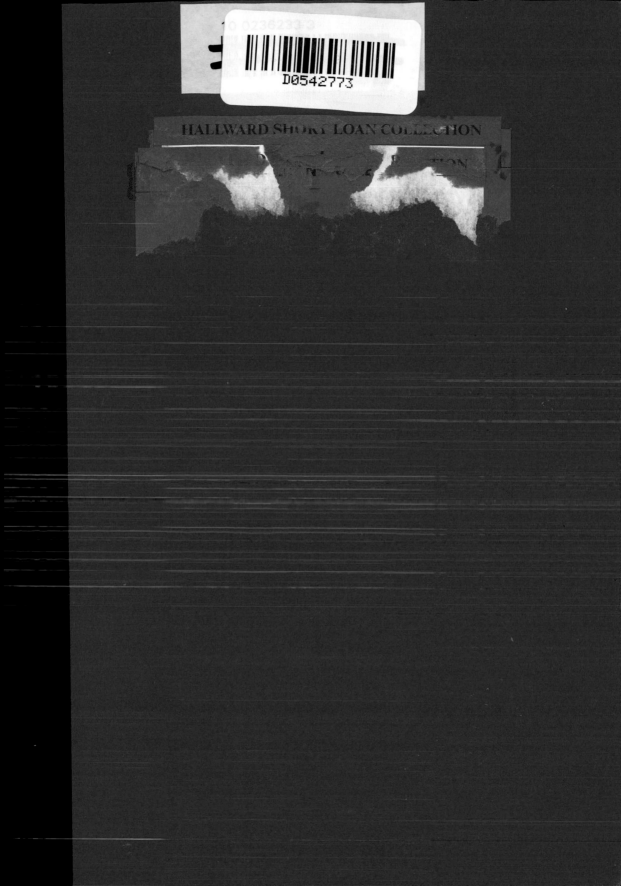

# The Tramp in America

# The Tramp in America

TIM CRESSWELL

REAKTION BOOKS

Published by Reaktion Books Ltd
79 Farringdon Road
London ECIM 3JU, UK

www.reaktionbooks.co.uk

First published 2001

Printed and bound in Great Britain by
Biddles Ltd, Guildford and King's Lynn


British Library Cataloguing in Publication Data

Cresswell, Tim
    The tramp in America
    1. Tramps – United States – Social conditions
    I. Title
    305.5'68

ISBN 1 86189 069 9

# CONTENTS

## ACKNOWLEDGEMENTS

I have been fortunate enough to have received a good deal of assistance with this book. Most of the work was done while at the University of Wales, Lampeter. My colleagues there were a wonderful and supportive group of people to work with and they have helped me form questions and interests that bear on this work. Thanks to all of them. David Atkinson insisted on more endnotes and taught me to be scholarly. Ulf Strohmayer has been a constant source of argument, inspiration and friendship and Catherine Nash helped with chapter Four through the loan of several books and constructive comments. Chris Philo provided support at the start and has always been a source of encouragement. I am indebted as ever to David Delaney who has been kind enough to intervene with the hardest questions to answer. Thanks also to Yi-Fu Tuan for continuing to show an interest. Some of the work for this book was supported by grants from the British Academy and the Newberry Library, for which I am grateful. The staff at the Newberry Library, the University of Illinois at Chicago special collections division, Smith College Library, the University of Chicago Special Collections department and New York Public Library have all been invaluable. Various parts of the manuscript for this book were much improved as the result of discussions and seminars at the Newberry Library, with the environmental history group at Harvard, the Wellcome Trust group at Glasgow and the geography departments at Keele, Bristol, Cambridge and Kentucky. The complete manuscript was read by Nathaneal Holt for reasons of intelligibility. Thanks also for the music. Finally, the biggest thanks of all to Carol Jennings, who read it all many times and has supported me all along as well as delivering babies throughout West Wales.

This book is dedicated to the memory of Joyce Mae Jennings. I miss her a lot.

# 1 Tramps, Knowledge and Mobility

By 1880 the United States had become engulfed in a moral panic that became known as the 'tramp scare' or 'tramp evil' as those people who had been displaced by a series of economic downturns took to the road in search of work.[1] Across the country these travellers met with verbal and physical abuse from local residents, they were pilloried in newspapers and arrested under new laws. Editors and letter-writers from Chicago to New Orleans prescribed radical measures for the unwanted wanderers. In his account of migrant labour in American life, Kenneth Allsop lists some of the media's more extravagant responses to the so called 'tramp'.[2] The *Chicago Tribune* of 12 July 1877 opined: 'The simplest plan, probably, where one is not a member of the humane society, is to put a little ... arsenic in the meat and other supplies furnished [for] the tramp. This produces death within a comparatively short period of time, is a warning to other tramps to keep out of the neighborhood, keeps the coroner in good humor, and saves one's chickens and other portable property from constant destruction.' Several months earlier a farmer had written to the *Cincinnati Commercial* suggesting that 'Some helpful hint, no doubt, could be taken from Russia's Siberia business. The only remedy for the tramp is occupation.'[3] By 1876 news of the rising panic had reached Britain. The London *Times* in an editorial of 5 October reported the depression in the United States and gave special attention to what it called a new feature of American life – the tramp. 'The tramp is not a picturesque character like the gipsy of the English lanes, and does not awaken sympathy like the "strapped" journeyman in search of a job. He is a low-browed, blear-eyed, dirty fellow, who has rascal stamped on every feature of his face in nature's plainest handwriting.'[4]

Although the 'tramp scare' was at its height in the 1880s and 1890s (and did not really end until the 1940s with World War Two), it began in the 1870s. The new figure of the tramp was described in terms common to other alarms, from health threats to agricultural and economic disasters. Familiar metaphors abounded. Tramps were pests, a disease. They descended on small rural towns like 'plagues of locusts'. They swarmed and stormed. They formed armies and invaded. They appeared closer to nature than to culture.[5] Such language prepared the ground for defensive measures. Plagues needed to be eradicated, armies defeated. An editorial comment in the St Louis Journal in 1879 was not atypical. It noted that 'the average freight car seems to have been invented for the purpose of conveying the average tramp from one locality to another'. Applying the tools of logic, the editor went on to note that 'a wrecked freight car invariably means a dead tramp', concluding that wrecking trains provides 'an expensive but effective way of getting rid of a very undesirable class of nuisances'.[6] Many schemes to discipline the homeless and jobless were proposed, ranging from poorhouses, to rural character-building labour camps to the whipping-post. Charity workers promoted more serious suggestions: importing the almshouse from Britain or the workcamp from Switzerland.[7] On a more everyday level, tramps were frequently beaten up and chased out of town as 'informal justice' became common. Such events were written up in popular magazines such as Atlantic Monthly, Harpers and The Century and illustrated by imaginative line-drawings (illus. 1).

The word tramp was formulated as a noun in the 1870s in America to describe homeless and mobile people. By 1940 their successors were known as migrants or migrant labourers. During this period from 1870 to 1940, a number of new ways of knowing were formulated and developed that bear on our subject, not least sociology, American vaudeville, eugenics, documentary photography and silent film. And what links these disparate ways of knowing, each with its own epistemology, ontology and representational strategies, is the figure of the tramp. This book is about these connections. It is both an account of the moral panic that gripped America from the 1870s onwards and an analysis of the relations between mobility, marginality and knowledge during the same period.

KNOWLEDGE, MARGINALITY AND THE TRAMP

The relationship between the tramp and knowledge was a mutually constitutive one. The tramp was 'made up', brought into being, by a body of knowledge it was claimed was actually about them. Sociology, eugenics, vaudeville comedy and documentary photography were all prominent novel ways of knowing and representing in the late nineteenth century and each was implicated, instrumental even, in the process by which the

1 'A Timber Lesson', from Josiah Flynt, 'Tramping With Tramps', *Century Magazine*, 47 (November 1893).

tramp was made up. But just as these forms of knowledge brought the tramp into being, so the tramp, as an embodiment of marginality, was central to the delineation of these new forms of knowledge. Practices as diverse as silent film and eugenics produced themselves through the production of the tramp and the marginality the tramp stood for. The idea of marginality was central to the process. 'Margin' is a relational term. As such the construction of margins needs to be understood alongside the construction of a core. I like the term marginality because it nicely conveys the spatiality of what might otherwise simply be termed deviance or referred to in the numerical concept of a minority. Investigations of the processes that inscribe something or someone as marginal simultaneously defines what is not marginal – what is accepted and expected.[8] Marginality and centrality, pathology and normality were two dualisms at the centre of late-nineteenth-century thought; they pervaded literature, art, medicine, politics and a plethora of other ways of knowing. The tramp was made up as a marginal figure. In the process, marginality itself was being constituted in relation to deeply held notions of what constitutes normality. In their very definition, the high includes the low, the centre includes the margin, and the normal includes the pathological.

It is useful at the outset to distinguish between surface and depth knowledge. Surface knowledge denotes things known in the everyday sense of the word and takes for granted the ontology of the things that are known about. Disciplines have their surface knowledges. Geographers may talk about places, distances, landscapes, territories, levels of development or flows of people. Maps showing the distribution of tramps in the United States or tables of flows between states would provide surface knowledge. Depth knowledge, on the other hand, defines the very terrain on which such concepts are discussed. What is a tramp? What made it possible to write about tramps, to count them and tabulate them? In *The Tramp in America* I am more concerned with this type of knowledge. In exploring depth knowledge, however, I hope to impart surface knowledge too.

In one of the few published sustained academic treatises on the tramp, the social historian Paul T. Ringenbach maintains that tramps, along with the concept of 'unemployment', were 'discovered' by social reformers in New York in the years after 1873;[9] the economic crash and subsequent panic of 1873 resulted in the presence of increasing numbers of jobless men on the streets of American cities. Social reformers noted this and came up with the new word – tramps – to describe them. The central argument of his excellent book revolves around the word 'discovery'. While previous observers had noted the existence of vagrants and blamed their condition on their own personality deficiencies, the new reformers stumbled across the explanation that the economy might have something to do with it.

Far from simply noticing something and then describing it, however, social reformers were one of the many groups of people who brought the tramp *into being* through the application of a particular kind of knowledge. My claim is not that the tramp and the mobility of the tramp were 'socially constructed', though I do not avoid this claim because it is untrue but because it is obvious. Human mobility, however it is embodied, can never be anything other than social. I am more interested in the approach taken by the Canadian philosopher Ian Hacking in his descriptions of the process of person construction in relation to a number of mental disorder diagnoses, particularly multiple personality disorder.[10] Hacking suggests a framework for thinking about the construction of individuals and social types that he calls dynamic nominalism, which he opposes to the arguments of realists and nominalists.

A realist argument rests on the assumption that conditions, categories and types exist in the world waiting to be patiently discovered and analysed. People come pre-sorted: 'Some are thick, some thin, some dead, some alive. It may be a fact about human beings that we notice who is fat and who is dead, but the fact itself that some of our fellows are fat and others are dead has nothing to do with our schemes of classification.'[11] Similarly, the realist will argue that stable human dichotomies such as male and female are simply facts to be noticed and discussed, but not invented. There may be some individuals, 'hermaphrodites', for example, to complicate the issue, but gender and sex, to the realist, are almost identical and real distinctions. In the opposite corner are the nominalists who believe in nothing but invention, arguing that all we have are names. Hacking cites Thomas Hobbes and his question 'How can any man imagine that the names of things were imposed by their natures?'[12] Following Hobbes, the nominalist believes that all classifications, categories and names are human creations, not 'natural' ones, and that once invented, they hang around and have effects. Dynamic nominalism insists that kinds of people 'come into being at the same time as the kind itself was being invented'.[13] In this respect, human types are like manufactured objects, such as gloves, and not like other things, such as horses. While horses existed prior to our thinking about them, and it would be strange to think that the only thing all horses have in common is that we call them horses, a glove can only be seen to exist hand-in-hand with the observation that we made them. The category 'glove' and the thing 'glove' emerged more or less simultaneously. From this perspective, categories and the people covered by them emerge together. So while water falls down a hillside regardless of our knowledge concerning water and gravity, human action is often dependant on, and created by, the things we describe it as, for 'if new models of description come into being, new possibilities for action come into being in consequence'.[14] The implications of such an argument are that individuals (as members of social groups) have new possibilities – new potential ways of being – when new categories are invented.[15]

Ringenbach's argument about tramps is that they were discovered, along with unemployment, by social reformers in New York. In this sense it takes a firmly realist approach to the relationship between tramps and knowledge – that tramps were there waiting to be discovered. My argument here is that tramps were not discovered but 'made up' in America around 1870. As we shall see, a number of categorical strategies conspired to make up the figure of the tramp as a super-mobile masculine figure.

This book is concerned with how tramps were made-up by various forms of knowledge. I am not arguing, however, that knowledge was the only factor regarding the existence of tramps. To return to Hacking's discussion of gloves as 'made up' entities, it is clear that even glove manufacturers need raw material with which to make their product. In chapter One I consider some of the economic, social and cultural factors that influenced the birth of the tramp. The most obvious one is that of political economy. Any discussion that highlights knowledge (and the related terms 'discourse' and 'representation') is liable to attack by those who see such discussion as idealist or dangerously anti-materialist. The usual inference made is that a discussion of things such as knowledge, photography, comedy and even science is opposed to interpretations of human life based on politico–economic factors. I reject this opposition for two reasons. First, my argument is not that political economy is an unimportant factor in the existence of the tramp, simply that a wider array of knowledges and their geographical constituents are important. Second, I am convinced that the rôle of knowledge in 'making up' the tramp is profoundly material. In this sense I am in agreement with Raymond Williams's observation that classical Marxism, for instance, is not *too* material, but not material enough. Factories, farms and other sites of labour and capital are not the only places where society is produced. It is also produced in universities, concert halls, records offices and medical labs. It is these sites of production that feature in the body of the book.

## MOBILITY AND A SEDENTARY METAPHYSICS[16]

Knowledge about tramps from 1870 onwards was informed by a morally coded set of geographical suppositions about mobility. On the one hand the tramp's mobility was seen as a clear indicator of the threat that he, or she, posed to respectable society. On the other, this mobility slotted quite nicely into an ideology that placed mobility right at the heart of American national identity. Running through this book is the delineation of moral geographies of mobility and, by the logic that governs all relational terms, place.

While a concept such as place has been central to arguments about identity, morality and 'the good life',[17] mobility has often played the rôle of a suspect 'other' threatening to undo the cosy familiarity of place-based communities and neighbourhoods.[18] In general terms, place, in its ideal form, is seen as a moral world, as an ensurer of authentic existence and as a centre of meaning for people. As its opposite, mobility is often the assumed threat to the rooted, moral, authentic existence of place.

Yi-Fu Tuan has described the attachment between people and the earth through the making of places as 'home'.[19] Whether through literature, art, architecture or the decoration of the favourite corner of a child's bedroom, Tuan highlights the effort people have expended in all cultures to create order and homeliness out of the apparent chaos of raw nature. The concept of place is central to our understanding of the ways in which people turn nature into culture by making nature their home. Indeed, the warm cosiness of 'home' as a general concept rubs off on the appreciation of place. Everywhere, the construction of places turns raw nature into a home for humankind. Place is a centre of meaning and a field of care. In Tuan's world the evidence for attachment and commitment is everywhere, from the greatest of monuments to the smallest aesthetic detail. What rôle does mobility have in this striving for commitment? His answer is an ambivalent one. Place, he argues 'is an organized world of meaning. It is essentially a static concept. If we see the world as process, constantly changing, we would not be able to develop any sense of place.'[20] The world of nomads, he suggests, might include a strong sense of place, for their movements often occur within a circumscribed area. 'Modern man', he continues, might be so mobile that he can never establish roots and his experience of place may be all too superficial.[21] Tuan's world is full of edifices material, aesthetic and moral that point towards place as an essentially moral concept. The implication here is that mobility and movement, insofar as they undermine attachment and commitment are antithetical to moral worlds. True, nomads may have a sense of place, but only due to the repetition of their travels and boundaries of their wandering – extend things too far and place commitments diminish.[22]

Philosophically, much of the moral value of place is rooted in the work of Martin Heidegger, who argued, through his conception of 'dwelling', that to be human is to have a place, to be rooted. Heidegger equated 'place' with 'being' through the concept of 'dwelling'. He was terrified by the speed and mobility of the modern world and chose, in theory at least, to retreat into a sense of rootedness in place in a Black Forest cabin. In this cabin he asserted the possibility of achieving a unity between people and things that is summed up with the word 'authentic'. The world of motion, to Heidegger and to his followers, was one that threatened authentic existence and was thus deeply suspect.[23]

When place is thought of in this way it becomes surrounded by terms such as 'involvement' and 'commitment' – terms that insinuate transience and mobility to be morally ambiguous at best. Place, home and roots are described as a fundamental human need: 'to have roots in a place is to have a secure point from which to look out on the world, a firm grasp of one's own position in the order of things, and a significant spiritual and psychological attachment to somewhere in particular.'[24] Place as home, then, is described as perhaps the most important significance-giving factor in human life. Place, home and roots are profoundly moral concepts in the humanist lexicon. By implication, mobility appears to involve a number of absences – the absence of commitment, attachment and involvement – a lack of significance. The more widespread associations of mobility with deviance, shiftlessness and disrepute come to mind.[25]

Place, as well as being a moral concept, is one that has close links to the notion of identity. These links have recently been open to question.[26] The concept of 'roots' connects types of people to particular places. The notion of identities rooted in the soil of home is profoundly metaphysical. In our incessant desire to divide the world up into clearly bounded territorial units we produce a 'sedentarist metaphysics'.[27] Fixed, bounded and rooted conceptions of culture and identity are linked to particular ways of thinking that are themselves sedentary. These ways of thinking then reaffirm and enable the commonsense segmentation of the world into things like nations, states, counties and places. This process is so ingrained as to be invisible. The consequences of sedentary metaphysics for mobile people are severe. Thinking of the world as rooted and bounded is reflected in language and social practice. Such thoughts actively territorialize identities in property, in region, in nation – in place. They simultaneously produce thoughts and practices that treat mobility and displacement as pathological. We will see how this applies to tramps. A similar process has surrounded the existence of the refugee as evidenced by this passage from a post-war study of refugees:

> Homelessness is a serious threat to moral behaviour ... At the moment the refugee crosses the frontiers of his own world, his whole moral outlook, his attitude toward the divine order of things changes ... [The refugees'] conduct makes it obvious that we are dealing with individuals who are basically amoral, without any sense of personal or social responsibility ... They no longer feel themselves bound by ethical precepts which every honest citizen ... respects. They become a menace, dangerous characters who will stop at nothing.[28]

A 'sedentary metaphysics' pervades both academic discourse and more routinized and everyday views of the world. Knowledge about tramps was significantly informed by such a place-based, anti-mobile view of the world. In this sense sociology, reform, eugenics and all the other forms of knowledge I consider are products, in part, of a geographical imagination.

The moral geographies of roots and rootlessness go back a long way, especially in reactions to people who have been seen to be without place. The discussions of knowledge and tramps that make up *The Tramp in America* need to be understood in the context of these wider suspicions of vagrancy and mobility. Given the apparent marginality of these people it is somewhat surprising that they appear so frequently in tales of the origins of the world we now live in. That which is expelled to the margins of society in a practical sense – the flotsam of modernity – becomes symbolic for the society that is expelling it.

Roguish vagabonds, according to Zygmunt Bauman, 'were the advanced troops or guerrilla units of post-traditional chaos … and they had to go if order … was to be the rule. The free-roaming vagabonds made the search for new, state-managed, societal-level order imperative and urgent.'[29] Vagabonds, in early modern Europe, were described by the guardians of a spatialized and increasingly disciplinary order, as anarchic mirror-images of order:

> What made the vagabond so terrifying was his apparent freedom to move and so to escape the net of the previously locally based control. Worse than that, the movements of the vagabond were unpredictable; unlike the pilgrim or, for that matter, a nomad, the vagabond has no set destination. You do not know where he will move next, because he himself does not know or care much.[30]

As with the tramp, the mobility of the vagabond was key. Unlike other mobile people, such as tourists and nomads, the vagabond's mobility was wholly unpredictable, and thus threatening. His wayward travels meant that he always had traces of elsewhere about him that disturbed those who had chosen a settled and rooted existence. The vagabond threatened to undo the comforts of place and transgressed the expectations of a sedentarist metaphysics.

A certain ambivalence constituted the key threat to order in emerging European nations. The struggle for order was a struggle against ambivalence. Order was imposed through a new and specifically modern form of knowledge called legislation. Legislation was, in part, a product of intellectuals who were crucial to the process of European state formation.[31] They were crucial because they developed and embodied the Enlightenment ideas of science and reason that the modern states claimed to be based on. The rise of intellectuals was set in the context of a large-scale transformation of Europe from feudal, close-knit and mostly local communities to a wider scale, more highly populated, society. One element of this transformation – from feudalism to early capitalism – was the displacement of thousands of people from the lands and the villages they had formally belonged to. These 'vagrants' and 'masterless men' created a new measure of uncertainty about the traditional patterns of rights and duties. In short, they were seen as people without place and therefore as a threat to the most fundamental forms of order. Certainty was replaced by a large measure of ambivalence. Vagrants, as embodied forms of this ambivalence and anarchy, became the principal targets of attempts to establish a new kind of modern order to replace the older feudal certainties. Because vagrants were rootless and moved beyond the bounds of the local, the older forms of control and order could no longer put them in their place. Thus when the modern state emerged, those in charge sought to produce effects of order and clarity over a much wider scale than that of the local. Zygmunt Bauman goes so far as to suggest that the modern state originated in the wide-scale control and regulation of vagrants and others who embodied ambivalence. The new class of intellectuals, as bastions of reason, were central to the war against vagrants and sought to separate and educate them through new disciplinary practices that ranged from the asylum to the poorhouse to the school. Less visibly, they were at the vanguard of the new practices of 'rational' ordering and classifying that existed both in and beyond the new spaces of discipline. Vagabonds, however marginal to the societies of an emerging Europe, were major, if unwitting, players in the establishment of modern order.

England experienced a panic regarding vagrancy as early as the late fifteenth century.[32] France went through a similar process in the late nineteenth century, at approximately the same time as the American 'tramp scare'. In the recent *Mad Travelers*, Ian Hacking describes the appearance and disappearance of the medical diagnosis 'fugue' in France in the period 1887–1909. Fugue was the label given to a disorder accompanied by amnesia and other symptoms of a disturbed mental state that involved sudden, uncontrollable urges to travel. First diagnosed in 1887, it was declared a dead issue in 1909.[33] Hacking's explanation for this revolves around four elements in the social context of France at that time that he calls 'vectors'. We need not concern ourselves with all of them, but one is significant. He describes a cultural polarity at the time between two social phenomena that were well-established in French culture. One was tourism, which stood for leisure and fantasy; the other was criminal vagrancy, which provided the bourgeoisie with its nightmares. Fugue, for the most part an affliction of the well-off working-class, existed uneasily between them. In the 1880s vagabondage was a well-established, respectable fear. France, like the United States, was instituting a series of strict anti-vagrancy laws. Many vagrants, those who were deemed irredeemable, were sentenced to transportation to a penal colony. The French were worried about racial degeneracy and the vagrant was perceived as a threat to the racial stock. Many medical and psychological pathologies were seen as connected to vagrancy. (One author has since described the medical incarceration of

French vagrants as a form of genocide.[34]) In a thesis for the medical faculty at Lyon on the relationship between vagrancy and madness, the candidate wrote that vagrants 'must be eliminated systematically from society, because they are noxious, but they must be cared for, because they are above all ill'.[35] The vagrancy crisis in France ended in 1909, and so did the diagnosis of fugue. We will see similarly dramatic calls in the American context in the same period.

Linking the stories of the vagabonds and vagrants of Europe with the tale of the American tramp is the conflict between the order and hierarchy of the state and its agents, and the threat posed by the mobile bodies of the vagrant, the vagabond and the tramp. The key process in all cases is the way in which people have sought to return the threatening vagrant into the fold of order and intelligibility. In France this took the form of a series of medical and psychological diagnoses that either criminalized or medicalized the vagrant. In Bauman's account of the rise of legislation this is expressed as the machinations of reason and intellect in the service of the state. It is important to know that the American 'tramp scare' was not isolated. In the following pages focused on the tramp in America there is constant interaction between the United States and ideas originating in Britain and France and in reactions to panics in Europe.


AMERICAN MOBILITY

Although America's tramp scare shares many features with the moral panics surrounding vagrancy in Europe there are some important differences. While it is largely true that mobility often plays off the suspect 'other' to the warm glow of place, in the American context mobility is often seen in more positive terms. Indeed, mobility has often been portrayed as the central geographical fact of American life, one that distinguishes Euro-Americans from their European ancestors. Jeffersonian imagery of America as a garden suggested that space might replace time as the central location of development in American life. While Europe had developed through time and in a limited space and had thus become overcrowded and despotic, America could simply keep expanding west. This would ensure morally upright and democratic citizens. Frederick Jackson Turner's Frontier thesis of 1893 also put movement at the centre of American history and identity. As Europeans moved west, the argument went, they confronted savagery and were converted into Americans in the process. The United States was different from Europe, it was claimed, because its people were less rooted in space and time and therefore were free from the shackles of both feudalism and industrial capitalism. A new American spirit was forged in the movement of people from other parts of the world and within the emerging nation. More recently, cultural commentators have argued that mobility and process are central to what it is to be American. Daniel Boorstin, for instance, has argued that 'Americans were a new kind of Bedouin. More than almost anything else, they valued the freedom to move, hoping in their very movement to discover what they are looking for. Americans thus valued opportunity, or the chance to seek it, more than purpose.'[36] Here mobility is given as a central freedom in American life that is connected to the idea of opportunity. John Kouwenhowen, in his classic essay 'What's American about America?' has made the break from Europe explicit. 'In the hierarchical civilisations of the past', he asserts, 'where systems of status kept people as well as values pretty much in their places, men were insulated against an awareness of process to an extent that is no longer possible. In an environment dominated by technology and democracy, a world of social and physical mobility and rapid change, we cannot escape it.'[37]

Few modern nations are so thoroughly infused with stories of wandering, of heroic migrancy and pilgrimage as are the Americans. Clearly, mobility as a geographical phenomenon in American life is linked to a number of ideological themes, including opportunity, democracy and modernity. Indeed, the equation that linked mobility, technology and democracy was one that for many people pointed to the very definition of American modernity. But there are other tales to tell, connected to, but not synonymous with, America's foundation myths. Just as Turner's frontier was said to be closing in the late nineteenth century, as railroads stretched from shore to shore, a new figure emerged on the American landscape, the tramp, or hobo. The story of the tramp is not a story of the pioneer or cowboy, it is a far less sentimental and more problematic one – a mobile body inscribed with multiple signifiers of deviance and transgression. The story of mobility in America needs to include less central stories, often untold: tales of marginality and exclusion, which cast a different light on the grand narratives of nationhood, of progress, of democracy and of modernity. A different kind of story emerges when we look at the marginal cases and use them to reflect on an undifferentiated and glorious story of 'America'. My aim is not to negate the comfortable stories of grounded and centred ideologies, but to problematize them, make them more complicated. While more complex stories are less certain and less glorious, they are also more profound. They highlight difference rather than sameness, discontinuity rather than seamlessness. The addition of complications, of unheard voices, to grand narratives is not simply an additive exercise, but one that changes the core of the story being told.[38]

Mobility in America, then, is a far from straightforward issue. Throughout this book knowledge about the tramp has to deal with the tension between mobility as a threat to the rooted and moral existence of place, together with its specific cultural manifestations of small-town America, hot apple-pie and white picket fences, at the same time as mobility, in some forms, is seen as a uniquely American geographical and historical experience guaranteeing freedom, opportunity and independence.

## A MULTI-REPRESENTATIONAL APPROACH

In this book I provide an account of the multiple ways in which the tramp was made up in the United States between the completion of the transcontinental railroad and World War Two. My interest in the way that knowledge constitutes its subject is reflected in five chapters that revolve around different knowledges. No individual or social group is ever entirely constituted by just one form of knowledge.[39] It is all too easy to draw a linear and determining line between a form of representation, such as medicine or law, and claim that it constituted a subject in a particular way. This is rarely, if ever, the case. It is for this reason that the diversity of ways of knowing discussed in these chapters represents the broad width of ways of knowing the tramp. I make no claims to a comprehensive survey. Such a task is impossible. It is the case, however, that the ways of knowing I consider were important public discourses about tramps in the period under consideration. In chapter Three I provide an account of some of the formal processes involved in 'making up' the tramp. I start, as do all good accounts, with a discussion of the definition of the tramp (and the hobo, and the bum). Once defined, it became possible to count, tabulate and classify the tramp. Chapter Three, therefore, also examines the social classification tables that claimed to provide knowledge about the tramp. Connected to these were the efforts of early sociology and law to supply 'solutions' to the freshly acknowledged problem. As with any kind of knowledge, there are always alternatives that have been forgotten or deliberately excluded from formal legal and academic accounts. As evidence of this I look at the work of the anarchist and hobo Ben Reitman, who was frequently in conflict with the Chicago School of Sociology over how to approach the tramp question. The matter of alternative knowledges points towards the incompleteness of ways of knowing. With this in mind, chapter Four considers the rôle of gender in the construction of the tramp, particularly the presupposition that tramps were male and were threatening women in domestic environments. I turn this around by considering the accounts of female tramps who took to the road disguised as men. A particular theme of this chapter is that of embodiment. I consider the theme of embodiment in relation to gendered mobility and apply this to the way in which the clothes, hairstyles and ways of moving ascribed to female tramps served to confuse anxious onlookers. The existence of female tramps provoked a crisis in knowledge as observers attempted to fit these doubly deviant characters into their carefully constructed categorization schemes.

In chapter Five I assess how medical and eugenicist discourse examined and constructed the body of the tramp as an untrustworthy and diseased body originating in unsound heredity. A key word in this chapter is 'pathology'. While medicine, psychology and eugenics were busy defining the tramp's body as pathological in a medical sense – as a product of unsound genetics and as a conveyor of disease – they were simultaneously instrumental in defining the tramp *as a pathology* in the more general body politic. Suggestions that tramps were vectors for syphilis were thus linked to calls for the exclusion of tramps from the body politic.

Not all forms of knowledge about the tramp were entirely negative. In chapters Six and Seven I consider two more sympathetic ways of knowing. In chapter Six I examine what I call comic knowledge. In particular I deal with the tramp as a cartoon strip figure, the tramp of the vaudeville stage and the classic tramp character played by Charlie Chaplin. I show how the body of the tramp, and especially the tramp's mobility, are used to create comic moments through the inversion of expectancies about 'normal' bodies and 'normal' mobility. The non-conformity of the tramp's appearance and behaviour coupled with the manifest deviance of 'his' lifestyle made the tramp an ideal figure for slapstick humour. While much of this humour made the tramp an incompetent figure of fun, Chaplin used the tramp as a source of irritation for agents of order in the modern world and thus produced a more sympathetic and heroic figure. In chapter Seven I examine the tramp as a subject of the documentary photography of Jacob Riis, John James McCook and Dorothea Lange in the context of the wider institutional efforts to produce knowledge of marginal people. Here I think through the ways of knowing encapsulated in the documentary photograph in relation to the tramp and the migrant. In particular I consider how Lange's photographs signify the transformation of the tramp into the flivver bum, the Okie and the migrant worker.

Before any of these, however, it is necessary to return to the tramp scare and say something of its context.

## 2 The Tramp in Context

What were the factors that made it possible for the tramp to be 'made up'? To say that various forms of knowledge made up the tramp for the period 1869–1940 is not the same as saying the tramp emerged fully formed from the fertile imaginations of medical officials, social reformers, documentary photographers and others. Categories are constructed in order to make the world legible. They take the raw material of the world and mould it into shape and form in ideological ways. In this chapter I account for the raw material necessary for the creation of the tramp. Two factors are particularly important: the increased mobility of the late nineteenth century enabled by the advent of a national rail system and the economic downturns that led to mass unemployment across the country. The nature of mobility and the state of the economy in the late nineteenth and early twentieth centuries are intimately linked. In addition to this I provide a brief outline of the broad characteristics of the population who came to be called tramps, who they were and how they lived.

### TIME–SPACE COMPRESSION, THE RAILROAD AND MANIFEST DESTINY

The phenomenon of time–space compression is key to understanding the context in which the tramp was brought into being. Time–space compression describes the effective shrinking of the world by technologies of transportation and communication. We have become accustomed to the idea of globalization that accompanies the ability to reach across vast distances in relatively short periods of time. In the 1870s the process that was to make this possible was just beginning to accelerate.[1]

On 10 May 1869 at Promontory Point, Utah, a major event in the history of time–space compression occurred when workers and officials cheered the placement of the last tie, a sleeper of laurel wood bound in silver, and the driving of the last spike, made of gold, of the first transcontinental railroad in North America. The ceremony marked the end of a perverse race between workers from the East, mostly of Irish origin, who built the Union Pacific track west from Iowa, and those from the West Coast, the majority of whom were Chinese, who laid the Central Pacific track from Sacramento to Utah. The connection of these two tracks at Promontory Point linked the West Coast to the Missouri River and thus to the East Coast. The railroad brought North American agricultural commodities, ore, lumber and finished goods to the ports of the West Coast and returned to the Midwest with foodstuffs and products not indigenous to the region. The landscape of the American West changed on a massive scale as wheat farms spread across the plains and irrigated fruit and vegetable plantations sprang up in New Mexico and California. By 1900 the Trans-Mississippi West possessed an intricate rail network connecting the United States to Canada and Mexico, and via the steamship routes of San Francisco, Los Angeles, Seattle, Portland and Galveston to Asia, Latin America and Europe. In 1850 the whole of the continental United States had boasted only 9,000 miles of track. By 1869 there were more than 70,000 miles. The railroad shrank space both for those who rode the trains and the agents of an increasingly interconnected global economy.

The railroad was central to the development of the national economy within a global system.[2] One railroad historian has gone so far as to state that 'The railroad encouraged and gave birth to what we so proudly refer to as the free enterprise system.'[3] It was also central to the definition of a modern American identity. As is often the case, the economic and the cultural were intimate bedfellows. Indeed, the development of the railroad was quite explicitly intertwined with the wider discourse of America's world rôle and destiny. One of the central strands in the rhetoric of American nationhood is that of 'manifest destiny' – America's inevitable westward movement ordained by God. This idea was promoted by William Gilpin, a journalist, who travelled the Oregon Trail in the 1840s. He was instrumental in preparing documents encouraging American westward expansion for the Senate in 1846:

The untransacted destiny of the American people is to subdue the continent – to rush over this vast field to the Pacific Ocean – to animate the many hundred millions of its people, and to cheer them upward ... to teach old nations a new civilisation – to confirm the destiny of the human race ... to emblazon history with the conquest of peace ... and to shed blessings round the world!

Divine task! Immortal mission! Let us tread fast and joyfully the

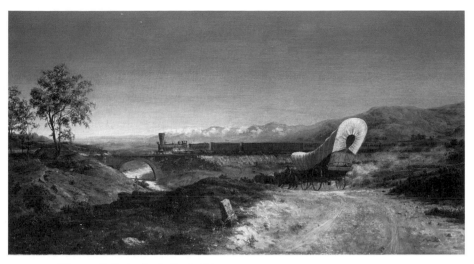

2 Thomas P. Otter, *On the Road*, 1860.

open trail before us! Let every American heart open wide the patriotism to glow undimmed, and confide with religious faith in the sublime and prodigious destiny of his well-loved country.[4]

This idea of manifest destiny was used in support of a vast network of railroad routes that would ensure both a strong economy and a moral landscape and society. Samuel Bowles in San Francisco made this quite clear in 1866 while supporting the construction of the first trans-continental railroad:

> You will feel hearts breaking, see morals struggling slowly upward against odds, know that religion languishes; feel, see and know that all the sweetest and finest influences and elements of society and Christian civilisation hunger and suffer for lack of this quick contact with the Parent and Fountain [the Eastern states] of all our national life.[5]

This almost metaphysical rôle the railroads served was reflected in landscape art used to promote westward expansion, an art replete with images of mobility, including wagon trains, steamboats and railroads. Thomas Otter's *On the Road* (1860) is widely believed to be the first work featuring the railroad in what was later to become its heroic central guise (illus. 2). The train is in the centre of the picture and contrasted with an evidently slow and cumbersome covered wagon. The most famous of the railroad pictures were those produced by Fanny Palmer for the print company Currier & Ives,[6] particularly *Across the Continent: 'Westward the Course of*

*Empire Takes its Way'* (1868), which shows a train racing into the distance, surrounded by a small settlement of pioneers in log cabins and watched by Native American Indians from a nearby hill (illus. 3). Not accidentally, these Indians are being submerged in the smoke and steam produced by the progress of technology into the West. Railroad pictures often used Indians as a counterpoint to progress. John Gast's *American Progress* (illus. 4) was painted to specifications provided by George A. Crofutt to be used with a travel guide for travellers heading west. The train moves west as the Indians retreat into the left margin of the picture. Floating overhead is a female figure carrying a book of law and a telegraph wire.

These images and many more implicated the railroad (alongside other technologies of mobility such as the wagon, the steamboat and the telegraph wire) in the project of westward expansion. They were often used directly to promote the development of railroads, particularly the transcontinental ones. They typically combined images of modern transportation technology with messages of progress, American destiny and might. They slotted right into the developing story and ideology of American mobility.

The association of American values of progress, individualism, democracy and technological know-how with the railroad did not die in the heady days of railroad boosterism in the 1860s, '70s and '80s. Railroad

3 Francis F. Palmer, *Across the Continent: 'Westward the Course of Empire Takes its Way'*, 1868.

4 John Gast, *American Progress*, 1872.

historian George Douglas has recently stated that 'The railroad was the agency that brought the United States of America into being.' Before the railroad, 'Travel between Boston and any interior city – Albany, New York let us say – less than two hundred miles away would be an arduous, physically punishing journey of several days and one that would never be undertaken lightly.'[7] The mere fact of connection between just about anywhere is said to have unified the American people in a way previously only dreamed of. These kinds of grand statements are, of course, linked to the even grander claims about the rôle of mobility in American life dating back to Jefferson, Gilpin and others. According to Douglas,

> Americans saw the railroad as inextricably bound up with their national destiny. Somehow, the railroad was an agency of freedom, and freedom was what America was all about … In Europe, there had been but one lot for the ordinary man – toil and drudgery. For centuries, he had been a serf, tied to the land. He could move nowhere. In the factory system of the late eighteenth century, he had gotten off the land but was tied to his workbench or some gloomy,

cavernous mine. But the railroad, America's chosen industry, was something different, something infinitely more romantic and agreeable. It provided a licence to move, a true declaration of independence. The railroad dramatized human freedom better than any other agency yet dreamed of by any human mind.[8]

The railroad, for Douglas as much as it was for Gilpin, is a symbol for a uniquely American form of mobile independence and freedom that helped ensure the fruition of a modern democracy: 'All previous forms of human endeavor had enslaved people, kept them wedded to toil. The railroad always represented the opposite. It was a form of energy suited to the appetites and dreams of a democratic people.'[9] Like most elements of national mythology, this has some truth to it, but misses the darker side of the alleged democratizing influence of the railroad.

### THE RAILROAD, THE TRAMP AND THE POLITICS OF MOBILITY

The technology of the railroad provided the conditions for the emergence of a new social type – the tramp. Most directly it gave homeless and jobless people the ability to travel vast distances in a short period of time. Passengers, whether legal or illegal, could be on the East Coast one week and the West Coast the next. Contemporary observers were quick to notice this. One railroad worker in New Mexico in 1877 despaired at the number of tramps on the line. 'The country was different before the railroads got in', he noted. 'Then it took a small fortune to get down here; stage fare was fifteen cents a mile, and every one who came had capital enough to start a ranch or go prospecting … the tramp had no show in the old stage coach days.'[10] It is quite clear that without trains, there could not have been tramps. Trains provided the means for travel across the continent. The automobile was still several decades away and there were only a few roads for wagons.

The necessary relationship between the tramp and the train led to serious conflicts between the railroads and the local authorities in areas crossed by the tracks. The crux of the problem was that the geography of the railroad overlaid a much older geography of bounded spaces and jurisdictions. With the spread of the continental railroad system, migrant workers and non-workers were enabled to travel previously extraordinary distances with comparative ease. While vagrancy had always been a local problem dealt with at town, county and, less often, state scale, tramps were on the move across the whole country. The mobile space of the railroad and the static space of the jurisdiction were often in conflict about how to deal with them. The railroads insisted that local areas should enforce vagrancy laws, while the local authorities along the line complained that they were effectively subsidising the railroads by policing a problem caused by them. As an editorial in the *Railroad Age Gazette* put it:

> County Commissioners in Beaver, Lawrence and Mercer Counties have all decided that the county treasuries shall not pay for the upkeep of the men whom the railways want punished for train riding. The commissioners say the train riders have committed no crime to warrant the county paying the expenses of keeping them and that the railways should meet the bond bills of the hoboes, as the railways and not the taxpayers get the benefit of arresting them for trespassing.[11]

Railroad leaders were adamant that responsibility for disciplining vagrants lay with the local jurisdictions that surrounded the railroads. The practice of 'passing on' was one they campaigned against, claiming it to be irrational. As President James J. Hill of the Great Northern Railroad noted, 'It is the almost universal custom for justices to order vagrants to leave town within twenty-four hours. When all neighborhoods are doing the same thing, the community receives exactly as much refuse as it gets rid of.'[12] The towns along the route, on the other hand, believed that it was unjust for their communities to be made responsible for the cost of maintaining tramps in jails and workhouses. Such action, they argued, benefited the railroads but was paid for by local taxpayers. Eventually, the ongoing conflict between the railroads and the municipalities led to the creation of a railroad police force.

The conflict between the new mobile space of the railroad and the older spaces that lay along it took many forms. Despite the huge amount of railroad boosterism, which was in turn tied to powerful national ideologies, people who lived and worked in areas the railroad cut through were frequently opposed to its effects. Trains were frequently responsible for damaging livestock, causing fires on agricultural land and killing people crossing the tracks at notoriously unsafe crossings. In addition, the railroads were known for charging unfair hauling rates where they had effective monopolies. To some the tramps were welcome nuisances to the power of the railroad companies. The lack of respect for the railroad led some municipalities to undermine railroad anti-tramp policies, as Orlando Lewis observed in 1907:

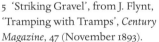

5 'Striking Gravel', from J. Flynt, 'Tramping with Tramps', *Century Magazine*, 47 (November 1893).

The Cumberland Valley Railroad must frequently subsidize local constables, and occasionally local justices, to obtain commitments. Some railroads give passes, hoping for reciprocity from city and county officials. Along the Big Four Lines, some town authorities warn vagrants not to get off the trains, and along the C., B. & Q. some town officials even assist tramps aboard trains, to facilitate their departure.[13]

Modes of travel tell us a lot about the constitution of a society. Few images better represent the constitution of American society in the last decades of the nineteenth century than that of a Pullman travelling though the landscape. Yet by the end of the 1870s many trains, both passenger and freight, would have been carrying a number of illegal passengers who, by then, were known as tramps or hobos. The development of an extensive and increasingly standardized network made travel for both legitimate and illegitimate passengers easier. As locomotives became more powerful and trains longer it became easier for a man or woman to get on board and hide. Standardized carriages made it possible to develop a working knowledge of the hidden spaces of a train regardless of the line in question.[14]

The modes of tramp travel were extraordinary. If they were lucky, tramps found an empty boxcar and remained undetected by the 'bulls', the railroad police. Often though, hobos would travel on the outside of a train, either between carriages, on top of them or underneath – riding the rods. In order to avoid being caught, hobos clambered aboard once the train was moving, for then the train was outside the disciplinary space of the station or yard (illus. 5). This was often a very dangerous undertaking, and many hobos lost limbs or died trying to climb aboard moving trains. Indeed, the majority of railroad related deaths in the late nineteenth century and early twentieth were those of tramps and hobos. Some estimates of death and injury per year to tramps gave a figure as high as 5,000.[15] Rumours suggested that some railroads kept unmarked mass graves in which the anonymous bodies of tramps were buried. In addition to the dangers of boarding a moving train, hobos frequently died from the cold or were struck by hot cinders and ashes as they clung to the top or bottom of a carriage. The most dangerous of all travel methods was 'riding the rods' underneath passenger or freight cars. Under boxcars and carriages were a series of underbraces or gunnels running lengthwise about eighteen inches below the car. Tramps would squeeze into this space and use a grooved board called a 'tramp's ticket' to latch on to the rods and then lie on it just inches from the ground (illus. 6). An additional danger here was the brakeman's spike. The spike was dangled on a wire underneath the train, so as to bounce off the sleepers as the train raced along and hit any tramps under the carriage. Jack London described this eloquently:

> The 'shack' (brakeman) takes a coupling-pin and length of bell-cord to the platform in front of the truck in which the tramp is riding. The shack fastens the coupling pin to the bell-cord, drops the former down between the platforms, and plays out the latter. The coupling-pin strikes the ties between the rails, rebounds against the bottom of the car, and again strikes the ties. The shack plays it back and forth, now to this side, now to the other, lets it out a bit and hauls it in a bit, giving his weapon opportunity for every variety of impact and rebound. Every blow of that flying coupling-pin is

6 'A Ride on a Truck', from J. Flynt, 'Tramping with Tramps', *Century Magazine*, 47 (November 1893).

freighted with death, and at sixty miles an hour it beats a veritable tattoo of death. The next day the remains of that tramp are gathered up along the right of way, and a line in the local paper mentions the unknown man, undoubtedly a tramp, assumedly drunk, who had probably fallen asleep on the track.[16]

As well as the space under the carriage there were numerous other nooks and crannies for tramps and hobos to latch on to. These included the 'iron plate', a small toehold on a steam car; the 'death woods', a narrow plank above the couplings (illus. 7); the couplings themselves; the 'blind', the space between the engine and the baggage car; or the top of the train. Now and again tramps fell asleep and tumbled from the moving trains, so some tied themselves to the carriage or boxcar in whatever way they could.

Compare all this to the mobility of those inside the train. The railroad certainly provided well for those who could afford to use it. Wealthy travellers could now travel in splendour and comfort and the railroad appeared to be tied to a glorious future marked by progress and opportunity. By 1891 the Pennsylvania Limited consisted of Pullman cars that included a barber's shop, bath and valet service for gentlemen and maids for women travellers. Extensive wine lists accompanied the food.[17] Advertisements for the new railroads made a great deal of both the phenomenon of time–space compression and the luxury and comfort available to paying customers. The Chicago and Northwestern Railway Time Tables for 8 May 1876, for example, announced with pride that

> The trains that run over this line are made of elegant new PULLMAN PALACE DRAWING ROOM AND SLEEPING COACHES, BUILT EXPRESSLY FOR THIS LINE, luxurious, well lighted and well ventilated Day Coaches, and pleasant lounging and smoking cars; all built by the company in their own shops. The cars are all equipped with the celebrated Miller Safety Platform, and Patent Buffers and Couplings, Westinghouse Safety Air Brakes, and every other appliance that has been devised for the safety of passenger trains. All trains are run by telegraph.
>
> This popular route is unsurpassed for Speed, Comfort and Safety. The Smooth, Well-Ballested and Perfect Track of Steel Rails, the Celebrated Pullman Palace Cars, the Perfect Telegraph System

7 'Riding on the Bumpers', from J. Flynt, 'The Tramp at Home', *Century Magazine*, 47 (February 1894).

of Moving Trains, the Regularity with which they run, the admirable arrangement for running Through Cars to Chicago from all point West, secure to passengers all the COMFORTS IN MODERN RAILWAY TRAVELLING.[18]

This advertising copy reads like a manifesto for modern mobility incorporating the latest technology to achieve speed and comfort. Compare this to the very different materiality of modernity's other travellers – the tramps. A Chicago journalist, in an article on hobos, reflected on the theme of power and mobility in the *Chicago News*:

> The world respects the rich man who turned to be a globe-trotter and uses first class cabins and Pullman cars, but has inclination to look over his shoulder at the hobo who, to satisfy this so strong impulse, is compelled to use box-cars, slip the board under the Pullman or in other ways whistle on the safety of his life and integrity of his bones.[19]

The politics of mobility around the train was also evident to the tramps and hobos. One anonymous hobo wrote that 'Inside the passengers sat, warm and soft on the upholstered seats, or lay sleeping in their berths. And on the prow of the giant land-ship stood three muffled figures, shivering but dauntless, carried on – through bitter cold and smoke and turmoil, danger of arrest or of beating – towards the harvest jobs that would earn them sustenance for a short space.'[20]

THE ECONOMY OF MOBILITY

To understand why men and women in large numbers chose to ride trains illegally, it is necessary to consider other structural conditions that helped make and situate the tramp. Many commentators, particularly those at the time, have identified the end of the Civil War in 1865 as a reason for the existence of a suddenly large and mobile group of homeless people. At the Conference of Charities held at Saratoga in 1877, the Revd E. Hale claimed that military life had produced men who were hardened to life outdoors, used to living off the land and disposed not to thinking too far into the future.[21] Men, the argument went, had been removed from their normal contexts and introduced to the possibilities of extended mobility. Josiah Flynt, a tramp turned investigator, was asked by the Pennsylvania Railroad to undertake an ethnographic investigation of tramp life on the railroad in order to ascertain the extent of the 'problem'. It was Flynt's view that the tramp was a product of the Civil War. Demobbed soldiers had become used to life on the road, including the railroad, and had simply continued to live in the manner to which they had become accustomed. By 1875, he claimed, 10,000 tramps would ride for free every night on America's railroads. 'The railroads', he claimed, 'spread the tramp nuisance over a much greater stretch of territory than would be the case if the tramps were limited to turnpikes. As matters now stand, however, you may see a beggar one day on fifth avenue in New York City, and a fortnight later he will accost you in Market Street in San Francisco.'[22] In order to underline the importance of the railroad to the new American tramp, he provided an illustration of 'A Comparison Between American and English Modes of Tramp Travel' in his essay 'The Tramp and the Railroads' (illus. 8). Although tramps were mobile by definition, some were more mobile than others.

While scholars and investigators of the late nineteenth century saw the Civil War and widespread personal deficiencies as the causes of tramping, it is surely the case that the principal reason for men and women jumping freight trains was the boom and bust cycles of the American economy. The existence of the people who came to be called tramps was closely linked to

8 'A Comparison Between American and English Methods of Tramp Travel', from J. Flynt, 'The Tramp and the Railroads', *Century Magazine*, 58 ( June 1899).

the changing nature of industrial capitalism and associated shifts in the labour market. The late nineteenth century and early twentieth were hit by periodic depressions, the worst of which were in 1873, 1893–4 and the 1930s. These depressions brought about significant increases in the number of workers taking to the rails in search of work. In addition to large-scale economic downturns, there were geographical transformations in industry, with an increasing focus on the Great Lakes region and an expanding number of jobs that required worker mobility. Railroad building, crop-harvesting and lumberjacking all necessitated the movement of tens of thousands of workers. For the first time the United States was home to a large pool of intermittently employed workers who were mobile on a continental scale.

The political economy of mobility is neatly illustrated by the rôle of the railroad in American economic life. The continent was an investment arena for European as well as American capital during the nineteenth century. Following the Civil War, financiers responded to recurring crises in capital accumulation at home by seeking new overseas investment arenas. One such that proved to be popular was railroad development in the American West. British and Eastern seaboard money opened up the West for economic expansion and geographical transformation. The existence of railroads west of the Mississippi led directly to the decimation of the bison and the confinement of Indian tribes on the Great Plains. Pastoral modes of existence were rapidly curtailed and the 'range' was opened up to the cattle industry that spread northward across the Plains.[23]

The development of a national economy rested on an enormous range and quantity of natural resources, including most of the minerals central to an industrial economy (coal, iron, copper, zinc, etc.), oil, agricultural products such as cotton and hemp and lumber for the production of houses. A combination of Federal policy and private enterprise encouraged an expansive and innovative capitalist economy. As William Robbins argues, this economy produced a quickening in the pace of change in the world economy marked by uneven development at a variety of scales: 'expanding systems of production in one area retarded similar production elsewhere and resulted in a great transatlantic and transcontinental movement of people.'[24] The time of the tramp scare was thus marked by sudden and dramatic transformations in American life and work, as traditions were disrupted by the shifts in capital and labour that characterized the developing capitalist economy.

The railroad was central to this transforming economy. In addition to enabling tramps to travel further and quicker, time–space compression also enabled the development of Western agribusiness, where fruit plantations demanded 200 workers one month and 20,000 the next.[25] The natural resources of the Great West were not resources at all until they could be transported and converted into profit with the help of venture capital. Capitalists needed to turn the trans-Mississippi West into a resource and investment arena by convincing people to move there. Both corporate business and the Government in Washington, DC, encouraged both railroad construction and settlement. In 1900, just 31 years after the first transcontinental railroad was completed, there were five trans-continental railroads. The largely pastoral economy of the American West had been transformed into an important part of the expanding world capitalist system. It had become a site of industrial agribusiness. It was linked to the East and to Europe both literally by transport networks and, less visibly, by an economic dependency.

The new landscape created by mobile capital and made possible by the railroad was quite different from the great Prairie it replaced. One element of this landscape was the bonanza farm. With the scattering of the Sioux in revenge for Custer's defeat at the Little Bighorn in 1876, North Dakota's Red River Valley was available for settlement. The Dakota territory was opened up to mining and extensive wheat farming. Several railroads, including the Northern Pacific and the Great Northern, encouraged settlement of the Dakotas. The huge wheat farms, marked by high levels of mechanization and absentee ownership, were located along these railroads providing connections to Chicago and the populated areas of the Eastern seaboard. Land companies had managed to buy huge tracts from the railroad companies and established huge farms that were enormously successful and profitable as long as the rains came. Large numbers of seasonal labourers were needed at harvest time in these factory like farms. Throughout the 1870s and early 1880s these labourers were tramps and hobos. By the end of the 1880s the farms had been hit by drought and falling wheat prices and the land was gradually parcelled off. People had to look elsewhere for work.

Shortly after the Civil War and the construction of the first transcontinental railroad came the financial 'panic' of 1873, itself a symptom of industrial transformation. This financial panic followed a period of massive stock speculation, rapid expansion of the agricultural West (a product, in part, of the new trans-Mississippi railroad network), a world-wide drop in prices and the collapse of Jay Cooke & Company, a powerful banking corporation and the financial agent for the Northern Pacific Railway. More than 100 banks collapsed, insurance firms closed and the previously booming railroad industry went into shock. Hundreds of thousands of rail workers lost their jobs almost immediately. The crisis was felt throughout the 1870s in an ongoing depression that threw hundreds of thousands more out of work. This was repeated in 1893, when the national economy was threatened by a series of bank failures and industrial collapses, contributing to the ever-growing band of homeless and destitute people looking for work, or just getting by. As with most depressions, the already poor and unskilled, on the margins of the economy, were disproportionately effected. As Eric Monkkonen has argued, working-class people 'incorporated tramping as a rational response to underemployment as well as unemployment'.[26] During the financial panic of 1873, for instance, work at the Great Northern Railroad terminal at Duluth, Minnesota, ceased and 3,700 of the city's 5,000 people left within a month.[27] In Philadelphia, the nation's third largest city at the end of the nineteenth century and the home of Jay Cooke & Company, the numbers of vagrants entering the Prison or House of Correction increased massively in 1873. In the period 1835–73 few of the wandering poor appeared on their books: throughout the 1860s, for instance, only three out of every 1,000 people in these institutions were classified as vagrants. But in 1873 the figure rose to ten.[28] It stayed high (over six) for the rest of the decade.

The existence of people who came to be called tramps as a result of time–space compression (notably the rapidly expanding railroad system that allowed them to travel illegally over long distances in short periods of time), and the development of communication and transportation technologies that facilitated the inclusion of much of the United States into a global capitalist system (a system that was, and still is, marked by rapid transformations from boom times to economic downturns) were indissolubly linked. The incursion of agribusiness into the Great West transformed the landscape and economy on a massive scale and produced new movements of both capital and labour. When sociologists, eugenicists and others began to use the term 'tramp' they were referring to people whose lives were made possible by this conflation of mobility options and economic pressures that occurred for the first time in the 1870s.


THE TRAMP'S WORLD

Most tramps of the late nineteenth century travelled alone either on trains or on foot. The majority were male, white and American-born. There are no reliable national statistics of vagrant populations from the 1870s. In 1911 James Forbes guessed a total tramp population of 350,000.[29] Edmond Kelly

in 1906 estimated a total of 500,000 tramps.[30] More recently Eric
Monkkonen has looked at the numbers of people staying in police station
lodgings between the Civil War and the 1920s and has estimated that
somewhere between 10 and 20 per cent of the population in the last two
decades of the twentieth century came from a family with a member who
had tramped in search of work.[31] Since accurate overall numbers are not
available, snapshots will have to do. Of those arrested for vagrancy in
Philadelphia in 1874–5, some 18.6 per cent were women.[32] These women
were far more likely to be married than men arrested on the same charge.
Most people described as tramps were white; Kenneth Kusmer's survey of
tramps and vagrants indicates that only 3.3 per cent of the males were
black.[33] He suggests that the majority of these were probably former slaves
who had migrated north following emancipation. Vagrancy laws could be
particularly severe when applied to black wanderers. Vagrancy and tramp
laws in Southern states were frequently used to sell black people into
servitude, thus reintroducing slavery through the back door. Georgia's
Supreme Court had stated in 1866 that vagrancy laws should be more
rigidly enforced against the 'colored' population because blacks were
thought more likely to lead idle and rootless lives. It is clear that mobility
meant something quite different to black people. They had been denied
the freedom of movement that whites generally enjoyed. Their movements north to the industrial heartlands of St Louis, Chicago and New
York were affirmations of new-found freedom in ways that the movement
of white people would never be. As Peter Kolchin has remarked, black
people often moved 'to affirm their freedom, because free movement was
one of the obvious earmarks of their new status. No matter what else
might happen to him, the Negro who could move was in an important
sense master of his own destiny.'[34] In addition, the movement of black
people was seen by whites in quite different ways. The black presence in
formerly white-only areas was seen as evidence for the end of white control and domination.[35]

It was a common misperception in the popular press that the tramp
population was predominantly foreign-born. Following the crash of 1873
and widespread unemployment, many American-born workers became
tramps. Indeed, it was not until the majority of those on the road were
those of American birth that people became worried about 'the tramp
evil'. By the 1890s in Philadelphia, well over half of the tramp population
was 'American', with the Irish as the largest foreign-born contingent.[36]
These figures match the data collected by John J. McCook in Connecticut.
In 1906 in Chicago, the hub of both the railroad system and the tramp net-

9 'Midnight in a Two-Cent Doss', from J. Flynt, 'The City Tramp', *Century Magazine*, 47 (March 1894).

work, as many as 85 per cent of the tramp population had been born in the United States. This figure is even more remarkable when compared with the percentage of native-born among all adult males in Chicago, which stood at only 46.5 per cent at the turn of the century.[37] In the same year nearly 60 per cent of the adult male residents of the New York municipal lodging house were 'American'. In these cities the majority of foreign-born vagrants/tramps were Irish, with the rest being predominantly German, English and Italian.[38]

The image of the tramp during the scare was one of a shiftless, idle hooligan who avoided work at all costs. The vast majority of tramps, however, did work. Many were employed in a number of different industries in the course of a single year, including construction, fruit-picking and mining. Tramping changed seasonally as people followed the availability of work. Winter jobs included cutting ice, tree-felling and moving coal. During the rest of the year a series of agricultural tasks requiring cheap and mobile labour were pursued. Tramps followed the harvests down the West coast, for instance, moving from apples in Washington state to beets and grapes in California. Others followed the wheat harvest through the Midwest from Kansas to the Dakotas. Even so, tramps spent long periods between jobs in major transport hubs such as Chicago, where they developed intricate informal infrastructures.[39]

Tramps slept just about anywhere they could. Most often they stayed in formal or semi-formal settings, such as bunkhouses by railroad or lumber camps or on the huge wheat farms of the upper Midwest. When in cities, they were put up in police stations, lodging-houses, flophouses (cheap hotels) and missions. Police stations provided one of the most important places for tramps to stay. By 1890, police stations in New York furnished nearly 150,000 lodgings annually.[40] Lodging-houses boomed in the last years on the nineteenth century. Twenty-five cents bought a tramp a tiny, inhospitable cubicle for the night. For ten cents he got to share the floor of a large and overcrowded room with many other men (illus. 9–11). If they were very fortunate, tramps could find an alternative provided by a philanthropist, such as the 'workingmen's hotels' of D. O. Mills in New York, which had clean single rooms, libraries and reading halls. Dr Ben Reitman provided a similar service at the Hobo College in Chicago.

Municipalities, along with charity reformers, took it on themselves to provide lodging houses, such as Boston's Wayfarers' Lodge (opened in 1879). These were particularly widespread in the North-east, but by the turn of the century were to be found throughout the country. These

10 *Seven Cent Lodging House, East Side New York, February 22, 1895.*

municipal lodging-houses were disciplinary institutions through and through, with strict curfew hours, rules prohibiting drink and various work duties, such as log-splitting and street-cleaning. The Wayfarers' Lodge was a place where the work ethic could be imposed on the tramp. Reformers believed that the system would encourage only the saveable tramps, who would work and repel the truly dangerous tramps who would not. Once in the Lodge, tramps would be well and truly regimented. The following are the rules of the Washington, DC, Municipal Lodging House that were printed on the back of the identification card given to every resident:

RULES

The house will be opened from 6 A.M. until 10 P.M. except for those who have registered, who are required to return by 8 P.M.

Breakfast served at 7 A.M.; Dinner, from 5 to 6 P.M.

No person under the influence of **liquor** will be admitted.

**No drinking, smoking or swearing will be allowed.**

All applicants admitted will be required to saw one-eight cord of wood for supper, bath, lodging and breakfast.

No person may remain longer than three days.

All persons having stayed one night, and wishing further accommodations are **required** to report not later than 2 P.M.

All meals for **Sunday**, must be worked for on a week day.

At the end of the **Gong** at 10 P.M. all talking will cease.

All **valuables** must be left at the office.

Any **violation** of these rules will debar a person from the house.[41]

Not surprisingly, these rules were not popular among the tramps.

Tramp life in the city during the day revolved around an area known as the 'main stem'. This was an area of lodging-houses, soup-kitchens and employment agencies close to downtown and not far from the railroad stations. San Francisco's South of Market area, Gateway in Minneapolis and New York's Bowery were all such areas. It is estimated that over 60,000 transient people a year overwintered in West Madison Street in Chicago's main stem in the first decade of the twentieth century.[42] In an area such as this, food, shelter and, occasionally, work could be found. Tramps, when arriving in a city, would search out the main stem and with it the company of people who shared their way of life. It was a space apart from the rest of the city where a unique subculture developed in relative autonomy.

The other space in which tramps met was the area known as the 'jungle'. The jungle was usually an area of disused land immediately adjacent to the railroad tracks. According to Nels Anderson,

> It should be located in a dry and shady place that permits sleeping on the ground. There should be plenty of water for cooking and bathing and wood enough to keep the pot boiling. If there is a general store near by where bread, meat, and vegetables may be had, so much the better. For those who have no money, but enough courage to 'bum lumps,' it is well that the jungles be not too far from a town, though far enough to escape the attention of the natives and officials …[43]

Anderson, who spent many years as a hobo, explains that there were both temporary and permanent jungles. Temporary ones were formed spontaneously by small groups looking for a place to rest, wash and eat before moving on. Large cities and important railroad junctions had more permanent jungles, where someone was always keeping the fire burning. Standard fare was the famous 'Mulligan Stew', a stew made over a fire out of whatever was available. Anderson describes these as uniquely democratic spaces where black, white and Mexican tramps mixed freely, telling one another stories and singing tramp songs [44]

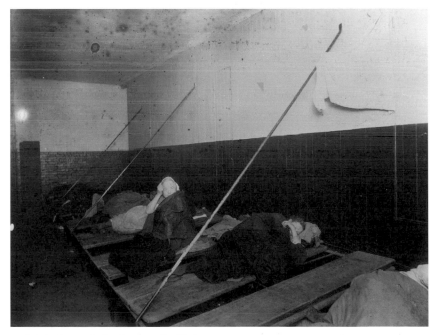

11 *Fourth Precinct Police Station, New York 1895.*

World War Two made a huge reduction in the number of people out of work. It also marks the point when the word 'tramp' fell out of common usage and was replaced by the term 'migrant'. Just as the advent of the railroad and the economic collapse of 1873 help explain the origins of the tramp, so the spread of the automobile and the Great Depression of the 1930s were implicated in the metamorphosis of the tramp into the migrant. Just as conditions in the 1870s gave rise to a large population of wandering people looking for work, so the Great Depression, combined with soil erosion and dust storms in Southern and Midwestern states (Texas, the Dakotas, Arkansas and Oklahoma), led to a new population of displaced people heading, for the most part, to California.

California was used to migration. Its history was based on the movement of people from the West, from the South and from the East. On many occasions the state had promoted immigration. In the 1840s the Gold Rush was heavily promoted, drawing migrants from the East. In 1869 Governor Henry H. Haight invited 'immigrants of kindred races who will constitute a congenial element and locate themselves and their families permanently upon the soil'.[45] The growth of Los Angeles was based on massive boosterism encouraging the growth of a city based on little more than high expectations.[46]

The farmers of the Great Plains had arrived in the Midwest in large numbers when the railroads opened it up in the late nineteenth century. Agricultural existence on the Plains was always a precarious affair. Major John Wesley Powell had warned that settlers would be subject to recurrent drought.[47] Many, convinced by the publicity generated by the railroad companies, ignored his advice and, believing that rain follows the plough, had set up homesteads. These farmers were accustomed to medium-size holdings and relatively humid climates. They were not familiar with the one-crop system of cotton or wheat that soon predominated on the Plains. Not surprisingly, the whole area entered into a series of boom and bust cycles, beginning with the cold winter of 1885–6 followed by droughts in 1890–91 and 1894–9. Good years, however, witnessed enormous production and encouraged further migrations. In 1906 and 1914 many more people moved onto the Plains following boom times encouraged by rain and war. General economic depressions hit the farmers in 1919 and 1925. They had made quick and seemingly easy profits during boom years and had overcapitalized in order to produce even more. These years were more often than not followed by droughts, economic downturns or surpluses of agricultural products, and farmers found themselves in ever greater debt. Many sold their land to corporations and became tenant farmers rather than owners. By the late 1920s the vast majority of wheat, cotton and corn production was in the hands of corporations, who proceeded to mechanize agriculture on a huge scale. This mechanization and monoculture production steadily wore out the soil and produced the conditions that led to the dust storms of the 1930s.

During the Great Depression, 100,000 people moved from Oklahoma to California. These migrants constituted one tenth of the total state increase during the 1930s. Although many came from Kansas, Arkansas and Texas, the migrants became known as Okies. Former tenant farmers, they had been displaced by the machinery of corporate agribusiness, recurrent droughts and intense soil depletion. The flow started rather modestly and had reached its peak by 1935. Despite the obvious enormity of the situation, migration to California was actually smaller during the Depression that in the decades before and after it. It is curious, therefore, that the migration of white Protestant Americans should have provoked such hysteria. California had constantly been selling itself as a location to migrate to. In addition to a history of positive messages emanating from the state, it was widely perceived to be a land of milk and honey, with a fine climate, economic prosperity and where it was easy to get relief by those without work. Californian agribusiness had become hugely successful (in contrast to the conditions on the Great Plains), and California's growers frequently encouraged workers from Oklahoma and the other Plains states to move there.

The Okies were certainly not the first group of mobile workers to head for California. Previous panics had centred on other sources of cheap labour in Californian agriculture.[48] In the 1870s California's crops had been transformed from wheat to labour-intensive fruit cultivation. The increasingly reliable railroad network meant that fruit could be shipped quickly over long distances. It also meant that labour could be transported into the state to take advantage of the relatively short periods of time in which labour was needed for the harvest. From the 1870s, tramps travelled to California by train to help bring in the fruit harvest. By far the majority of these 'fruit tramps' worked and travelled individually, and most were men. In the early part of the twentieth century, they were vigorously, although not entirely successfully, recruited by the International Workers of the World (IWW).[49] Fruit tramps (sometimes called 'bindle stiffs') worked up and down the West coast, following the harvests from apples and orchard fruits in the Pacific Northwest to the fruits of California.

Tramps were outnumbered, however, by non-white migrant labour. The Chinese, whose labour had been crucial when the trans-continental railroad was under construction, were thought to be docile and compliant, and growers employed them in large numbers. After a series of anti-Chinese riots in the 1890s, however, growers were forced to end their reliance on Chinese labour. Japanese beet pickers were treated in a similar way. Mexican labour became increasingly important to the growers and was comparatively invisible as a more or less established part of the landscape. While the wheat and corn harvests of the Midwest were failing repeatedly, the Californian fruits and vegetables industry, through Mexican labour, was able to cash in and transform the nation's diet. The Mexicans were only required for harvest times. During the remainder of the year they lived on the outskirts of towns such as Fresno, Bakersfield and Los Angeles. But by the late 1920s there were increasing worries about the amount being spent on relief for Mexican labourers during the off-season, and in 1930 a campaign for voluntary repatriation began that was to result in 150,000 labourers being returned to Mexico within seven years.[50]

The loss of so many potential harvest workers presented the growers with a problem. Who would replace them? Agricultural journals predicted severe labour shortages that did not immediately develop in the early years of the 1930s. By late 1933, however, the growers were experiencing reductions in production levels and a diminished supply of labour. In 1933 there were 186 workers for every 100 available agricultural jobs, but by 1934 the number had decreased to 142. Many people preferred to remain on relief rather than work for low agricultural wages.[51] Farmers were convinced there was an under-supply of labour. This was combined with anxiety about the increasing militance of the remaining Mexican labourers, who were able to make the fears of a decreased labour supply work to their advantage. Luckily for the growers, this coincided with the first large waves of migrants from the Dust Bowl states.

The Okies saw an opportunity in California and started to make their way along Highway 66 through New Mexico and Arizona, stopping on the way to pick cotton. Typically, they travelled in family groups in cars known as 'Jalopies'. They headed for the fields of the Sacramento Valley in the north, the Imperial Valley in the south and the cotton fields of the San Joaquin Valley. In addition to cotton, which they were used to, they learned to pick citrus fruits, beets, peaches, grapes and potatoes. It did not take long for them to replace the Mexican workers who had remained. As Stein has remarked, the Okies were a new phenomenon.

The Okies were not bindle stiffs or single men. They were families, and they wanted to relocate permanently in California. They had never intended to become migratory agricultural laborers, carrying their few belongings from place to place, incessantly following the crops in a never-ending cycle of grinding harvest labor ... As their numbers increased, they threatened to become a serious social and political dislocation in counties that could not possibly absorb a new population of such magnitude within sufficient time to avoid misery for the newcomers and expense for the older residents.[52]

Unlike the Mexican workforce, the Okies did not disappear to the edges of the cities in non-harvest times. Instead they remained in the rural counties and became an embarrassment to the local communities and the state in general.

The new migrant labourers of the 1930s differed from the tramp in two main ways. Again time–space compression was central. Just as it contributed to the birth of the tramp through the technology of the railroad, so it marked the end of the tramp through the popularity and accessibility of the automobile. The migrants of Steinbeck's *Grapes of Wrath* and the songs of Woody Guthrie travelled in cars. As the photography of Dorothea Lange was to show (see chapter Seven), these cars were packed full with the paraphernalia of domesticity, including large and extended families. As Stewert Holbrook, a somewhat sentimental historian of the American railroads, remarked, the 'railroad tramp will never return ... The automobile, in one form or another, is taking him off the steamcars. It is one effect of the motor age that has been of considerable benefit to the railroads.'[53] The second, connected, difference was that the Dust Bowl migrants were entire families who had been displaced and were looking to resettle. They were not single men, not tramps.

# 3 Knowing the Tramp

How were the tramp and the hobo known in the late nineteenth century? In answering such a question we are confronted with questions of knowledge and the history of knowledge. In this chapter we will see how a curious ontological symbiosis existed between the tramp and the emerging disciplinary knowledge of sociology. Before that, however, it is prudent to reflect on the definition of the tramp and the rôle that definitions play in the process of making up the tramp.

## DEFINING THE TRAMP

Every student knows that one of the most basic forms of knowledge is the definition. Definitions are supposed to make things clear, to provide exactness and precision. The connected word 'definitive' also denotes authority – the *definitive* text. The definition of the tramp, then, is a supposedly precise and authoritative marker that tells us who we are talking about when we talk about tramps.

The definition of what constitutes a tramp is, however, far from distinct. The first time the noun 'tramp' appeared in *The New York Times* was in February 1875 and was used to describe the homeless unemployed.[1] The term only became common usage in the United States in the period following the crash of 1873. The most famous and often repeated (formal) definition is said to originate from the work of the Chicago anarchist and occasional tramp Ben Reitman. Reitman claimed that the general condition of vagrancy is divisible into three main classes: tramps, hobos and bums.

> A tramp is a man who doesn't work, who apparently doesn't want to work, who lives without working and who is constantly travelling. A hobo is a non-skilled, non-employed laborer without money, looking for work. A bum is a man who hangs around a low class

saloon and begs or earns a few pennies a day in order to obtain drink. He is usually an inebriate.[2]

This definition was a version of the one used by men on the road and repeated in a number of contemporary accounts. Nicholas Klein, President of the Hobo College in Chicago, wrote the following:

> A hobo is one who travels in search of work, the migratory worker who must go about to find employment ... The name originated from the words 'hoe-boy' plainly derived from work on the farm. A tramp is one who travels but does not work, and a bum is a man who stays in one place and does not work. Between these grades there is a great gulf of social distinction. Don't get tramps and hobos mixed. They are quite different in many respects. The chief difference being that the hobo will work and the tramp will not, preferring to live on what he can pick up at back doors as he makes his way through the country.[3]

As far as hobos were concerned the hobo was a migratory worker, the tramp a migratory non-worker and the bum a non-migratory non-worker. Such subtle differences were often lost on outside observers, though, who took anyone riding a freight train to be a tramp and dealt with them accordingly. Similarly, texts concerning tramps often slip between the words tramp and hobo for no apparent reason.

If there were no people called tramps before the 1870s then there were no tramps. The act of definition is a foundational moment in the making up of a social type. I do not mean by this that tramps were simply fabricated. I mean that both the meaning and the materiality of the life of people who came to be called tramps changed when the word tramp and its meanings started to be used. A new model of description came into being and new possibilities for action arose as a consequence. These working definitions of the tramp combined the geographical fact of mobility and ideas about work to differentiate between mobility that was to be applauded and mobility that was suspect.

Arguments over definitions are rarely simply semantic. Consider the way in which definitions become reified in law. It is important to make this point because the general definition of the tramp that emerged in the 1870s quickly became part of the legal fabric of nineteen states, and, as such, had stark effects on the lives of those so defined. Once tramps have been defined, they can be dealt with, argued over, confined, made to work on log piles and disenfranchised. Again, arguments over mobility and work are key.

In 1876, seven years after the completion of the trans-continental railroad, the first of many state 'Tramp Laws' was passed in New Jersey. A tramp was defined as an idle person without employment, a transient person who roamed from place to place, and who had no lawful occasion to wander.[4] Tramp laws were not the first laws at the state level to intervene in the lives of the mobile unemployed. Indeed, vagrancy laws had been on the books of most states since their foundation. For the most part these had been borrowed wholesale from Great Britain, which had a long history of anti-vagrancy laws.[5] The legal concept of vagabondage originated, in England, in the long-standing distinction between able-bodied and non-able-bodied poor. As early as the fourteenth century, Parliament had made it an offence to have no master (and thus no 'place').

Legal codes around vagabondage and vagrancy proliferated in England in the fifteenth and sixteenth centuries. These codes rested on the ability to work. An Act of 1531 defined the vagabond as 'any man or woman being whole and mighty in body and able to labour having no land, master, nor using any lawful merchandise, craft or mystery whereby he might get his living.'[6] An Elizabethan 'Acte for the Punishment of Vacabondes', for instance, defined all wanderers as rogues. These acts had been updated in the Vagrancy Act of 1824, which made it an offence to be in the open, under a tent or in a coach or wagon without any visible means of support.[7] This Act was aimed at a diverse range of people thought to be likely to commit crime. These included vagabonds, gypsies, itinerants who refused to work and prostitutes. It was seen to go hand in hand with the Poor Laws designed for the so called 'deserving poor'. The Act applied to the undeserving poor. It was a combination of the 1824 Act and earlier ones concerning vagrancy that formed the basis for most state vagrancy laws in America before 1876. Similar laws existed across Europe. In France, for instance, the penal code of 1810 (article 270) stated that 'Vagabonds or people without a place [*gens sans aveu*[8]] are those who have neither an assured domicile nor means of existence, and who generally have no trade [*metier*] or profession.'[9] Here, as elsewhere, the legal definition of vagrancy hinges on both geography – the lack of a home – and work. In addition, these vagrancy laws typically specified three further characteristics of vagrants: that they were able-bodied, poor and potentially dangerous. As A. L. Beier has remarked in relation to early English vagrancy laws, the underlying fear was that of a generalized form of disorder which threatened the ruling elites.

The history of vagrancy law in the United States reflects the variety of European, particularly English, legislation. Vagrancy laws in colonial

America were used as tools to deal with perceived moral threats to small, isolated communities: 'drifters challenged both the moral character of small-town society and the delicate web of mutual obligation that provided relief for the poor in country settings.'[10] The problem of vagrancy was, for the most part, a local or regional problem. Local institutions were obliged to care for their own poor, but not for the poor from somewhere else. During the nineteenth century, vagrancy laws were increasingly used to counter the threat of an industrial poor gathering in nearby cities during economic downturns hoping for relief. As they increased in number and visibility, vagrants were more likely to be seen as a threat to social order. Thus moral standards and vagrancy legislation were used to attempt to disperse the perceived threat. The laws were very broadly written and used to apprehend a diverse array of potential trouble-makers.

One notable chain of events occurred in Buffalo during the depression of 1893–4.[11] The State of New York had passed a Tramp Act in 1879 in response to the increased number of jobless wanderers following the depressions of 1873 and 1877 and the railroad strike of 1877. Following the depression of 1884 it was revised in 1885 to become a 'model' Tramp Act.[12] The Act was used extensively in Buffalo against both the wandering poor and the more vulnerable members of the working classes in the area. It was also used to arrest and repress working-class organizers and agitators who were often moving between sites of industrial struggle and could thus easily be described as 'tramps'. Buffalo was a large city on Lake Erie, the eleventh largest in America, and, like Chicago, it was an important hub in the transportation network and a focus of industrial employment in the Great Lakes region. Twenty-six railroads served the city, which was also a major port. It was a node in both the shipment of raw materials from the American West and manufactured goods from the East. The depression of 1893–4 hit Buffalo severely and the city suffered unemployment on a grand scale. The 1885 Act was used to arrest 2,110 'tramps' in 1891. This constituted 11 per cent of the arrests for that year. Before 1891 the law was never used to arrest people despite the existence of an anti-tramp act since 1879. In 1894, in the height of the depression, 4,716 people were arrested as tramps. When this was added to the number of people arrested as vagrants, the arrests represented 40 per cent of all arrests made that year.[13] By 1893 the police had been ordered to arrest and lock up all tramps on sight. The Tramp Laws were being used by an increasingly pro-business police force as a form of class control. Tramps were said to be troublemakers in league with strikers. The spring of 1894 brought with it large-scale unemployment and the threat of a national railroad strike. The authorities in Buffalo became increasingly nervous about the increasing numbers of tramps who were said to be attracted to troubled times and places.

One reason for the unease was the increasing number of 'industrial armies' of the unemployed who marched towards Washington, DC, to petition for federally financed work schemes.[14] One such army was that of 'Count' Joseph Ryakowski. This group consisted of Polish and Bohemian canal workers from Chicago who entered Buffalo and received considerable support from the city's Polish community and from local trades unions. Ryakowski's 175-strong army were defined as tramps by the Buffalo police force and were met with outright violence. Two were shot, twenty were seriously wounded with clubs and 120 were arrested and jailed for periods up to six months. The court managed to convict 70 of the 'tramps' in just two hours. Clearly the consequences of being labelled a 'tramp' had potentially fatal consequences.

American vagrancy laws, like British ones before them, often included many types of offender against society, including vagabonds, wanderers, rogues, prostitutes, pimps, gamblers and people who refused to work for wages. Some laws were explicitly referred to as vagabond laws and were marginally more specific than vagrancy laws. Illinois' laws of 1874 defined vagabonds as 'idle and dissolute persons who went about and begged, runaways, pilferers, drunkards, night-walkers, lewd people, wanton and lascivious persons, railers and brawlers, persons without a calling or profession, visitors of tippling houses and houses of ill-fame, and wanderers.'[15]

The question arises as to why nineteen states found it necessary in the ten years following 1876 to rewrite their established vagrancy laws as 'tramp laws'. No law explicitly defined tramps until New Jersey's law of 1876, which was little changed from earlier vagrancy laws on both sides of the Atlantic.[16] Attempts to differentiate tramps from vagrants were occasionally made in court. In 'Des Moines v. Polk County' in 1899, the court held that tramps were a division of the genus vagrant, which included the usual range of 'worthless and wandering people'.[17] Further elements of definition, however, began to differentiate the tramp from the vagrant. Key to this differentiation was a specifically geographical factor – the newly extended possibilities of mobility on a continental scale. The new technologies of modernity – so connected in American myth to democracy and Manifest Destiny – also created new forms of deviance and new repressions.

Most states went to great lengths to define precisely who counted as a tramp. Chapter 159 of the general statutes of Connecticut, 1902, for example, states that 'All transient persons who rove about from place to place begging, and all vagrants, living without labor or visible means of support, who stroll over the country without lawful occasion, shall be deemed tramps.'[18] Section 1337 makes the link with excessive mobility explicit by stating that 'Any act of begging, or vagrancy, by any person not a resident of this state, shall be *prima facie* evidence that such a person is a tramp.' Finally, Section 1341 points out that 'These provisions shall not apply to any female, or minor under the age of 16 years, nor to any blind person, nor to any beggar roving within the limits of the town in which he resides.'[19] Technically, and interestingly, Connecticut's tramp laws excluded women, children, blind people and local vagrants, who legally could not be tramps. Punishment for convicted tramps varied from 90 days hard labour in New Mexico to being sold into servitude for up to a year in Kentucky. In Missouri, the tramp could be hired out to the highest bidder with cash in hand. Tramps were usually released with no provision for the future, thus making them liable to be immediately re-arrested on the same charges. Being defined as a tramp had severe consequences.

Tramps were not wholly without support. A prominent supporter of their rights, Governor Lewelling of Kansas, reacted to the 'tramp evil' by issuing a circular (which became known as the Tramp Circular) to his police chiefs suggesting they be lenient on tramps. Lewelling maintained that 'the right to go freely from place to place in search of employment, or even in obedience of a mere whim, is a part of that personal liberty guaranteed by the constitution of the United States to every human being on American soil. Even voluntary idleness is not forbidden.'[20] This defence of tramps was subjected to ridicule by newspapers in Kansas and across the United States. Newspapers accused Lewelling of consorting with anarchists and Communists and increasing the risk of tramps flooding into Kansas from other states.

A contemporary observer, Elbert Hubbard, supported Lewelling and satirized the tramp laws that were being formulated around the country. He pointed out that the tramp laws were rooted in English common law designed centuries earlier to suppress vagrancy. Section 1 of the Kansas Vagrancy Act read:

> All beggars and vagabonds who roam about from place to place without any lawful occupation, sleeping in barns, sheds, outhouses or in the open air, not giving a good account of themselves, and all persons roaming about commonly known as gypsies, shall be deemed vagrants and be liable to the penalties of the act.[21]

The penalty for those found guilty was imprisonment in jail or hard labour not to exceed 60 days. On release the person could be re-arrested immediately for the same crime. If a person wished to contest the sentencing he was entitled to redress by jury after paying a bond of approximately $500. Hubbard found the whole process ridiculous:

> Beside not being able to 'give an account of himself,' if it can be proven that he 'slept in the open air' the night before his arrest, and that, being hungry, he asked for food, both counts are construed against him as a proof of his guilt. The state legally regards him as a criminal, and being such, the state has the right to confiscate his labor. The taking of food by force to satisfy the demands of hunger is not a crime, but the asking for food is. Hunger in the United States of America, is crime.[22]

And further:

> In this country we say every man is assumed to be innocent until he is proven guilty. This applies only to men who have money. No peaceable decent man with money is asked to 'give an account of himself.' But let him have no place to lay his head, and ask for a cup of cold water, immediately we may legally assume his guilt and drag him before the notary, who shall demand that he 'give a satisfactory account of himself.' Satisfactory to whom forsooth?[23]

Unusually for the time, Hubbard argued that tramps were a symptom of economic downturns and legal formulations. He pointed towards the downturn of 1873 and seasonal agricultural work in states such as Delaware as reasons for the wandering tramps. In Delaware, he argued, migrants would arrive to work during the fruit season and offer to work for lower wages than Delaware workers. As a result of this Delaware introduced a Tramp Law in 1879. Section 1 of this law defined a tramp as 'Any person without a home in the town in which he may be found wandering about without employment.'[24] A person no longer had to beg, sleep in the open air, or have no money to be convicted. So a person who did not beg, was seeking work and carried a little money could now be arrested, be found guilty of being a tramp and sent to work for up to 30 days. In other words, just to have no home and seek employment was a crime. 'A tramp may be a criminal and he may not', Hubbard wrote. 'If he is a criminal punish him for his crimes, but do not punish him for being a tramp; to do this may be only to chastise him for his misfortunes.'[25] Lewelling's circular, in Hubbard's view, was a bold and noble refusal to create a whole class of criminals out of people who had already been subjected to great misfortune.

Lewelling's was a voice in the wilderness at the time when tramp laws were being made across the states. As legal discourse they had very material effects on those defined as tramps. The laws also made the explicit connection between tramp identity and long-distance travel, usually on trains. The main characteristics of the tramp were thus mobility over a large, possibly continental, area, and lack of work. It was the mobility, in particular, which distinguished the tramp from the earlier figure of the vagrant. People didn't use the word tramp to refer to homeless people before people were able to travel the kind of distances that the new rail-roads allowed. If someone could be defined as a tramp for the purposes of law they could receive far more severe sentences than if they were merely a vagrant and thus deserving of public charity. Definitions, as a form of knowledge, have their consequences, particularly when they become embedded in legislation.[26]

## LEGAL KNOWLEDGE AS A SOCIAL CONSTRUCTION

Legal knowledge was a particularly powerful form of knowledge because it had direct and pernicious effects on the way people defined as tramps were treated. The term 'social construction' is often used to describe how objects, beliefs and actions are the product of society and not simply 'natural'. The implication of using this term is that the thing (the tramp) is the product of a society. It is not just society in a generalized sense, however, but particular parts of society that are implicated in this process of production. Some people have more power to name and to act than others. Those who create laws and then prosecute people for transgressing them are particularly powerful, for they, in a limited but important way, define the things people can and cannot do. The issue of social construction, in a legal context, is quite literal.[27] There is a tendency to think of law, in a liberal Western tradition, as in some way separate from society – as a high-minded and independent abstraction. Recent work in critical legal theory has questioned this assumption and argued instead that law is embedded in society. This is the case both in the sense that law plays an important part in making society what it is and in the sense that law is itself constructed within particular arrangements of power within a given society. As David Delaney has argued, 'Legal and social phenomena are inseparable whether the point of their interpretation [...] is on the street, in the workplace, in the home, in law schools, or on the bench.'[28] This is particularly clear in issues regarding 'vagrancy', which is nothing if not a construction of the law. The legal definition of vagrancy, however, is not free-standing but linked to the more commonplace definitions based on mobility and work.

Work and mobility play familiar rôles in the definition of the tramp. The moral geography of roots and progress marked by a sedentary meta-physics is mixed with the moral imperative of work to form a nexus of meaning around the figure of the tramp/hobo. As with most characteristics of tramp definitions, the issues of work and mobility were imported from Europe. Vagabondage had become a particularly acute question in late-nineteenth-century France for instance.[29] Particularly prevalent was youth vagabondage. Young people would escape the countryside (and the work that went with it) to flee to the city. The threat of the vagabond taxed the minds of experts across France. Social reformers, medical experts, educators and psychologists all came up with classifications, diagnoses and disciplinary strategies relating to the problem. Their ideas were soon to find their way across the Atlantic and be taken up with varying degrees of enthusiasm. The 'problem' of the vagabond was one that mirrored that of the American tramp. 'Outside of the society that it frightens and repels', wrote one French observer, 'lives a class of individuals for whom there is no family, no regular work, no fixed domicile. That class is the class of the vagabonds.'[30] Vagabondage had no existence apart from that of a legal infraction. Vagabonds in France were constituted by law and made by the action of their arrest. The threat of the vagabond and the tramp is a virtual threat, for they have not committed any crime above and beyond that which makes them a vagabond or a tramp. Their 'way of life', Kristin Ross argues, 'places them in a state of *eventual* violation of laws: vagabonds are always virtual, anticipatory'.[31] A. L. Beier refers to vagrancy as a 'classic crime of status, the social crime *par excellence*'.[32] In Europe since the four-teenth century, vagrants had been arrested and punished not for an action they had committed but because of who they were and the threat to order they represented. The 'crime' of vagrancy is importantly not a quality of an act a vagrant commits but a consequence of the application of rules and sanctions to an offender. Law and legal definitions created the legal type *vagrant*, just as it would the legal type *tramp*.

Given the severe consequences of being deemed a tramp, it is not surprising that a good deal of energy was expended on defining the tramp and the hobo by individuals who called themselves hobos. One retrospectively wrote:

> To the vast majority of Americans, the men who came to beg food at back doors were as likely to be classified as 'no good bums' or tramps or vagrants as they were to be called hoboes. To the

respectable residents of small town America there was no difference. To the men who were 'throwing their feet' asking for a handout, there were important distinctions among hobo, tramp and bum. In the argot of the road 'a hobo was someone who travelled and worked, a tramp was someone who travelled but didn't work, and a bum was someone who didn't travel and didn't work.'[33]

It was, therefore, in the interests of those called 'tramps' to make distinctions between the deserving and the undeserving poor. Jeff Davies, apparently both King of the Hobos from 1908 and Emperor of the Hobos from 1938, indicated that the word *hobo* originated in the eighteenth century and was derived from *hoe boy*, which apparently meant a bonded servant who did nothing but hoe soil all day. After migrating to America, hoe boys, he argued, became construction workers, linemen, labourers, lumberjacks, printers and an assortment of other hard-working occupations. By the late eighteenth century he was simply called a hobo. According to Davies, a tramp was a 'thieving vagabond – never would work – always believed the world owed him a living'. To confuse the two was a slur on the hobo. The issue of definition was clearly a contentious one. Several pages later the same author again attempts to pin down the definition of the hobo, clearly hoping to avoid the consequences of being called a tramp. In this, his second, definition Davies describes a hobo as a 'gentleman of the road' and claims that the term derived from the Latin for 'good man' (*homa* and *bonas*) and relates to the hobo's predilection to 'share his last nickel with one less fortunate'. He goes on to outline the characteristics of the two mobile varieties of vagrant. The hobo is a victim of circumstances, such as economic down-turns, who 'if because of reverses ... takes to the road he keeps to the right of the road and does his best to keep out of trouble'. The tramp, on the other hand, is 'one who hits the road thinking that the world owes him a living'.

> It is the tramp who steals the farmer's chickens – the hobo gets the blame. It is the hobo who prevents the railroad wreck – yet newspapers, unthinkingly will give credit to the tramps. But credit or no credit – facts are facts. Hoboes are hoboes – tramps are tramps – and bums are bums.[34]

Davis continues by taking issue with Jack London, author of *The Tramp*, insisting that London had made an error in his title. London wrote of his tramp that 'When out of work and still discouraged he has been forced to "hit the road" between large cities in his quest for a job', to which Davis replied: 'when Jack London wrote that last line "in his quest for a job," that fellow was no tramp – for if he hit the road between large cities in his quest for a job – then naturally that fellow was a hobo.' Clearly, the definitions of the tramp and hobo held with them a whole host of meanings associated with work and mobility. To a self-confessed hobo like Davis it was an ontological error of some proportions to call a hobo like himself a tramp.

SOCIOLOGY AND THE TRAMP

Definitions, once in existence, provide the preconditions for any number of forms of knowledge about the thing that is defined. Every social definition or category is implicated in the construction, or making up, of people as parts of the 'real world'. Such categories are haunted by the plethora of meanings associated with them.

The English language categories of 'stone', 'tree' and 'hand' invoke a variety of shared connotations about these objects that add to whatever may be their reality as brute facts. But these cultural

12 'Tomato-Can Tramps', from J. Flynt, 'The City Tramp', *Century Magazine*, 47 (March 1894).

13 'The Tramp Hangout', from J. Flynt, 'The Tramp at Home', *Century Magazine*, 47 (February 1894).

connotations do not manufacture themselves out of thin air. The cultural categories of marriage, money, theft, on the other hand are created solely by adherence to the constitutive rule systems that define them. Without these rule systems these objects would not exist.[35]

Vagrancy, vagrants, tramps, etc., are what some people, in positions that enable them to define others, say they are. In law this means that a tramp could be so defined in a court of law and acted on accordingly. Law, as a form of knowledge, acted on and was constructed through the newly defined tramp. Needless to say, other forms of knowledge – other ways of categorizing – were directed at the tramp in the same period. Sociology, as a new form of formal academic knowledge in the United States, was born at around the same time as the tramp. It was accompanied by methodologies of statistics, classification tables and ethnographic fieldwork. As with law, sociology defined the tramp in relation to work and mobility.

Before sociology established itself as an academic discipline, many figures engaged in what would later be called participant observation. It was not unusual for people to act as tramps and write books about their experiences. Conversely, some tramps also wrote. Indeed, there is a minor genre of 'life on the road' accounts produced around the turn of the century.[36] The most influential of these has been Josiah Flynt Willard's *Tramping with Tramps* (1899), written under the pseudonym of Josiah Flynt to save his aunt, a noted Christian Temperance activist, from embarrassment.[37] Flynt was keen to get away from the confines of his Puritanical upbringing, and several times as a child ran away from home. He began writing about the life of the tramp and hobo in 1891 and frequently went on excursions dressed as a tramp in order to gather information. He successfully led a double life as a tramp and as a figure on the margins of literary circles. He travelled widely in Europe as well as in the United States. He liked to dress up, to play out different rôles, and had a remarkable linguistic ability.[38]

Flynt's accounts of tramps and hobos became the most influential reports on tramp life in the 1890s and were widely read in academic circles. He also produced a constant stream of illustrated articles in popular outlets such as *Century Magazine* and *Atlantic Monthly*. His *Tramping with Tramps* informed the work of the Chicago School of Sociology, particularly Nels Anderson. They were particularly impressed with his methodology, which he had commented on in the introduction to his book. He reflects on how he observed scientists observing micro-organisms and then writing up the results as 'valuable contributions to knowledge' and then compares this to his own work: 'In writing on what I have learned concerning human parasites by an experience that may be called scientific in so far as it deals with the subject on its own ground and in its peculiar conditions and environment, I seem to myself to be doing similar work with a like purpose.'[39]

Flynt was particularly keen to study the tramp in his own 'habitat'. In this sense he was opposed to the dominant methods in criminology that looked at criminals once they were in prison. Criminologists of the day, influenced by the work of Lombroso in Italy, advocated anthropomorphic methods that involved the careful measurement and comparison of criminals' ears, cheekbones, noses and the like. Flynt, by comparison, advocated what would later become known as ethnography. This involved, as he put it, living the tramp life: 'I must become joined to it and be part and parcel of its various manifestations.'[40] His popular magazine articles focussed on various tramp habitats and had titles such as 'The Tramp and the Railroad', 'The City Tramp' and 'The Tramp at Home'. They were heavily illustrated with line-drawings of tramps. Some were of particular sociological types, such as the 'Tomato-Can Tramp' (illus. 12), while others were used to indicate the habitat of the tramp – the world that his *in situ* methodology sought to explore. In 'The Tramp at Home',

14 'A City Tramp at Work',
from J. Flynt, 'The City
Tramp', *Century Magazine*, 47
(March 1894).

for instance, he explores the world of the jungle – the informal 'hangouts' that sprang up beside railroad tracks and away from the police (illus. 13). These illustrations closely mirror the photographs taken by John James McCook during the same period (see chapter Seven). Examples include tramps riding the trains in a number of different styles and 'flopping' in lodgings. Some were more sensational, feeding on some of the fears central to the tramp scare. Hence his articles included images of tramps in cities begging off women or seducing children into tramp life through their stories of adventure and travel (illus. 14–16). It was Flynt's methodological experimentation that impressed the sociologists who were to make up the Chicago School. Excerpts from his book made their way into the reader that Robert Park and Ernest Burgess used in teaching their courses.

Perhaps the best known account of tramps and hobos in American academic history is that of Nels Anderson, an individual directly influenced by Flynt. Anderson reviewed Flynt's book while a student at Brigham Young University. He wrote an unfavourable assessment, claiming that Flynt had not taken into account the many homeless men who spent most

15 'A Tramp's Depot', from J. Flynt, 'The Tramp and the Railroads', *Century Magazine*, 58 (June 1899).

of their time looking for work – the hobos. Much later, Anderson corrected this oversight in *The Hobo*, one of the key ethnographic monographs on the subject of the early twentieth century.[41] It is marked by an uneasy tension between formal academic and moralistic tendencies and a deep sympathy for the objects of his enquiry – the hobos. Anderson's ethnographic monograph, like the others produced by Chicago students, has to be understood in relation to the grand theories of W. I. Thomas, Robert Park and Ernest Burgess. While their students were busy discovering life in the neighbourhoods of Chicago, these three were inventing the diagrams and hypotheses that sought to explain the many and varied observations of their students. The development of the Chicago School is widely regarded as the key moment in the origins of American sociology, and of social science in general. Anderson's work on tramps and hobos needs to be understood within the overarching framework of Chicago School urban theory.[42]

16 'Telling Ghost-Stories', from J. Flynt, 'Tramping with Tramps', *Century Magazine*, 47 (November 1893).

The University of Chicago had barely come into existence (1892) when the first American department of sociology was founded. In its early years it was led by William Issac Thomas, who developed the idea of systematic study of social groups through empirical investigation. He focused on the concept of 'social disorganization', 'the decrease of the influence of existing social rules of behaviour upon individual members of the group'.[43] It was this idea that most strongly influenced the direction of study for the department's most famous member, Robert Park, and others who were to follow him.

Park had an unusual career for an academic. He had worked as a journalist for the *Minneapolis Journal*, where he developed a perspective on city life that resulted from his investigative reporting on the urban underworld of opium dens, gambling houses and alcoholic haunts.[44] It is probably not entirely irrelevant to his later work that he claimed to have 'covered more ground, tramping about in cities in different parts of the world, than any

17 Robert E. Park.

other living man'.[45] Following his stint of journalism he moved to
Germany where he was was taught by Georg Simmel (among others),
eventually receiving a PhD from Heidelberg. On his return to the United
States he worked for Booker T. Washington at his institute on race relations in Tuskagee. It was in 1911 that W. I. Thomas saw Park at a conference
on race and encouraged him to join the department at Chicago, where he
stayed for twenty years (illus. 17).

A key concept that Park formulated while in Chicago was that of
'moral order'. How, Park asked, do people preserve a positive conception
of themselves in an urban milieu where relationships were shallow and
based on money rather than habitual association? The city, to Park, was a
mosaic of little worlds each with its own moral code, which could support
a diverse array of different forms of behaviour:

> The processes of segregation establish moral distances which make
> the city a mosaic of little worlds which touch but do not interpene-
> trate. This makes it possible for individuals to pass quickly and easily
> from one moral milieu to another, and encourages the fascinating
> but dangerous experiment of living at the same time in several
> different contiguous, but otherwise widely separated, worlds.[46]

It was the description of these moral worlds that formed the bedrock of the ethnographic monographs that Park was to supervise, including Anderson's study of Hobohemia.

Park's work was foundational for the Chicago School, but it must be seen alongside that of Ernest Burgess and, in particular, the idea of 'human ecology'. Consider Burgess's well-known concentric ring diagram of the city (illus. 18). The model is a form of knowledge that reproduces in diagrammatic form a number of hypotheses about city life and structure. The underlying belief that structures this model is encapsulated by the term 'human ecology' and follows the basic rule that humans are like plants insofar as they behave in 'natural' ways. This 'natural' behaviour is evidenced primarily by competition for space – a competition that results inevitably in the strongest people getting the best places, a process referred to as 'ecological succession'. As a result of this competition the city gets divided up into distinct sub-areas determined by market forces and inhabited by similar people (natural areas). Over time these areas break down as people are assimilated by movements up the social hierarchy and outwards towards the suburbs. This results in a series of concentric rings around the city. By developing human ecology the Chicago School was

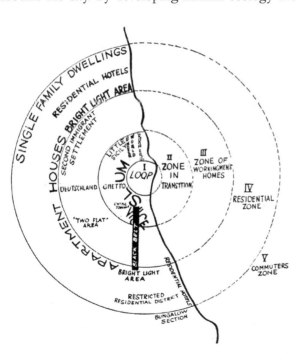

18 Ernest Burgess's Concentric Ring Model of 'Urban Areas', from Robert E. Park, 'The Growth of the City' (1925).

making an apparently chaotic city legible and understandable, finding regularity in confusion by applying the metaphor of nature. Using nature to explain the city has several implications. 'Nature' in Western thought implies something that is beyond human control – that just is. The nature/ ecology metaphor removes the processes of the city from the realm of history and human agency. No-one is to blame and nothing can be done. The city, when seen through the prism of this diagram and its implications, is not merely an artefact, it is an organism. Its growth, fundamentally and as a whole, is natural, uncontrolled and undesigned by any accountable agents.

This model is probably familiar to the vast majority of British children who have taken geography at school. It is also used almost universally in the United States, at least at college level. Most textbooks on urban geography feature it at some point or another. I have taught in a small Welsh town with two main roads and some 3,000 people. Every year we would set our incoming students an exercise that involves getting a feel for the place by using the knowledge they have gained from school and from sources in the local area. Every now and then some of them would *try* and understand the town (Lampeter) by applying the concentric ring model. The model, of course, is almost universally criticized at all levels for reasons that are almost as familiar as the model itself.[47]

Hobos and tramps do not appear as such on Burgess's concentric ring model. They are, however, mentioned in the text of 'The Growth of the City'.

> In the expansion of the city a process of distribution takes place which sifts and sorts and relocates individuals and groups by residence and occupation. The resulting differentiation of the cosmopolitan American city into areas typically all form one pattern with only interesting minor modifications. Within the central business district or on an adjoining street is the 'main stem' of 'hobohemia', the teeming Rialto of the homeless migratory man of the Middle West.[48]

Within the Chicago School's discussions of moral order was a clear preoccupation with the worrying effects of mobility, particularly in Hobohemia. A characteristic assertion of the Chicago School sociologists was that the city, unlike the country, was characterized by mobility. 'The City', Nels Anderson wrote,

> is more mobile, mobility being a characteristic of its life just as stability is characteristic of rural life. Main Street and Broadway are at cultural extremes, differing in the tempo of life, yet each is the

natural product of a situation. Main Street repeats itself day after day and resents disturbance. Broadway is bored with repetition. Main Street is hemmed in by the elements of nature more intimately than Broadway. The environment of Broadway is cultural, being man-made and mechanised; and being mechanised, the urban environment has a mobility of its own quite distinct from the movement of people.[49]

Mobility, to the Chicago School, was always a socio-spatial phenomenon denoting movement through geographical space *and* social space. This is best encapsulated by the general hypothesis visualized in the concentric ring model, that as people moved up the social scale they moved out from the Central Business District until they reached the suburbs. In 'The Growth of the City' Burgess makes mobility a central part of his ecological model of city form. He contrasts mobility with movement. While movement is 'a fixed and unchanging order of motion, designed to control a constant situation, as in routine movement',[50] mobility is a change of routine movement in response to new stimuli and situations. So while movement appears to be a relatively mundane and everyday activity, such as commuting, mobility is more exceptional – moving house or having adventures. The activities that Burgess labels *mobility* have implications for progress or regression, opportunity and threat. Burgess saw mobility as a central stimulus to the successful growth of both the individual and the city, but warned that when the mobility of individuals becomes detached from and unorganized by the whole (city, society) it becomes dangerous and pathological – a narcissistic vice. It is, of course, the 'zone in transition' that is most marked by this unattached mobility.

> The mobility of city life, with its increase in the number and intensity of stimulations, tends inevitably to confuse and to demoralize the person. For an essential element in the mores and in personal morality is constancy, consistency of the type that is natural in the social control of the primary group. Where mobility is the greatest, and where in consequence primary controls break down completely, as in the zone of deterioration in the modern city, there develop areas of demoralization, of promiscuity, and of vice.[51]

Burgess was clearly fascinated with the consequences of mobility on the city, as he believed that areas of high mobility were characterized by multiple pathologies such as prostitution, gangs, crime, poverty, wife desertion and alcoholism. He recounts how train rides per capita in

Chicago had risen from 164 in 1890 to 320 in 1910. Someone standing on the corner of State and Madison (areas of extremely high land values that lay alongside the area most frequented by tramps and hobos), he believed, would be passed by 31,000 people per hour on average over a day.

Mobility was also connected to the overwhelming concern with deviance, or social disorganization, as W. I. Thomas had termed it. Mobility, not for the first time, was theorized in opposition to place. Morally, mobility was a double-edged sword to Anderson. On the one hand there could be no urban civilization without mobility and, on the other, mobility threatened to undo place to such a degree that the city was threatened by chaos.

> The mobility of the city detaches and undomesticates the urban man. By it he is released from his primary group associations, the family or the neighborhood. With this independence comes a loss of loyalty. Urban man gains freedom, but the individualism he achieves is often at the cost of his locus.[52]

Mobility between and within cities produced new types of people and particular urban 'pathologies'. Given the twin interests of urban growth and social pathology, it is not surprising that the figure of the tramp/hobo looms large in the Chicago School's writings. In addition to Anderson's book and field notes there is the – often overlooked – short essay written by Park called 'The Mind of the Hobo: Reflections upon the Relation between Mentality and Locomotion'. In this essay Park considers the rôles of both place and mobility in constructing what he calls 'human mentality'. The well-known debt of the Chicago School to Darwinian evolutionary theory is evident in the essay, as Park considers the correlation between mobility and higher forms of life. Animals are distinguished from plants, he asserts, by their mobility. The rootedness of many people is represented as a kind of vestigial feature linking people to vegetables.

> This is evident in the invincible attachment of mankind to localities and places; in man's, and particularly woman's, inveterate and irrational ambition to have a home – some cave or hut or tenement – in which to live and vegetate; some secure hole or corner from which to come forth in the morning and return to at night.[53]

Insofar as humans continue to vegetate by remaining attached to place, Park suggests, people 'will never realize that other characteristic ambition of mankind, namely, to move freely and untrammelled over the surface of mundane things, and to live, like pure spirit, in his mind and in his imagination alone'.[54]

Park linked the human fact of motion to the other human characteristic(s) of intelligence and imagination. 'Mind', he argues, 'is an incident of locomotion'. It is only through the ability to change location – to be mobile – that humans were enabled to develop the ability to think abstractly. Park enlarges this argument still further by asserting that it is in 'locomotion' that forms of organization between and among individual people develops. Thus mobility, in addition to being responsible for abstract thought, is implicated in the development of the social. The social, to Park, is made up of individuals capable of locomotion.

Where, then, does the tramp and the hobo enter this equation? Clearly Park was familiar with the vast armies of tramps and hobos passing though Chicago who in many ways embodied the 'locomotion' he believed constituted both mind and society. Why then, he asked, were these itinerants not more philosophical? His answer revolved around the idea of directedness and destination. While the hobo was certainly mobile, he was not going anywhere in particular. His life was marked, Park thought, by a lack of vocation, direction and destination. His mobility was for its own sake. Park invoked the semi-medical diagnosis of wanderlust to label this type of mobility:

> Wanderlust, which is the most elementary expression of the romantic temperament and the romantic interest in life, has assumed for him, as for so many others, the character of a vice. He has gained his freedom, but he has lost his direction.[55]

> ... Society is, to be sure, made up of independent, locomoting individuals. It is the fact of locomotion, as I have said, that defines the very nature of society. But in order that there may be permanence and progress in society the individuals who compose it must be located [...] in order to maintain communication, for it is only through communication that the moving equilibrium which we call society can be maintained.[56]

So, despite the claims he makes for mobility, Park finally returns to place and locality for a sense of continuity and progress. The problem with the tramp's mobility, in Park's terms, was that he never stopped. Because of this the tramp was doomed to live an aimless life on the margins of society without the benefits of organization and association.

Park's ideas concerning the connection between mobility and mentality appear to be derived from the grandfather of the Chicago School, W. I. Thomas. Park quotes at length from Thomas's *Source Book of Social Origins* in his classic paper 'The City'. Park noted how Jewish people were associated with both intellectualism and radicalism, and connected this to their mobility.

> The 'Wandering Jew' acquires abstract terms with which to describe the various scenes which he visits. His knowledge of the world is based upon identities and differences, that is to say, on analysis and classification. Reared in intimate association with the bustle and business of the market place, constantly intent on the shrewd and fascinating game of buying and selling, in which he employs the most interesting of abstractions, money, he has neither opportunity nor inclination to cultivate that intimate attachment to places and persons which is characteristic of the immobile person.[57]

Throughout the work of Park, Burgess and Anderson there is a clear concern for the negative effects of mobility on city life. While directed mobility was clearly an important factor in the production of everything from city form to society itself, mobility in its extreme forms was linked to the idea of pathology and vice. It was therefore important for an investigator of hobo life such as Anderson to consider the life of the tramp and the hobo in terms of the pathological potential of mobility.

OTHER WAYS OF KNOWING

The formal sociologists of the Chicago School were not alone in producing sociological knowledge of the tramp. Just down the track, in Hobohemia's underworld, other forms of knowledge were being produced by the infamous hobo, agitator, doctor and anarchist, Ben Reitman (illus. 19). Academia is characterized by a distribution of power that tends to lead to the marginalization and exclusion of work that challenges established forms of academic knowledge. This may be doubly true when the excluded work is itself about, by and on the behalf of excluded groups in wider society. As David Sibley puts it:

> There are certain parallels between the exclusion of minorities, the 'imperfect people' who disturb the homogenised and purified topographies of mainstream social space, and the exclusion of ideas which seem to constitute a challenge to established hierarchies of knowledge and, thus, to power structures in academia. In both cases, there is a distaste for mixing expressed in the virtues of pure spaces and pure knowledge. In both cases, it is power – over

19  Ben Reitman in 1912.

geographical space or over the territory marked out by groups within an academic discipline – which is under threat.[58]

Sibley documents this with reference to the work of Jane Addams and W.E.B. Dubois, who worked at the same time and on the same issues as the Chicago School of Sociology. Theirs' was not the only excluded knowledge in Chicago at the time. Dr Ben L. Reitman was a contemporary of the Chicago School, who lived the life of an agitator, activist and independent scholar. Reitman existed as an uneasy bridge between formal knowledge with all its moral judgements, demarcated boundaries and purified spaces and the messy and often invisible world of Chicago's streets. Reitman produced knowledge that frequently led him into conflict with science, medicine and sociology as he transgressed the boundaries of acceptable thought and action.

On 17 November 1910 in the Pacific Hall on West Broadway, New York, Reitman orchestrated an event he called 'Outcast Night'. Anarchist intellectuals, who included Emma Goldman, witnessed a discussion featuring various types of social outcasts, among them hobos, prostitutes, 'homosexuals' and criminals. The hall was crowded and the event had attracted the press. The audience were treated to a number of appearances by various 'outcasts', from Hippolyte Havel, the Outcast Psychologist (speaking on why the outcast is the most important member of society), to Arthur Bullard, the Outcast Moralist (speaking on the religion of the outcast), and Sadakichi Hartman, the Outcast Poet (reading his unpublished sex drama, 'Mohammed'). At the end of the evening Reitman took the opportunity to reveal his 'social geography' – a talk based on a large map (entitled 'Reitman's Social Geography') of an imaginary peninsular and islands painted on a piece of canvas. The text of the lecture has disappeared, but the map is filed carefully in Reitman's archives at the University of Illinois at Chicago.[59] Here is a map of an imaginary space in which many of the exclusions and differences of contemporary social and cultural geography are depicted.

Reitman was one of the more curious figures of turn-of-the-century America's public life. He led the life of a radical and, in his time, had upset almost everyone he had come into contact with.[60] For many years he had been a hobo, travelling with others from coast to coast looking for seasonal employment. On several occasions he had been crowned King of the Hobos. He had formed hobo colleges in Chicago, seeking to educate his fellow travellers in philosophy, religion and politics. For a while he was the lover of Emma Goldman, the American anarchist who was later deported to Russia. He was jailed several times for his anarchist activities, which included promoting free love and birth control. Later he trained as a doctor and opened clinics for Chicago's down-and-outs. He was particularly concerned with the treatment of venereal diseases. Towards the end of his life, campaigns against syphilis took up an increasingly large part of his energies. His map of the outcast islands is given added meaning in the context of his life.

'Social geography' is not a phrase that tripped off the tongues of many people around 1910. Indeed the sub-discipline was hardly in existence until the 1960s at best.[61] Reitman's map depicts a large number of excluded social groups, including prostitutes, the poor, the sick, the disabled, the insane, the homeless, disadvantaged races, the old, the parentless and the politically radical (illus. 20). All these groups live on islands disconnected from the mainland apart from possible ferry services. In the bottom left-hand corner are two symbols for ideals marked 'freedom' and 'utopia'. In many ways this depiction of 'social geography' is quite visionary, differing from contemporary views of society in important ways. The map presents many

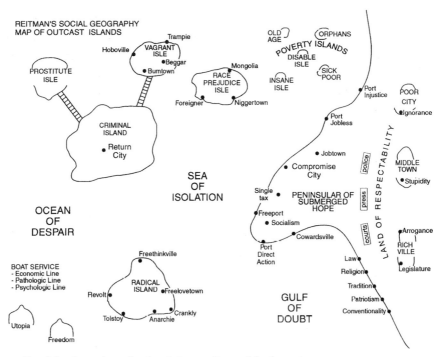

REITMAN'S SOCIAL GEOGRAPHY
MAP OF OUTCAST ISLANDS

Trampie

OLD AGE

ORPHANS

POVERTY ISLANDS

Hoboville   VAGRANT ISLE

DISABLE ISLE

Mongolia

•Beggar

•Burntown

SICK POOR

PROSTITUTE ISLE

RACE PREJUDICE ISLE

INSANE ISLE

Port Injustice

POOR CITY

Foreigner   Niggertown

•Ignorance

Port Jobless

CRIMINAL ISLAND

•Return City

•Jobtown

MIDDLE TOWN

•Compromise City

•Stupidity

SEA OF ISOLATION

Single tax   PENINSULAR OF SUBMERGED HOPE

OCEAN OF DESPAIR

•Freeport

•Socialism

•Arrogance

•Cowardsville

RICH VILLE

Freethinkville

Port Direct Action

Law•

•Legislature

BOAT SERVICE
- Economic Line
- Pathologic Line
- Psychologic Line

Religion•

RADICAL ISLAND   •Freelovetown

Tradition•

Revolt•

GULF OF DOUBT

Patriotism•

Utopia

Tolstoy   Anarchie

•Crankly

Conventionality•

Freedom

LAND OF RESPECTABILITY

police   press   courts

10 Sketch by the author after Ben Reitman, *Outcast Islands*, c. 1910

of the ideas of social exclusion prevalent in the social science of the 1990s.

Exclusion, of course, invokes the idea that someone somewhere is doing some excluding. It is an active expression. This is quite different from the idea that social geography is simply the 'mapping' of society or the result of natural forces, ideas central to the Chicago School and others.[62] Sure enough, Reitman's map indicates the rôle of the press, the police and the courts in populating his outcast islands. If newspaper reports are to be believed, he condemned and cursed almost every branch of respectable society involved in the construction and protection of the 'Land of Respectability'. The map stands in sharp contrast to the diagrams of Burgess and his colleagues. One wonders what would happen if Reitman's islands, rather than Burgess's rings, were part of the secondary school geography curriculum.

On the far right of the map are three cities/towns that form a fairly classic triumvirate of class-based identities: Poor City (working class), Middle Town (middle class) and Richville (upper class). These are marked respectively by the attributes of ignorance, stupidity and arrogance. Together they make up the 'Land of Respectability'. The remainder of the mainland forms the 'Peninsular of Submerged Hope' and is separated from 'The Land of Respectability' by a three-part barrier made up of the police, the press and the courts. The Peninsular includes a number of failed reforms and reforming movements, including socialism, single tax, direct action and compromise. All of these were being promoted in the United States during Reitman's career. All, the map would suggest, had failed to make a difference. The hope invested in each of them was metaphorically submerged. Finally, the map shows several ports and entry points on the mainland's coastline. The ports appear to be both departure points and possible entry points. Port Direct Action, Port Injustice and Port Jobless all point towards ways in which formerly respectable people could be banished to the outcast islands. Unemployment, involvement in direct action and injustice at the hands of the establishment all provide routes out of respectability. On the lower half of the coast there are a number of piers or jetties that might provide ways back in to the Land of Respectability. These include formal and informal mechanisms of inclusion and assimilation, including law, religion, tradition, patriotism and conventionality.

The outcast islands represent an array of groups excluded (by choice or accident) from the mainland. The location of the islands appears to be significant in relation to the various ports along the shore of the peninsular. Nearest to the mainland is a group of islands labelled Old Age, Orphans, Sick Poor, Disable Isle and Insane Isle. Collectively these are called the Poverty Islands. The nearest port to them is Port Injustice, suggesting that Reitman believed that various forms of injustice created the outcast. This can be compared with Radical Island (at the bottom of the map), which appears to be most closely linked to Port Direct Action, perhaps pointing to the way various groups become outcasts due to their activist rôles. Included on Radical Isle are anarchists, free-love advocates and Tolstoy. (As a self-confessed anarchist-sociologist, this was probably Reitman's isle too.) It is interesting that the inhabitants of Radical Isle are outcasts, while advocates of socialism and the single tax are placed on a Peninsular of Submerged Hope, among strategies and struggles that have failed or become submerged. Reitman was always keen to dissociate himself from socialism and Communism. The other islands are home to non-white racial groups, criminals, vagrants and prostitutes, all made outcast by injustice and joblessness. The links made on this map between criminality, vagrancy and prostitution, including bridges returning vagrants and prostitutes to Criminal Island, are interesting. Vagrant Island includes four towns that reflect the by now familiar triumvirate of bum(town), tramp(ie) and hobo(ville) in addition to 'Beggar'. The links with prostitution are particularly noteworthy, as vagrancy and prostitution are often connected in the imaginations of social commentators (see chapter Four).

In the bottom left-hand corner of the map are two curiously shaped symbols denoting utopia and freedom, located as far away from the Land of Respectability as possible but not too far from Radical Isle. Also, three ferry services linking the mainland and islands are marked. These transitional lines of communication seem to indicate the ways of becoming outcast – economically, pathologically and psychologically. In 1910 'pathological' meant deviant, to indulge in inappropriate activities (prostitution, vagrancy, sex outside of marriage); 'psychological' pointed towards literal insanity and other lesser mental infirmities; 'economic' indicated the processes of employment and unemployment most often overlooked by social reformers and formal social scientists at the time.

Although we do not have the text of Reitman's Outcast Night lecture, we do have an extensive collection of papers that indicate the thinking underpinning the map. Indeed, this was not the only time that Reitman referred to his work as 'geography'. On 21 July 1939 he gave a lecture – 'The Geography of the Underworld and Mental Topography of the Educator' – at the University of Chicago to a group of educators. (This lecture was linked to one of the tours of the underworld Reitman frequently led for the benefit of scholars at the University.) In his lecture Reitman angrily remarked on the lack of connection between the actuality (as he saw it) of the 'Geography of the Underworld' and the ideas of educators in formal education (their 'Moral Topography'). He portrays the Geography of the Underworld' as one of destitution, unemployment, vice and disease. He reels off statistics ranging from 12 million unemployed to two million gamblers, arguing that 'one out of every ten of the pupils that you will try to educate will go into the world to kill, steal, lie, cheat, and peddle their bodies in order to secure food, shelter and other things.'[63] He goes on to berate the audience for having failed to make the conditions of their pupils any better. 'For all the good that you do', he asserts, 'the majority of your students would be just as well as if they had never come into contact with you.'[64] Reitman was never one to make half a criticism though, and in his conclusion he accuses the teachers of being in some way responsible for an unfair and exploitative society. He does this by pointing out how many people were being robbed, not by petty criminals, but by America's banks and businesses. 'Where do you suppose the bankers and the brokers and the business men and the exploiters of labor get their first idea of trimming the public? Why, from you lovely teachers of course – the ideals you taught them helped them to be better stealers and crooks.'[65] In addition, he suggests that the teachers in his audience inculcated a sense of patriotism in their students that bred war and warmongers and diverted both attention and money from dealing with the issues of exclusion. He ended with the plea that they change the ideals and values – the Moral Topography – they introduce to their students:

> You teachers taught your students to be stupid patriots, exploiters, successful and superior. Now teach your students to have genuine high ideals – to be co-operative, democratic and to build a world without jails, hospitals, relief organisations, where every man and woman has an opportunity to earn an honest living.[66]

In this lecture it is clear that Reitman was pointing towards a mismatch between the 'Moral Topography' of the teachers and the geography of the world many of their students were about to enter. While it was his view that the former revolved around idealized families, the idea that education was sure to solve problems in and of itself and patriotic ideas of nationhood and citizenship, the latter was a world of exploitation, exclusion and destitution that remained unchallenged by the morality and education of the teachers.

Both the map of the Outcast Islands and the facts of Reitman's life indicate a number of similarities with current social and cultural thought. Most importantly, Reitman was concerned with marginalization and difference. While it may be argued that the formal sociology of the Chicago School (for instance) was concerned with these themes, it is also clear that Reitman looked on them rather differently. While Chicago sociologists produced colourful and evocative accounts of the lives of 'deviants' such as hobos, gangs and taxi-dance-hall girls, these ethnographic monographs were subsumed within overarching theories of arrival and assimilation based on ecological root metaphors.[67] The assumption was that the various subcultures in the city would and should assimilate to dominant mores and moralities. So the suburbs in Burgess's model of the city were the inevitable end-point for all deviant groups. The Land of Respectability, on the other hand, is a place marked by arrogance, ignorance and stupidity – not a social space to aspire to, nor one that inevitably assimilates all difference. The Land of Respectability is a space that consistently excludes and rejects, creating islands of outcasts.

The identities and voices of marginalized people were important to Reitman. Recall that the lecture on social geography was part of a programme of outcasts presenting their views on society to an interested audience. As well as being a hobo for many years, Reitman spent much of his life getting marginal voices heard in a number of places, including at his own Hobo College. His work was also notable for the number of different groups he sought to work with, for and on. The map of Outcast Islands indicates a plethora of groups from prostitutes to the disabled, from the insane to the homeless.

Finally, Reitman's geography is notable for the attention paid to the forces that lead to and maintain exclusion and, inversely, encourage assimilation. Injustice, unemployment and political activism are all seen as forces leading to outcast status, while law, religion, patriotism and tradition all encourage assimilation. In addition, Reitman's map points to the defensive barriers of the media, the police and legal system placed around the Land of Respectability. Clearly, the processes of inclusion and exclusion are multiple and non-deterministic, but they are sharply and pointedly defined.[68]

As with law and classification tables, diagrams and other forms of visualisation in the social sciences are important ways of constructing knowledge about people and their practices. Reitman's map is indicative of how different his knowledge was from that of Burgess and other Chicago School theorists. In its emphasis on marginality, its concern for the voices of 'others' and its consistent indication of the multiple forces of inclusion and exclusion, Reitman's map, in the context of the rest of his work, prefigures some of the distinguishing features of social and cultural thought in the 1990s. His comments on the 'Moral Topography' of the educator were indicative of his uneasy relationship with formal social and scientific enquiry. In addition, the evidence of Reitman's relationship with formal social enquiry underlines the very different moral geographies of Reitman and his established contemporaries.

A number of letters Reitman wrote make it quite clear that his relationships with formal and acceptable academic knowledge were uneasy. He was, on occasion, certainly excluded from the halls of formal academia and science. In several letters he comments that he has a less than comfortable relationship with the Department of Sociology at the University of Chicago. In a letter to Harvey Locke, a sociologist at Indiana University, on the subject of homosexuality, he explained that 'I see Burgess and Blume and the rest of the sociologists occasionally. I am not quite anathema but I always make them uncomfortable when I ask them to let me lecture to their students.'[69] In another letter, to Victor Evjan, he recounts an occasion when he was literally excluded from an Urban Problems class he had previously been invited to speak at:

Last night I was engaged to conduct a sociological tour for the Urban Problems class at the University of Chicago, and President Hutchins and Dean Gilkey of the University forbade the lecture at the last moment. They don't like my method of doing things. In public and in print I have said Edith Abbott and the Social Service Administration were training students to be efficient social workers and in order to get jobs for all the students they needed plenty of poverty, misery, slums, insane and sick. On another occasion I said that President Hutchins was a Fascist and the University of Chicago had no desire to prevent syphilis but wanted a lot of syphilis so their students could make diagnosis and cure the disease.[70]

Reitman also had a relationship with formal social reformers that was tenuous at best, for he believed them to be acting in the interests of the establishment rather than of those they aimed to serve. One social reformer, Graham Taylor, was particularly active in Chicago, working there with Chicago Commons and Jane Addam's Settlement House. Reitman wrote to him after reading his book on social reform, *Pioneering on Social Frontiers*.

My dear Mr. Taylor:

Your evaluations of the rich and powerful men is bourgeois if not servile. Without meaning to be I am sure your defence and explanation of the rich give evidence that you have enjoyed their favor.

Your explanation of the anarchist and the radicals is patronising but not illuminating.

To me your book sounds like a speech before an exclusive lady society where you have to be careful what you say ...

The man from Mars reading your book would think that the Chic. [Chicago] Commons, the Hull House, and the University Settlement had made a contribution to human suffering and has solved some social problems. When you know perfectly well that there is more unemployment, delinquency, perversion, police brutality, than when you, Jane Addams, and Mary McDowell started.

You will admit that when you came to Chic. there was the nucleus of a revolutionary movement in America that bid fair to overthrow the present economic order in society. And if that revolutionary movement is dead or distorted the capitalistic society have you and your colleagues to thank more than anyone else.

Down thru the years you have always been most kind and

friendly to me. And I have always had a kindly feeling towards you. And so when I say to you that the record of your life to me is the story of a colossal failure, I do so with genuine regrets.[71]

On another occasion Reitman took issue with a review in the *Chicago Daily News* that Taylor had written of Reitman's book about pimps, *The Second Oldest Profession*, in which Taylor paid homage to the forces of law and order:

Were you thinking? when you wrote page 136.

Neither by my own or other's questioning opinions have I swerved in my abiding loyalty to law as not only the indispensable basis and bond of any social order, but also as the best friend of each and all ...

I reach out my hand to you and say I think the Government and the Rich are more wicked and Powerful because you Pioneered on Social Frontiers.

There was not a complete barrier between Reitman, the Chicago sociologists and Social Reformers. Clearly Reitman contacted them frequently, even if the communications were marked by hostility and anxiety. He was asked to give lectures in the University of Chicago, and sometimes he did give them. He also arranged for Hobo orators to talk at the same university. Professor Mike Smith of New York ('Chinatown Whitie' to his fellow hobos) gave a talk on unemployment and Frank Gibbons ('Chicago Red') discussed the customs of insects in lodging-houses.[72] Reitman himself claimed that he wanted to reform both sociologists and social workers in order to make their work more useful and relevant to those they studied. In an address to the American Sociological Congress in 1935 he explained that 'My present work is to encourage citizens of the underworld to reform, I'm also trying to reform sociologists. I'm trying to teach them to concentrate less on research work and more on the application of their studies to the people I know.'[73]

Reitman was a bridge between the worlds of formal social enquiry and the lives of marginal(ized) people in Chicago's Hobohemia. He was instrumental, for instance, in getting Nels Anderson admitted into the Department of Sociology in order to undertake PhD research on the American hobo. Anderson had been a frequent visitor to the Hobo College in Chicago both as a hobo and as a newspaper seller. Anderson heard Reitman give a speech in which Reitman condemned social workers for taking a cold and scientific view of the poor, thus promoting impersonal relationships. Anderson and Reitman had coffee after the talk and agreed that there needed to be compassionate research into Chicago's homeless. Reitman then encouraged Dr William Evans, head of Chicago's Public Health Department, to fund Anderson's studies of the hobo. Reitman appears several times in Anderson's monograph, most prominently in the chapter 'Personalities of Hobohemia', in which he is 'King of the Hobos'.[74] Thus Reitman ironically became part of the subject-matter of the formal social science that he found so difficult to live with.

Reitman's knowledge and the social geography he invoked was clearly contrary to this circumscription of the proper that lies at the heart of scientific rationality.[75] Reitman lived a life that frequently ignored the boundaries of propriety. He would give up his medical practice to become a hobo; consort with anarchists, promote birth control, lead demonstrations and frequent the spaces of the city that 'official knowledge' chose to ignore or deride. It is not surprising that his analysis of the social system, as made visual in his map, also failed to fit into the neat boundaries of academic ordering. His social geography is not a part of our formal intellectual heritage because Reitman was not part of a discipline or a department, unlike the more familiar (and equally fantastic) diagrams of Ernest Burgess.

THE CLASSIFICATION OF TRAMPS

A characteristic endeavour of early social science, including that of the Chicago School and Ben Reitman, was to construct tables and lists of categories and classes. The degree to which tramps and hobos were subject to the classifying gaze of social science was extraordinary. Almost all taxonomies began with the tripartite division of hobo, tramp and bum described earlier. Anderson uses this scheme in *The Hobo*: 'There are three types of the genus vagrant: the hobo, the tramp, and the bum. The hobo works and wanders, the tramp dreams and wanders and the bum drinks and wanders.'[76] This is but one variant of the distinction. Another is attributed by Anderson to St John Tucker of the Hobo College in Chicago:

> A hobo is a migratory worker. A tramp is a migratory non-worker. A bum is a stationary non-worker. Upon the labor of the *migratory worker* all the basic industries depend. He goes forth from the crowded slavemarkets to hew the forests, build and repair the railroads, tunnel mountains and build ravines. His is the labor that harvests the wheat and cuts the ice in winter. All of these are hobos.[77]

Anderson based his own classification schemes on this well-established tripartite division elaborating on it to produce five 'types': the seasonal worker; the transient or occasional worker or hobo; the tramp who dreams and wanders and works only when it is convenient; the bum who seldom wanders and seldom works; the home guard who lives in Hobohemia and does not leave town.[78] Anderson was well aware that the word 'tramp' had become a blanket derogatory term for all homeless men and he sought to provide a stricter definition of the term:

> He is usually thought of, by those familiar with his natural history, as an able-bodied individual who has the romantic passion to see the country and gain new experience without work. He is a specialist at 'getting by' ... He is typically neither a drunkard nor a bum, but an easy-going individual who lives from hand to mouth for the mere joy of living.[79]

Before Anderson's work on the hobo, the classic text on the subject was Alice Solenberger's *One Thousand Homeless Men* (1911), in which she claimed that:

> Almost all 'tramps' are 'homeless men' but by no means are all homeless men tramps. The homeless man may be an able-bodied workman without a family, he may be a runaway boy, a consumptive temporarily stranded on his way to a health resort, an irresponsible, feeble minded, or insane man, but unless he is also a professional wanderer he is not a 'tramp'.[80]

*One Thousand Homeless Men* is an extremely thorough and exhaustive account of homeless men in Chicago in the first decade of the century. It was the first systematic survey of vagrancy in the United States. Her observations were gathered from men who used the Chicago Municipal Lodging House. What stands out in the book is the care she put into a comprehensive categorization of vagrants. Rather than simply separating the men into the worthy and the unworthy or the able-bodied and the disabled, Solenberger organized them into categories such as the 'crippled and maimed', the insane, the aged, the epileptic and runaway boys. Some 220 out of the 1,000 men are described as 'tramps'.

Once sociologists and social reformers started to study the tramp, the original division of vagrants into tramps, hobos and bums became infinitely more complicated. The issues of work and mobility still formed the bedrock of sociological classifications but other differences were introduced until classification tables were constructed that seemed inordinately long. Anderson, mixing an ethnographic desire to excavate the tramps' knowledge about themselves with the impulse to classify, asked some tramps and hobos to produce their own systems of classification. One such table was provided by James Moore, 'the Daredevil Hobo':[81]

I TRAMPS OF SOCIETY

(Those who have some graft or excuse)

1 Missionaries – organized beggars or parasites.

2 Professional beggars.

3 Tourists and autoists; these have taken the place of the old wagon tramp. Tramp families may go about in autos; gypsies, for example.

4 Vacationists.

5 Street fakers; those who work some selling game.

6 Loiterers; those who stay home but do not work – the idle rich.

II TRAMPS OF TRAMPDOM

(Those who roam the country without funds and do not work unless forced to. They aim to be parasitic.)

1 Bundle stiff; he carries his blankets and equipment on his back, and stops where he likes, as long as he likes.

2 Yegg; is a rogue and a desperado.

3 Gay cat; one who serves as a scout for a yegg. a young yegg.

4 Jungle buzzard; any kind of tramp may be a jungle buzzard if he spends his time cooking food or washing his clothes in the jungle.

III HOBOES AND WANDERERS

(Those who aim to work, but not long in any place)

1 Pikers – those who wander the highways.
   a) mush fakers = those who mend umbrellas.
   b) Hand organ man; often foreigners.
   c) Grindstone man; those who sharpen tools and file saws.

2 Rattlers; those who ride freight trains only.

3 Ramblers; those who ride passenger trains only.
   a) Foxes; those who steal hat-checks and flim-flam the conductors.
   b) Wolves; those who ride outside.
      x) Catchers – ride the 'blinds,' the engine, etc.
      y) Danglers; ride underneath.
      z) Roofers; ride the decks exclusively.

IV BUMS

(Those who will not work, the dregs of society.)

1 Moocher – begs money on the street.

2 Panhandler – begs 'lumps' and 'set-downs' at back doors.

3 Floppers; live in flop houses and around parks and poolhalls.

4 Jockers; train boys to be crooks and beggars.

5 Road kid; a boy who serves a jocker.

6 Punk – a boy who has broken away from his jocker.

7 Pokey bum; so-called because he 'pokes' along with no interest, is stupid and sometimes weak-minded, begs and picks up food.

8 Proper bum; thinks toil is a disgrace, keeps clean, and is seldom drunk; he is a 'manager.'

9 Marauder bum – does destructive things.

10 Mission bum – will get on his knees for a ham sandwich.

V OTHER CLASSES

(Insane, venereals, dope-heads, women, men with fits.)

1 Cripples
    a) Wingle – one arm off.
    b) Peggie – one leg off.
    c) Halfie – two legs off.

2 Stew bum; begs meat from slaughter houses, bread from bakeries; will steal potatoes, corn, fruit, or such, from the farmer; will milk the farmer's cow; lives in the jungles.

3 Sponger – a man who sponges off his fellow bums.

4 Distillery bum; hangs around distilleries and breweries.
    a) White line bum – drinks pure alcohol.
    b) 'Alkie' – one who takes his alcohol half-and-half.
    c) 'Rummy' – drinks anything he can get.

5 Women tramps.
    a) Prostitutes.
    b) Dope fiends and drunks.
    c) Mental defectives.

6 Men who have fits or diseases, and leave home for shame.

7 Old men.

This table is not unlike others of the time. As with any attempt at classi-fication it is constructed around a set of characteristics that are used to progressively differentiate between groups of people who fall under one general description. The key characteristics that are used here are work, mobility, bodily attributes and social relations. The distinction between bums, tramps and hobos is maintained but then elaborated. Mobility, for instance, is broken down into ways of being mobile, such as riding on freight trains or not; riding on the inside or outside; on the back or the front; on top or underneath. Similarly, work and its alternative are sub-divided into categories, such as those who mend umbrellas and those who sharpen knives. Anderson discusses other categories designated by work, such as a skinner (a man who drives horses or mules), a 'rust-eater' (a man who works laying tracks) and a 'splinter-belly' (a man who does rough carpentry work). Bodily attributes play a key rôle. The risks engendered by riding freight trains were clearly considerable and tramps and their observers typically had a litany of names for tramps with bodily impair-ments resulting from accidents. The three provided by James Moore can be supplemented by dozens of other names such as Fingers (a train rider who lost one or more fingers), Mitts (a train rider who lost one or both hands), Righty (a train rider who lost both the right arm and leg) and so on.[82] Social relations between tramps were also important in the creation of these tables. James Moore's table includes references to Jockers, Punks and Gay Cats, who are all defined by their (often implicitly homosexual) relationships to each other.

The drawing up of categories, typologies and classification tables was a characteristic endeavour of early social science. Tables of vagrants and vagabonds had existed for a while before tramps became a category. Once established as a category, people referred to as tramps could be counted, subdivided, analysed and objectified. Sociological categoriza-tions, like legal definitions, are forms of knowledge that were implicated in making up the tramp. Categories have a way of becoming the taken-for-granted commonsense bedrock of the social world, and yet they are also social products.[83] Sociology (and other social sciences) records itself as much as it records the world. The production of ethnographies and taxonomies is part of the way in which society produces a set of social problems that are seen as self-evidently worthy of debate. The pro-duction of categories by academics is a way of 'officializing' a problem and making it a matter of public concern. Sociology in particular needs to have 'social problems' in order to legitimize itself and generate oppor-tunities for funding, contracts and the production of research bodies. Anderson's book is a case in point. The title-page states that *The Hobo* is 'a study prepared for the Chicago Council of Social Agencies under the direction of the Committee on Homeless Men'. The preface to the book includes a statement by the Committee, which includes the following:

> The object of this inquiry, from the standpoint of the Committee, was to secure those facts which would enable social agencies to deal intelligently with the problems created by the continuous ebb and flow, out of and into Chicago, of tens of thousands of foot-loose and homeless men. Only through an understanding both of the human nature of the migratory casual worker, and of the economic and social forces which have shaped his personality, could there be devised any fundamental program for social agencies interested in his welfare.[84]

Clearly, Anderson's work was, in part, implicated in the production of the tramp as a social problem and, as such, produced, through his work, the problem he was allegedly reporting. Many of the objects of social science are 'social problems' made formal in an academic arena. We need only think of contemporary catch phrases such as 'globalization' or 'social exclusion' to realize that the products of social science are quickly institutionalized into social facts that are subsequently used to legitimate themselves. Just by directing funding at a problem it is possible to create it as a social fact. Many of the norms of social science both at the time of the Chicago School and now are implicated in quite unconscious ways into the production of social reality. Pierre Bourdieu invites reflection on

> all those things that have become so common, so taken for granted, that nobody pays any attention to them, such as the structure of a court of law, the space of a museum, a voting booth, the notion of 'occupational injury' or of 'cadre', a two by two table or, quite simply, the act of writing or taping. History thus conceived is inspired not by an antiquarian interest but by a will to understand why and how one understands.[85]

Taxonomies and categorization tables are one such taken-for-granted way in which understanding is formed. Tramps and hobos were minutely differentiated by early sociologists and became a sociological problem produced by the collective work of the construction of social reality. Anderson, Park and others were deeply implicated in the production of problems that needed experts to solve them and committees to fund the research. Sociology, through the production of the tramp, was producing itself.

I began this chapter with the question 'How were the tramp and hobo known in the late nineteenth century?' Clearly the tramp and the hobo were the objects of many forms of knowledge. Lay definitions, legal codes, sociological taxonomies and Chicago-style ethnography were all ways of knowing the tramp, as were the ideas of radical anarchists such as Reitman and the tramps themselves. What is clear is that each type of knowledge plays a rôle in making up the tramp. Following Ian Hacking's pragmatic and sceptical definition of 'dynamic nominalism' I believe that tramps are more like gloves than horses. That is to say that the category 'tramp' and the thing 'tramp' emerged simultaneously ('if new models of description come into being, new possibilities for action come into being in consequence'[86]). The implications of such an argument are that individuals (as members of social groups) have new possibilities – new potential ways of being, when new categories are invented. Some time during the 1870s in the United States it became possible to be a tramp. Being a tramp meant far more than simply being called one. Definitions and categories are far more than mere words to describe. Rather they are ways of acting on those who are being defined. The consequences of being a tramp were potentially severe, and it is therefore no surprise that some of those so labelled sought to distance themselves from tramphood.

# 4  Gendering the Tramp

On the 11 June 1886, many readers of the *Minneapolis Tribune* would have noticed a small item at the bottom of page 5 which explained that

> Last evening a poor Swede girl, aged 23 years was arrested for being found dressed in man's clothing. She was in the employ of a dairy-man named Farnquist, who lives about 4 miles out of the east side. He paid her $10 a month, and her duties were to herd cattle and do a man's work. Finding a dress inconvenient in the brush she put on a man's suit of clothes, without knowing that she was offending against the law.

In all likelihood the nameless woman was a migrant labourer – one of the millions who travelled the country looking for work during the cycle of depressions that hit America between 1873 and 1939. Her story – one that is all the more poignant for its brevity – invites us to investigate some of the trouble that gender and mobility causes for the logic of the category 'tramp'. This woman in a man's clothes encapsulates one of the problems women faced at the end of the nineteenth century. Female tramps and hobos led lives on the edge. The ways they managed their existence and the reactions others had to them differentiate these women from both the men who they shared the boxcars with and other categories of women who travelled.

The marginal position of the poor and wandering woman is also evident in the classification scheme of James Moore – 'the daredevil hobo'. There is a section at the bottom of his list labelled 'other classes'. This section includes 'insane, venereals, dope-heads, women, men with fits'. This curious hodgepodge of people labelled 'other' comprises those who did not fit into the definitions of bums, tramps and hobos provided higher up the table. Women tramps form section Five under 'other classes', and they are further subdivided into: (a) prostitutes, (b) dope fiends and drunks and (c) mental defectives. The need to place female tramps under the heading of 'other' is indicative of the problems posed by the presence of wandering women for those who sought to understand the world of the tramp. In this chapter I consider the frequently invisible world of female tramps and the problems their existence posed to anxious observers who were keen to maintain their expectations of who tramps were. To many, including those who wrote tramp laws, tramps were male by definition; so the possibility of a female tramp was discounted from the outset. To others, though, the possibility of female tramps caused a great deal of anxiety, for they appeared to have transgressed many of the boundaries that separated the masculine world from the feminine one. Exploring the nascent category of the female tramp reveals a great deal about the process of making up the tramp in general, about the connection between power and mobility and about the gendering of spaces and the practices associated with them. But first, let us consider the position of women outside of domestic space in general in the nineteenth century.

### THE *FLÂNEUSE*, THE PROSTITUTE AND THE LADY TRAVELLER

The problematical existence of the female tramp and the attempts to produce knowledge about her were linked to a wider context of anxiety about women outside the home that pervaded nineteenth- and early twentieth-century consciousness. We need hardly be reminded that women were firmly placed in the domestic, private sphere, while public and mobile space was considered masculine. The transgressions of women moving through public space called into question these associations. It might be argued that women who did move through the public spaces of these times experienced a unique kind of freedom and emancipation from the constraints of home, but work done on 'public women' suggests that the link between mobility and freedom for women was a highly ambivalent one. Three figures dominate the literature on women and mobility in the Victorian era – the *flâneuse*, the prostitute and the lady traveller. Studies of them reveal how feminine mobility rarely achieves the kind of transcendence associated with masculine travel and adventure.

The *flâneur* is a male literary figure associated with the poet Charles Baudalaire.[1] The opening up of Paris and the construction of the boulevards created new, archetypally modern, space where pedestrians could stroll anonymously, taking in the displays in the new shop windows, gazing at fellow strollers and revelling in the everyday. When the activities of these pedestrians were added to a bohemian desire for the low and the marginal the *flâneur* was created. This imaginary figure has been seen by some as a 'modern hero' moving easily through the spaces of modernity.[2] Feminist critics, however, have pointed out that the freedoms were clearly masculine ones.[3]

Both the use of the pedestrian as the hero of modernity and the celebration of the *flâneur* have been criticized for their essentially masculine orientation. Only men could really inhabit the streets as pedestrians, enjoying freedom of movement in modernity's new public spaces. The freedom of the *flâneur* depended on the ability to move alone in public, to look and not be looked at. Women in the nineteenth century (and arguably even now), could not simply stroll around on their own without being noticed and gazed at by men.[4] It is widely acknowledged that women today do not have the same freedom to walk around the city, especially at night. While it is no longer disreputable for women to inhabit public space, it is now considered to be dangerous. Although it is the case that most violence against women happens in the supposedly safe confines of the home, there is still a geography of fear that suggests public spaces are unsafe for women (but, conversely, that they are safe for men).[5] Despite this, there are many instances when women have ventured forth as pedestrians and enjoyed the freedom and exhilaration of walking the city streets.[6] In *The Sphinx in the City*,[7] Elizabeth Wilson has argued powerfully for the liberatory effects of city life on women's lives. She suggests that the women strolling though nineteenth-century department stores were more or less enjoying the freedom of strolling in the city. Even prostitutes were, in Wilson's opinion, compatible with the character of the *flâneur*. It seems safe to say, however, that women in the United States at the end of the nineteenth century could not easily venture out alone, and if they did it was only at certain times and in certain clearly defined spaces. Modernity and mobility were both marked as masculine. A sure sign of the restrictions placed on women across the Atlantic in Paris were the actions of George Sand, a female literary figure, who dressed up as a man in order to enjoy the streets of the city: 'no-one knew me, no-one looked at me ... I was an atom in that immense crowd'.[8]

One of the problems for a woman venturing out alone was that she might be mistaken for a prostitute. The figure of the prostitute was seen as threatening by respectable observers on both sides of the Atlantic. In Britain, where William Acton had published his survey of prostitution in 1857, social reformers and commentators described prostitution as the greatest evil of the age, one that threatened to undo society. Prostitutes were metaphorically linked to the French Revolution as a symbol of the overturning of 'natural' hierarchies, and all manner of devices, procedures and institutions were created and suggested to solve the problem.[9] In France prostitution was perceived in even more extreme ways, and prostitutes had been investigated at length by Alexandre Parent-Duchatelet in 1836. The French social historian Alain Corbin has argued that the body of the prostitute in France represented the threat of death, disease and decay and necessitated the kind of controls proposed by Duchatelet and others.[10]

In America, discussions on prostitution became common in major cities such as New York. Prostitution became increasingly visible during the mid-nineteenth century. And what disturbed observers

> was not just the number of women who bargained with men for sex, but the identity of those women. Moreover, the entire context of the transaction was changing, as prostitution moved out of the bawdy houses of the poor into cosmopolitan spaces like Broadway … Prostitution was becoming urbane. The trade was quite public in the business district as well as in the poor neighbourhood, a noticeable feature of the ordinary city landscape.[11]

The spatiality of commercial sex had changed from a predominantly private phenomenon to a noticeably public one. Certain areas of the city, particularly around Broadway and Five Points, were increasingly identified by the visibility of commercial sex. The public spaces of New York became points of exchange for sexual services. Prostitution gave women a relatively independent income through a very public form of trade that proved to be an affront to patriarchal expectations. The existence of prostitution on the streets was particularly offensive in a world in which women were associated with the home and the domestic as a sphere of influence. Public space was gendered as male and the existence of women there, whether in Paris, London or New York, brought the erotic into public view.

At a time when women were most closely associated with the private realm, prostitutes were the clearest examples of 'public women'. Elizabeth Wilson has gone so far as to suggest that perhaps all women who inhabited the new public spaces of the city – pavements, cafés, theatres – were, metaphorically at least, prostitutes: 'The very presence of unattended, unowned, women constituted a threat both to male power and to male frailty.'[12] It is not surprising, therefore, that female tramps were frequently mentioned in the same breath as prostitutes.

At the other end of the class spectrum was the 'imperial lady traveller'.[13] This character has been the object of much speculation and her mobility has been held up as a sign of new, if ambivalent, freedoms available to respectable, middle-class women from imperial centres.[14] (These women were almost all of middle-class origin from the imperial centre of Britain.) Their desire to travel was based on a number of motives, including the twin tools of capitalist imperialism – science and trade. Travellers such as Mary Kingsley and Isabella Bird were able to shake off some of the constraints imposed on them at home by engaging in various travels to colonial margins or national frontiers. Their mobility allowed them to produce new kinds of knowledge through their travel writing that often contradicted or revised commonly held assumptions that had been the product of masculine exploration. The freedom their mobility gave them was ambivalent insofar as these women were usually from imperial centres and carried the privileges of home with them. In some senses these privileges were experienced as constraints rather than freedoms, for women were forced to take 'home' with them as they moved. One way that these privileges were expressed was in dress: the women typically retained a sense of propriety by dressing in Western feminine clothing. The blessings of a good thick skirt have become metonymic for Mary Kingsley's insistence on retaining a feminine appearance for the sake of her gender and nation: 'I never even wear a masculine collar and tie', Kingsley wrote, 'and as for encasing the more earthward extremities of my anatomy – you know what I mean – well, I would rather perish on a public scaffold.'[15]

Kingsley was certainly not alone in her choice of feminine clothing. Birgitta Ingemanson has commented on the odd disjuncture between the increased freedoms associated with the mobility of women in Edwardian and Victorian times and their reluctance to rebel against the inhibiting clothing of Victorian homelife. 'Even in a period of dress reform and budding interest in women's sports', she points out, 'the great women travellers coolly persisted in donning their corsets and hats, dining in open nature on white linen cloths, and taking their stoves and often-intricate household utensils – in effect their homes – with them.'[16] Ingemanson's suggestion is that these polite lady travellers were pursuing a strategy of using a 'facade of propriety' to hide and legitimate the freedom that came with their mobility. The paraphernalia of 'home', including clothing, enabled the women to be mobile by providing a disguise that helped to overcome the obstacles to their mobility. The adoption of feminine clothing by otherwise rebellious travellers was also a way of distancing themselves from the cause of female emancipation.[17] Well-known travellers such as Kate Marsdon and May French Sheldon confirmed Mary

Kingsley's attitude and were opposed to wearing clothes that were more practical for the rigours of adventurous travel. Another Victorian traveller, Daisy Bates, was quite clear about her dress code while living in aboriginal Australia:

> It was a fastidious toilet, for throughout my life I have adhered to the simple but exact dictates of fashion as I left it, when Victoria was Queen – a neat white blouse, stiff collar and ribbon tie, a dark skirt and coat, stout, and serviceable trim shoes and neat black stockings, a sailor hat and fly-veil, and, for my excursions to the camps, always a dust-coat and a sunshade. Not until I was in meticulous order would I emerge from my tent, dressed for the day.[18]

Mobility and travel, like anything else, are marked by structures of gender, class and race in addition to the forces of nationalism, imperialism and colonialism. The adoption of feminine clothing by these generally middle-class women reaffirmed their whiteness and thus supported a racial distinction between themselves and the inhabitants of the countries they explored. As we shall see, the material mobility of female tramps was quite different from that of lady travellers and the *flânerie* of George Sand. While the maintenance of femininity provided a guise for the travels of Mary Kingsley, the guise of masculinity helped poor, white, female tramps avoid some of the dangers of the road. The clothing that women wore in order to enable mobility helps us to differentiate between forms and experiences of mobility. What, then, of the tramp?

GENDERING THE TRAMP SCARE

The assumption that tramps were men was codified in the legal definitions of tramps instituted by nineteen states in the ten-year period following 1876. In chapter Three I pointed towards the way in which nineteenth-century tramp laws and the discovery of classification schemes helped bring the tramp, as a social category, into being. In terms of legal definitions, tramps were, in most states, men. Section 1341 of the Connecticut tramp law of 1902 states that 'These provisions shall not apply to any female, or minor under the age of 16 years, nor to any blind person, nor to any beggar roving within the limits of the town in which he resides.'[19] More fixedly, the 1897 code of Iowa, section 5134, asserts that 'Any male person, sixteen years of age or over, physically able to perform manual labor, who is wandering about, practising common begging, or having no visible calling or business to maintain himself, and is unable to show reasonable efforts in good faith to secure employment, is a tramp.'[20] Technically, then, the majority of tramp laws did not apply to women who, legally, could not be tramps. In the eyes of the court tramps were men.

As far as the courts were concerned, tramps had to be male and there were literally, therefore, no female tramps. It was not only the formality of law that found it difficult to admit the possibility of women riding the rails. People found it hard to accept the existence of the female tramp. To understand why this was so problematical, we must consider the key rôle of gender in the moral panic that surrounded the tramp. The threat of the 'tramp scare' was, in part, a threat to home and women. The tramp was clearly supposed to be male. Knowledge is not simply the tool of specialist fields such as law and sociology. Knowledge is something we all have. Often it is the case that the ways of knowing enshrined in formal codes that include law and sociological treatises are nothing more (or less) than formalized versions of what passes for common sense. One way that knowledge has typically been structured is through dualisms that serve to make the world intelligible in a seemingly commonsense way. One of the most pervasive dualistic ways of thinking is one that divides the world in terms of gender. The division of the world into masculine and feminine in Western thought has been connected to other pervasive dualisms, such as nature (feminine) and culture (masculine), or inside (feminine) and outside (masculine).[21] Recent feminist theory has convincingly pointed out that this dualistic way of knowing the world is a masculinist way of knowing one that promotes one half of the dualism above the other.[22] Dualisms attached to masculine/feminine almost universally claim the greatest importance for the masculine half of the binary. Thus it is often thought that the public (outside, active) is more significant than the private (inside, passive). These dualistic and masculinist ways of knowing are particularly clear in reactions to tramps, both male and female.

Stories appeared in many states in local newspapers about the 'tramp scare' during the years following 1870. In many instances the general sense of danger was reduced to a specific threat against domesticated women and the homes they inhabited. The *Philadelphia Press* of 14 July 1907 reported that for the preceding two-week period, 'the newspapers have each day printed one instance, and often two, of women walking on county roads in and around Philadelphia, or in the rural districts of Eastern Pennsylvania or Southern New Jersey, who have fled in terror from some tramp or vagrant.'[23] Newspapers were replete with stories of young girls walking in the country being exposed to tramps, or women at home being threatened by a tramp appearing at their doors asking for food or money. These stories were repeated by charity workers and politicians in their quest to have labour camps created or whipping-posts restored. Professor Francis Weyland of Yale, in a report on tramps delivered to a Conference of Boards of Public Charities in 1877, had described the tramp as 'a lazy shiftless, incorrigible, cowardly, utterly deprived savage ... he seems to have wholly lost all the better instincts and attributes of manhood. He will outrage an unprotected female, or rob a defenceless child, or burn an isolated barn ...'[24] Weyland went on to dismiss the possibility of rehabilitation for the tramp. Even the hardened criminal, he argued, could be saved by 'the strength and sacredness of family ties, the love of mother or wife, or child'.[25] The tramp, however, by definition had no such hope of redemption, for he had cut himself off 'from all influences which can minister to his improvement or elevation'.[26] A correspondent to the Committee on Tramps reported the reaction of a Massachusetts minister to the presence of tramps in his area. 'Twenty years ago', he asserted, 'any woman within two miles of his church would have been willing to come, without escort, to any evening service in it, and to return home in the same way'; now, however, 'no woman in the town would willingly go alone after dark a quarter of a mile from home.'[27]

The incident that was portrayed as the biggest threat to women during the tramp scare was the moment when the tramp arrived at the door of a house to beg for food or money. The woman at home, without a husband, was seen as particularly vulnerable. Henry Rood in the *Forum* in 1889 observed that there are 'few mothers and fewer daughters who, under such circumstances, would refuse to give food or clothing to a burly, unkempt tramp, who accompanied his request with threatening expression'.[28] He continued to recount the story of a Representative in Congress whose wife insisted that he leave the door to his safe unlocked, for she had seen too many tramps around to feel safe, and would rather be burgled than be confronted with a tramp in the middle of the night.

The tramp was constituted as a threat that was gendered as masculine. Tramps are portrayed as primarily young or middle-age white men. Discourses on respectability at the time painted a happy picture of secure family life as the source of a moral culture that was the bedrock for social stability. By their homelessness, tramps threatened one of the central images in American ideology and national mythology. The home was seen as the locus for moral individuals and good citizens. The mother and the home combined to ensure the moral education of the young. It was the time of *Ladies Home Journal* and the rise of 'domestic science'.[29] The masculine tramp, rootless and wandering, was thus a particularly menacing

21 The Historical Society of Pennsylvania, 'The Man
Who Came to Your Door Last Night'.

image. What was threatened was, among other things, the bodies of
women and children.

As well as appearing in editorials and learned papers, the tramp was a
favourite figure for cartoonists and illustrators (see chapter Six). He
appeared either as a foolish clown or a hostile threat and sometimes as
both at once. The tramp was made to appear threatening in these cartoons
by being placed at the boundary of the home, usually occupied by a
mother and/or child. Consider the illustration from the Exhibition of
the Philadelphia Society for Organising Charity in Philadelphia of 1916
(illus. 21). It is a typical example of the menacing image of the tramp that
prevailed in the United States between the mid-1870s and the 1930s. In it we
see the dark figure of the tramp at the door of the home, the hearth …
filled with bright whiteness and inhabited by the silhouette of a woman.
What constitutes the menace here, and what is being menaced? Most literally the woman is being threatened – the body of the woman is threatened

22 Illustration from *Harper's* magazine (1876).

with rape, the inside by the outside. The body of the anonymous woman is, of course, a sign for a huge array of other comforts imagined from the point of view of men. The home, morality, stability, innocence – all that is sweetness and light. Another illustration, this time from *Harper's* magazine in 1876, paints a similar picture (illus. 22). Here the tramp is both pathetic and threatening: a bedraggled man asking for money or food. The woman, this time less sexualized, protects her child and brandishes a wooden spoon. Outside we can see more men walking past, while inside dinner is cooking and the table is laid – a vision of homeliness. These two images represent the often split (but logically linked) representations of female sexuality through their respective bodies. While one appears primarily to signify a sexual body, the other is encoded as first and foremost a mother in a stable home and hearth. Both of these – the sexualized body and the maternal body – are threatened by the tramp at the door.

While there is no doubt that women would have felt threatened by the presence of tramps, there is also little doubt that this fear was developed and drawn on by men in order to amplify the tramp evil and support the need for desperate measures. Such methods may also have had the effect of dissuading women from being outside the home by creating a geography of fear that associated 'outside' with threatening mobile men.

The construction of the tramp evil, then, was dependant in part on a resource of familiar categorizations derived from and reinforcing assumptions about the proper place of men and women. The existence of tramps was understood in terms of already existing schemes of perception. An assumption that prevails in this construction of the tramp evil is that tramps and hobos are all men – an assumption that fits into a more general association between public space, mobility and masculinity.

## FEMALE TRAMPS – ADVENTURES IN CROSS-DRESSING

The fact is that not all riders of the rails were men; indeed, a very large number of women took to the road after 1870.[30] Thomas Minehan, in 1934, suggested that 'Never does a freight pull out of a large city without carrying some girls, disguised in overalls or army breeches, but just as certainly and just as appallingly homeless as the boys.'[31] A number of social reformers did mention the existence of female tramps in passing, often noting that between five and fifteen per cent of tramps were female. Based on observations made in 1933, Theodore Caplow explained that 'Both prostitutes and female hobos were on the road in considerable numbers at this time. In addition, between 10 and 25 per cent of the child tramps were girls.'[32] James Forbes noted the increase in the number of women among the tramp population. 'Of late', he wrote, 'even women have definitely abandoned the discipline of employment and lived as outcasts and wanderers, in defiance of society. But so far the number of female vagrants is negligible, and there seems little danger of individual tendencies developing into a popular movement.'[33]

Ben Reitman did spend some time attempting to gather statistics and information on women on the road. Figures he obtained from the Federal Emergency Relief Administration indicate that around five per cent of transients under care nationwide were women. A survey of 93 women transients recorded by Chicago's Cook County Service Bureau for Transients shows them originating in 31 states with the largest number (thirteen) from California.

*Sister of the Road* is Reitman's record of the life of Bertha Thompson, alias 'Boxcar Bertha'.[34] Boxcar Bertha was the nearest a female hobo came to becoming a romantic heroine. Publicity material for *Sister of the Road* emphasised the shock value of women on the road. The book was described as 'The frank uncensored story of a wandering woman of the underworld. Intimate facts of a woman hobo's methods and habits: a life story that has no parallel.'[35] The material also featured a list of 'facts' to draw in the reader:

23 Promotional material for Ben L. Reitman, *Sister of the Road* (New York, 1937).

DO YOU KNOW THAT —

In one year over 5,000 women hoboes attracted the attention of the United States Government?

Your own daughter or sister, given certain stimuli, may become a 'sister of the road?'

... Practically any woman without sex scruples can cross the continent almost any time and not pay a cent for transportation?

Women hoboes, not professionally prostitutes, depend in large measure upon their sex to gain food and lodging while 'on the road?'

A poster for the book features a woman dressed in a skirt and sweater walking along the road (illus. 23). It is accompanied by a text which tells us that

> In her roving career she has been not only a tramp, but also a woman of the underworld, companion of shoplifters and dope fiends, doctors, professors, anarchists, criminals and a poet. She has been a social research worker and the mother of a child of an unknown father. She saw one lover hung and another killed under the wheels of a freight train ...

Clearly the female tramp/hobo is being marketed here as a sensational account of deviance. This is indicative of the way in which the marginal and deviant so often become the object of romance and curiosity for an audience who can maintain a safe distance.

*Sister of the Road* itself provides some interesting observations of the rôle of travelling women. Bertha certainly recounts many meetings with other female hobos on her travels. Particularly notable are the numerous references to the ambiguous gender and sexual identities of the sisters of the road. Women that Bertha meets are more often than not dressed as men or look like men in some other way. 'Dorothy Mack', for instance, 'was a stout girl of twenty-four with dark brown eyes and hair combed back from the face like a man's'.[36] Two other women 'had their hair cut short like men's and at first glance they didn't look much like women'. Indeed, one of them was dressed in 'torn men's trousers and shirt'.[37] Chicago was the central meeting-point for sisters of the road, as it was for men. According to the author of *Sister of the Road*, 'They came in bronzed from hitch-hiking, in khaki, they came in ragged in men's overalls, having ridden freights, decking mail trains, riding the reefers ...'[38] The observations of women dressed in men's clothing is supported by other social commentators and tramps-turned-writers, such as James Forbes:

> 'Good people' deprecate the admission of women to their ranks. Yet the 'hay bag' (female tramp) is by no means an uncommon type. The best known of her kind is 'Peg Leg Annie' or 'Cow-Catcher Annie' who lost a leg while riding on the pilot of a locomotive. Female tramps usually wear men's clothes to avoid detection by the police.[39]

This gender ambiguity reflected in clothes, haircuts and the act of being mobile itself brings us back to the story of the Swedish woman in Minnesota. Railway magazines and newspapers during the late nineteenth and early twentieth centuries were replete with stories of tramps and the threat they posed to trains, passengers and railroad property. Usually the menace was masculine. Occasionally a reference to a female tramp would appear. On 23 April 1880, in the *Railroad Gazette*, the simple heading 'Tramps' was followed by the report that 'A tramp captured at Rahway New Jersey on the platform of a Pullman car on a Pennsylvania train, turned out to be a woman in men's clothes, and was handed over to the police.'[40] More colourfully, the *New York Times* of 7 August 1901 told the story of 'Jimmie McDougall the handsome leader of the large and dreaded band of marauders and tramps who have been the terror of Monroe County farmers' who had been caught and put safely behind bars. He turned out to be a woman. 'Jimmie', the story went on, 'was attired in white cloth shoes, several sizes too large, blue overalls, and a red flannel shirt'. Jimmie claimed that she had 'adopted men's attire to beat her way from Cleveland to Rochester'.[41] Finally, there was the case of Miss Shelly reported in the *Railway Conductor* magazine in 1901:

> Dressed in a ragged pair of trousers, blue flannel shirt and thread-bare coat, she would slouch into town in the typical hobo gait, and there levy on the citizens for food, clothing and money in true tramp style. She delighted in having the police on her trail and seemed to get greatest enjoyment out of their peremptory orders to move on to another town.[42]

The description of Miss Shelly focuses on a body that crosses categories. Her bodily movements are described as a 'typical hobo gait', reproducing the traditional image of a slouching, furtive tramp/hobo, never described as 'upright' and certainly not indicative of expectations of female bodily comportment. In addition her clothing is 'unfeminine', signifying a further threat to traditional categories of masculine and feminine. In many ways the story could have been about a man or a woman. The judgements of her actions, however, are quite different from the usual tales of threat and fear that arise from the transgressions of male tramps.

> Pity alone was perhaps the incentive which induced trainmen to permit her to remain upon their trains, but it is safe to say that they felt no necessity of offering her any protection because of her sex. Thus it will be seen that she was wholly without protection,

and, if possible, more obnoxious than the male hobo whom she impersonated.[43]

There is a clear sense in this report that Miss Shelly had committed a kind of gender treachery and had thus abrogated her rights as a woman. The trainmen no longer felt it necessary to afford her the protection that her 'sex' would normally demand (the protection, we can assume, which included all the moral trappings of home). Women were supposed to be threatened by and protected from tramps – not to be tramps themselves. Miss Shelly was worse than a male hobo. If publicity posters and cartoons used the female body and the threat of rape as symbols for the threat posed by masculine mobility, then Miss Shelly's disguised body is thoroughly deserving of whatever it gets. Stephanie Golden's suggestion is that her status – lower than that of a hobo – was that of the prostitute.[44]

## PROSTITUTES, LESBIANS AND SEXUAL IRREGULARITIES

Recall that James Moore's classification scheme listed three types of female tramps, the first of which was the prostitute. In fact, many commentators during the period 1870–1939 referred to female tramps and prostitutes in almost the same breath, often making the assumption that the two were more or less the same. Frank Laubach claimed that a principal reason women do not become 'vagrants' in as great a number as men is that 'they do become the female kind of vagrant, namely, prostitutes, in many instances'.[45] Other commentators were more forthright. In reference to female tramps C. W. Noble wrote: 'They seem to have no idea of personal purity whatever. I knew of one instance of a woman tramp who was supported by several male tramps with whom she travelled',[46] and further that 'the women on the road seem to be much more irreclaimable than the men. They have less true politeness, less sense of honor, and if dishonest are much more subtle … Male agents, as a rule, will be fair with each other and have a strong esprit de corps, but for the female agent everything is fish that comes into her net.'[47] Bertha Thompson in *Sister of the Road* notes that many female tramps sell sex for money. Indeed, her 'autobiography' recounts time she spent as a prostitute in Chicago. The theme of prostitution links the experiences of the female tramps with the discussions of the *flâneur/flâneuse*. Feminist scholars have pointed out that one of the ways women were able to inhabit the streets of Paris in the nineteenth century was as a prostitute.[48] The mobility of both the street prostitute and the female tramp was thus an ambiguous mixture of freedom and constraint that was expressed in the presentation of their bodies as objects of consumption. Their bodies can never be interpreted as presentations of pure will and intentionality.

The matter of what clothes to wear when riding the rails was wrapped up in the strategies for dealing with sex and sexual abuse used by women on the road. Rape was apparently a common feature of life for these women. One female tramp recounted her life to a curious reporter:

> With a suitcase and a bundle she started on a Southern swing from Washington D.C., riding the rails, picking up rides in trucks, walking the highways ... She never had a female companion on the road. She has slept in the open, starved for days, ridden in box cars with as many as fifty men, camped out at night alone and with men. She has been attacked and raped on several occasions and has given in on several more. She has asked for food, clothes and a chance to wash. She has shared food and money with men. But she has never begged for money, never stood in bread lines, and never taken money for sex.[49]

The interviewer, Walter Reckless, was clearly fascinated by tales of sex on the road and encouraged his interviewee to expand on the subject. Following a series of stories about meetings where she is either attacked or agrees to sex, she tells him that sex is a constant feature of life on the road for female hobos. 'Men on the road never have a woman and when there is a woman they always come around every time', she says. 'It ain't the looks of me but it's just because I'm a woman ...'[50] He asks her 'Why don't you travel in knickers?' to which she replies: 'I only used them once and gave them away. I would rather travel in a dress. All other women I see on the road wear knickers or pants. I like dresses. They (other hobo women) wear pants so they won't be molested and pass off for men in getting on and off trains.'[51]

Female tramps constantly had to negotiate their positions *vis-à-vis* men while on the road. Strategies adopted included travelling with a male companion, working as a prostitute and disguising themselves in men's clothes. Occasionally women would also travel in groups, and there are accounts of a secretive lesbian subculture among female tramps. Ben Reitman wrote a series of descriptions (Outcast Narratives) of the tramps he met in his work. One of these concerns a female tramp called Eve:

> Eve was a short, red-headed Jew girl,
>     Born in Russia 25 years ago.

She has a pale, freckled, masculine face
With an ambitious nose and restless chin.
... She got tired of the New York factory life
And decided to tramp around the country.
She had several experiences with men
But soon found that they had no joy to give her.
Quite accidentally she slept with a lovely eighteen year old
And suddenly life began to take on new meaning and purpose.
    She worked like hell and hoarded her money
Until she found some female of the right type;
Then she would pursue and lavish presents and affections
        upon her.
She travelled around the country in search of types
And had about twenty affairs with the ladies
She said, 'Why do you object – what harm am I doing?'[52]

In Reitman's encyclopaedic appendix of types of female tramps and the causes for their lifestyle, he lists among his 'secondary factors' such 'vices' as drink, dope and 'sex irregularities' – 'the nymphomaniacs, the masturbators, those who run away to have an abortion, well marked homosexualists, perverts'.[53] *Sister of the Road* is full of references to the sexual activities of both men and women. For the most part, references to a lesbian subculture are hints rather than clear descriptions. At one point Bertha gives an account of homosexuality on the road, pointing out that the tea-shops and bootleg joints of the near north side of Chicago were something of a node for homosexual tramps. She became acquainted with one such tramp who called herself 'Yvonne the Tzigane'. Yvonne claimed to be a gypsy and migratory entertainer originally from Paris:

> Her first trip from coast to coast in 1925 took her eighteen days.
> When she was thirteen years old she was seduced by a woman and
> lived with her for two years. Since then she had several lesbian rela-
> tionships which lasted various lengths of time ... She said there
> were a number of lesbians on the road and usually they travelled in
> small groups.[54]

In addition to lesbians, Bertha notes a high incidence of bisexual women who led a tramping life. Occasionally such people had 'women sweethearts' but earned money through prostitution. Bertha indicates that the number of lesbian couples on the road together was quite high.[55] These hints at a lesbian subculture begin to reveal something of the subversiveness of the female tramp. While the gendering of the tramp scare was based (in part) on familiar sets of categorizations and assumptions about private and public space, home and away, the women tramps were developing identities that challenged the core values of American society in ways that even the male tramp could not.[56] The majority of these women, though, constantly had to negotiate their sexuality in relation to the men they would undoubtedly meet. Their sexuality was often controlled in 'an objectified and externalised way'[57] while trying to avoid rape and in using their bodies as a form of mobile capital.

A footnote here, of course, is that the contemporary use of the word tramp to describe a woman meant prostitute. Note though, that Miss Shelly did attract the trainmen's pity and was allowed to remain on board. Even though they felt no need to protect her because of her sex they did react differently to her as a woman than they would had she been a male hobo. As is usually the case with women on the road, reactions are riddled with ambivalence and ambiguity as observers try to maintain the categories they are accustomed to, even as such categories are transgressed before their eyes.

## LOATHSOME BODIES

The very idea of a female hobo was ludicrous to some observers. Cliff Maxwell, writing in *Scribner's* magazine made the connection between the hobo lifestyle and its masculinity quite explicit. 'The hobo', he declared,

> deliberately chooses a life of hardship, privation, poverty and ostracism; because, without the money to pay his way he must beat it, and beating his way on the railroads he becomes in the eyes of the law a minor criminal and is treated as such by the municipal authorities and citizens alike. In short his life as a hobo is everything that life shouldn't be. This, in itself, is argument enough against any woman ever becoming a chronic hobo.[58]

The hobo lifestyle then, was one for men that was logically inappropriate for women. It was thus impossible for a woman to be a hobo. 'Show me a 'lady hobo', he wrote, 'and I'll show you an angular bodied, flint eyed, masculine travesty upon her sex.'[59]

Maxwell appears to have been faced with a crisis in the logic of the category. Female hobos, if they existed, would be 'travesties' – bodies that mixed unlike attributes to produce an unnerving and unlikely hybrid. Perhaps Maxwell's thoughts indicate his belief that female tramps were lesbians. Returning to Miss Shelly again it is surely possible that the anxious commentator in the *Railroad Gazette* was suggesting not so much that she was a prostitute but that she was a lesbian. Marjorie Garber's wonderful history of cross-dressing, *Vested Interests*, maps the ongoing cultural anxiety produced by bodies whose gender is not immediately identifiable. It is suggested that the transvestite and the female dressed as a male embody an ongoing crisis of a dualistic categorization at the heart of human culture – that of man and woman.

> ... one of the most important aspects of cross-dressing is the way in which it offers a challenge to easy notions of binarity, putting into question the categories of 'female' and 'male,' whether they are considered essential or constructed, biological or cultural.[60]

Mobility adds another layer to this observation, for women were not supposed to lead a life on the road, just as they were not supposed to wear men's clothes. The combination of clothing and the spatiality of these women's lives led to fundamental crises in the ability of onlookers to categorize them. Labels such as prostitute and lesbian allowed observers to regain a sense of order. For women to take to the road was, in the eyes of Maxwell and others, essentially to renege on being a woman. The categories that existed in early twentieth-century America had no space for the poor female wanderer.

Bodies, as much recent cultural and social theory has indicated, are central sites for the reproduction of culture.[61] Meaning is inscribed onto them, and bodies, through practice, make social codes material. Clothing is just one way in which bodies are marked in a way that binds them to 'systems of significance in which they become signs to be read'.[62] Mobility also provides meanings and norms that allow social categorizations to be incorporated into the very physiology of the body.[63] The presence of the disreputable bodies of female tramps triggers a categorization crisis. Embodied codes, norms and ideals were transgressed by the female tramps, and observers sought to instate understandings – reinscriptions – that brought the women back into the realm of legibility. Categories such as lesbian and prostitute served to fit the tramp's bodies back into texts and codes that were in some sense known. Another way of reinscribing the bodies of female tramps with social meaning was to label their bodies deviant with reference to both the insides of their bodies – diseases and psychological problems and their external appearance – dress and variations of ugliness.

One attempt to classify female tramps – to codify their bodies – is Ben Reitman's in *Sister of the Road*. He focuses on both the external and internal characteristics of their bodies. Reitman was clearly fascinated by women on the road, and attempted an explanation of the causes of their vagrancy. In *Sisters of the Road* he supplies an appendix of over 30 pages of female hobo classifications. In line with his radical thinking, Reitman is quick to point out that there is little that differentiates a poor woman on the road from rich women with any number of vices apart from the status of tramp, hobo or vagrant. He makes it quite clear that the major reason for their homelessness is economic: 'Many women on the road are sick and diseased. But if they had plenty of money, they wouldn't be on the road. They would be going to the spas of Europe and Hot Springs.'

Drink also is listed among the causes of vagrancy. But the rich and middle class drink much more than the poor women, and they never have to go on the road or apply for charity, no matter how drunk and disorderly they are.

> There is really not much difference between those who become vagrants and others. The upper classes have all the vices of the sisters of the road, and perhaps more, but no matter how lewd, vulgar, promiscuous or immoral they are, they never get on the road or become public charges, and are seldom disgraced.[64]

This is followed by a host of information about female tramps, suggesting that secondary reasons for women taking to the road include age (adolescent or senile), ill-health, appearance, vices (drinking, gambling, drug addiction, 'sexual irregularities'), social inadequacy and even a preference for the lifestyle it offered. These are all further subdivided into various headings. Under ill-health, for example, he lists:

> 1) Infectious diseases such as tuberculosis, syphilis, amoebic dysentery, malaria, gonorrhoea and tubo-ovarian infections.
>
> 2) Constitutional diseases – heart, kidney, liver, diabetes, respiratory, dropsy, asthma, cirrhosis of the liver, etc.
>
> 3) Emaciation, wasting diseases – starvation, general weaknesses.
>
> 4) Handicaps – blindness, deafness, dumbness, crippled, injuries, paralysis, etc.
>
> 5) Glandular disturbances – hypo and hyper thyroid; Addison's Disease.
>
> 6) Insanity and psychoses.
>     a) The hysterical.
>     b) The neurasthenic.
>     c) Flights and fugues.
>     d) Dromomania.

e) Melancholia depression.

f) Dementia praecox.

g) Epilepsy.

h) Alcoholic insanity.

i) Childbirth insanity.

j) Illusions, delusions and hallucinations, that constitute mis-
construed grievances and persecutions. Running away from
supposed enemies.[65]

Other headings have similarly comprehensive subheadings that add up to
a picture of persons marked through and through by abnormal and
deviant attributes and behaviours. Internally they are, in Reitman's eyes,
likely to have syphilis, wasting diseases, handicaps and 'glandular distur-
bances' in addition to a whole host of psychoses. Externally they are
marked by 'deformities and lack of physical attraction'. His list includes

1) Consciousness of lack of attraction and beauty.

2) Deformities, handicaps and injuries.

3) Extremes of leanness and stoutness.

4) Extremes of shortness or tallness.

5) Extreme awkwardness –'Miss Gawky.'

6) Cross-eyes and eye lesions.

7) Hyper-trichosis (excessive growth of hair) and Hypo-trichosis
(slight growth of hair).

8) The tiny and massive breast.

9) A natural appearance of being unkempt, tough and unpleasant.[66]

The body is central to dominant cultural designations of certain groups as
'Other'. Such groups are frequently constructed through their bodies and
according to standards that designate them as 'drab, ugly, loathsome,
impure, sick or deviant'.[67] The distinction between the ugly and the beautiful is often an aesthetic dualism that underscores the difference between
the observer and the observed.[68] Ugliness frequently denoted both
immorality and disease. Once again the tramp was pathologized. Reitman
commented on the physical impairment of male tramps but only used
descriptions of ugliness to refer to and classify female tramps.

The general propensity to label 'others' with reference to bodily attributes has a more specific relevance in the nineteenth and early twentieth
century, when it was firmly believed that moral character was inextricably
linked with biology. This was the time when discourses of rationality and
order reigned supreme, and everyone from census officers to lawyers to

biologists to the police were busy sorting out different types of people into hierarchies of perfection and imperfection. As Jennifer Terry and Jacqueline Urla have remarked:

> Efforts to measure the ears of criminals, the clitorises of prostitutes, and the facial contours of 'perverts' fuelled a feverish desire to classify forms of deviance, to locate them in biology and thus to police them in the larger social body. The somatic territorializing of deviance, since the nineteenth century, has been part and parcel of a larger effort to organize social relations according to categories denoting normality versus pathology, and national security versus social danger.[69]

Deviance is often located in the body. Socially transgressive behaviour is coded into bodily attributes as a cause of the deviance (i.e., tramps are tramps because they are disabled or venereal or just plain ugly), as a symptom of deviance (i.e., female tramps look like men because of their deviant life) or, as Terry and Urla put it, as a 'suggestive trace'.[70] Recall how Cliff Maxwell, in his denial of the possibility of female hobo, suggested that such a person would be 'angular bodied' and 'flint eyed' and in doing so provided material bodily markers of the manifest deviance of the female hobo's 'impossible' lifestyle.

Female tramps, when acknowledged, clearly puzzled contemporary observers. The ways of knowing in America in the late nineteenth century and early twentieth were heavily structured around schemes of perception that incorporated the basic division of the world into masculine and feminine with all its host of associated binaries. The law was not alone in defining the tramp as masculine. The strongest evidence about the invisibility of female tramps is probably the comparative lack of material on them. Most sources say nothing about women on the road despite the fact that there must have been many thousands of women who were, as Minehan put it, 'just as appallingly homeless as the boys'. When presented with female tramps, some observers found the subject difficult to deal with, or they denied it altogether. Some found it helpful to use familiar markers of female deviance, such as prostitution and lesbianism, in order to make the female tramp socially intelligible. Others went to great lengths to argue that these women were, as Maxwell put it, 'travesties' – not real women at all, but masculine forms of womanhood marked by male dress, unkempt appearance and a 'hobo gait'.

These observations resonate with feminist and post-structuralist accounts of the gendered body. For Judith Butler, for instance, the key question is how configurations of power construct the subject through the binary relations of man and woman. 'What happens', she wonders, 'to the subject and to the stability of gender categories when the epistemic regime of presumptive heterosexuality is unmasked as that which produces and reifies these ostensible categories of ontology?'[71] In the observations of female tramps I have recounted, 'these ostensible categories of ontology' are clearly being brought into question. The discovery of cross-dressing tramps and the questioning of their sexuality produced panic in anxious observers. In the troubled words of Cliff Maxwell and others there is a clear attempt to reinstate dearly held categories before they fall apart. Such 'gender trouble' allows us to begin what Butler, following Foucault, calls a genealogical critique – an investigation of 'the political stakes in designating as an origin and cause those identity categories that are in fact the effects of institutions, practices, discourses with multiple and diffuse points of origin'.[72] Categories (such as man, woman, tramp) are naturalized through repeated performance. Gender and the moral geography that equates mobility with masculinity is constructed through performance and practice. Cross-dressed female tramps are using their bodies to perform a transgressive rôle that disrupts the easy inscription of gendered bodies and thus produces a categorization crisis. 'Gender trouble' occurs when bodies are not compliant, and the bodies of Miss Shelly and others were out of compliance in a number of ways that connected mobility to clothing and to sexuality.

As I noted at the beginning of this chapter, female tramps appear as an 'other' in James Moore's classification of tramp types. The category of 'other' so central to post-structuralists at the end of the twentieth century indicates just how marginal female tramps were in the investigations of tramp observers. Women on the road appear to have produced a categorization problem for James Moore in much the same way they did for Maxwell and Miss Shelly's captors. They were simply too deviant to contemplate.

The female tramp simply did not fit in. She produced in anxious male observers a crisis of the male/female binary and a crisis of category itself. Female tramps were clearly outside the normal spaces and social rôles ascribed to women, nor did they fit into the male world of the tramp/hobo. Female tramps were perceived as a community of double outsiders – a neither/nor group on the margins of a margin.

# 5 Pathologizing the Tramp

As an appendix to *The Feebly Inhibited*,[1] the early twentieth-century American eugenicist Charles Davenport provided details of a hundred family histories of people he called 'nomads'. These read as bizarre litanies of pathological traits allegedly linked, through the logic of heredity, to nomadic lifestyles:

> 4. Propositus is a *restless visionary. He has always been shifting from one position to another. Left home some months ago saying he was going West; has not been heard from since.* Sibs: 1, female, died 14 years. 2, male, died in infancy. 3, female, works in a factory; is getting divorced. 4, male, has a *roving disposition*; is a nurse and companion; accompanies various patients on their trips for health. 5, female, has long been lawless and violent in her actions; *she ran away from home* while in a commercial school; had been their only a few weeks when she got the principal to refund her tuition, which had been paid in advance; with this money she went to L—— and became a telephone operator, later she *ran away again to marry*, and since her marriage she has *run away*; she loses her temper.
>
> *Father*, unknown.
>
> *Mother*, unknown. Sibs: 1, male, unknown; 2, male, drowned when 7 years old.
>
> *Mother's father*. Was a stage-driver between Salem and Boston and kept a tavern or 'roadhouse' in what is now an outskirt of L——. Some of his descendants suggest that the *wanderlust* and frequently erratic character of his descendants come through this ancestor.
>
> *Mother's mother*, unknown.[2]
>
> 11. Propositus, born 1895 in Missouri, is (1914) a wanderer and *has left home repeatedly and been away for months at a time*, returning home for

rest and clothes, then he goes away again; works some, but does not save or provide for the future – a disobedient boy ... Smokes a pipe and cigarettes, drinks whiskey, and has used cocaine considerably ... Is irregular and uncertain in his habits, *does not like to stay in one place long; likes to bum and tramp around to see the world* ... Has flat feet, crooked toes, crooked spine, and one shoulder is higher than the other ...[3]

In these family histories, anything from headaches to drinking to having crooked feet is considered evidence for the pathological nature of human wandering. The hundred entries are a remarkable map of the prejudices and paranoias of early twentieth-century social science. The extensive use of italics points towards the significance, for Davenport, of mobile episodes in the lives of these people as well as uncontrolled sexuality and excess alcohol consumption. In this chapter I consider these eugenicist diagnoses alongside a loosely connected array of vague diagnoses ranging from 'wanderlust' to 'railway fever'. Through an examination of these diagnoses, and other observations that linked tramps to the spread of syphilis, it is possible to map the ways in which normality was being defined in relation to the pathological mobility of the tramp.

We have already seen how reactions to tramps, whether male or female, tended to define this new social type as an 'other' – as a marginal character whose unsavoury characteristics served to help define what constituted health and normality. The body of the tramp was seen as one of the clearest indicators of his or her reprehensible nature. Classification schemes consistently referred to the various bodily deficiencies of the tramp in addition to ideas surrounding mobility and work. One of the ways that female tramps were simultaneously defined and denied was with reference to their deviant (ugly and masculine) bodies. It is a characteristic technique of 'othering' to define a category of people or forms of behaviour as 'pathological'. Words such as *pathological, deviant, normal* and *abnormal* haunt the early days of social investigation, and all of them swirl around the new figure of the tramp.

THE NORMAL AND THE PATHOLOGICAL

The kinds of knowledge about tramps being constructed at the turn of the century in the United States rested on earlier, pre-twentieth-century developments in knowledge that made possible the use of terms such as pathological, normal and deviant. Such is the momentum that words of this kind carry with them, we are often left unsure as to where they came from. Our understandings of the word 'normal' have histories. There are two distinct understandings of the word. One suggests that normal is average, not particularly interesting but in some way representative. But normal is also used to mean 'good'. To be labelled 'abnormal' is rarely a compliment. 'Normal' only acquired its present meanings in the 1820s. Before that it had been used to refer to a right-angle in geometry – a synonym for orthogonal. Even at this stage the term had a normative function. Ian Hacking has traced the origins of words such as this one and makes his point well:

> It is just a fact that an angle is a right angle, but it is also a 'right' angle, a good one. Orthodontists straighten the teeth of children; they make the crooked straight. But they also put the teeth right, make them better. Orthopaedic surgeons straighten bones. Ortho-psychiatry is the study of mental disorders chiefly in children. It aims at making the child normal. The orthodox conform to standards . . .[4]

The word 'normal' came to have its two quite distinct meanings in the nineteenth century. To the arch-positivist Comte, normal was an idea derived from his medical hero Joseph Victor Broussais, a physiologist who was a proponent of the organic theory of disease. To Broussais the task of medicine was to find out how some form of 'excitation' leads to deviation from what he called the 'normal state' and constitutes an abnormal, diseased state within the body. Disease here is caused by some form of excess or lack of 'excitation'.[5] Comte took up this idea that the pathological is no more than the 'normal state' over-amplified with a vengeance.[6] He translated this idea into the social sphere, suggesting that social pathology was simply a variation on normality.[7] But, as Hacking makes clear, the idea of normal changed in its social usage from the ordinary healthy state to an ideal purified state to which social beings should aspire: 'In short, progress and the normal state became inextricably linked.'[8] Suddenly the normal becomes an aspiration, something to be achieved rather than something that is everyday. This shift marked the invention of a contradiction in the meaning of the word that we have inherited. Normal means both an existing average – the ways things are – and an ideal towards which we should aim. To Durkheim, the normal is the good and deviation from it is termed 'pathology', while to others, particularly eugenicists, one end of the normal distribution was not pathology but excellence. As Hacking points out:

> Words have profound memories that oil our shrill and squeaky rhetoric. The normal stands indifferently for what is typical, the

unenthusiastic objective average, but it also stands for what has been, good health, and for what shall be, our chosen destiny. That is what the benign and sterile sounding word 'normal' has become – one of the most powerful ideological tools of the twentieth century.[9]

The modern (post-1820) use of the word quickly moved out of the realm of medicine and colonized many other areas of life in the nineteenth century. It is a word that joins together fact and value, claiming that the normal and the right are the same thing.

The opposite to normal in the Durkheimian framework is pathology. This is a word that also underwent a curious mutation in the early nineteenth century as it changed from a term denoting the study of diseased organs (rooted, as with 'normal', in the body) to one used to mark the deviation from the normal state, a limitless variety of possibilities. Most famously, Durkheim used pathological to refer to extreme deviation from a norm or average that was thought of as good. In this sense pathology became linked to 'deviance' – a word with its origins in statistics, marking the difference from the mean along a normal distribution curve. Not surprisingly, the roots of statistics in the social sciences were firmly connected to social and eugenicist concerns with marginal members of society in Western Europe, particularly vagrants. Early statistical enquiry first discovered law-like regularities among populations thought of as deviant. Suicide, vagrancy, prostitution and crime were all early subjects of statistical science that paradoxically helped produce the very methods that sought to count and regulate them. Central to these early statistical endeavours was the urge to improve and control people – to bring people back into the fold of the normal.

The relations between the normal and the pathological are somewhat contradictory. As Georges Canguilhem has argued, we might expect 'pathology' to be an idea derived from the idea of the 'normal', and yet we often only become aware of the normal (so often left unstated because unquestioned) when we experience the 'pathological'. Experientially, the pathological is necessary in order to make clear what normality is.[10] This is true of biological science as much as it is of everyday social experience:

> every conception of pathology must be based on prior knowledge of the corresponding normal state, but conversely the scientific study of pathological cases becomes an indispensable phase in the overall search for the normal state.[11]

What then of the tramp? My argument here is both that observers sought to encode the bodies of tramps as pathological, as diseased and genetically unsound, and that tramps were metaphorically a pathology in the wider social body.

## EUGENICS AND THE TRAMP

Many of the discussions of the tramp in turn-of-the-century America revolved around the then respectable world of eugenics. A great deal of intellectual labour was invested in the search for the origins of the tramp problem. In the late nineteenth century very few people were willing to point towards an economic context as a reason for taking to the road; most commentators laid the blame firmly within the individual. Eugenics was in full swing, and it was explanations of heredity that held sway. Particularly influential was the analysis of a family known as the Jukes, whose family line had been studied by R. L. Dugdale. Dugdale had studied six sisters and 709 of their descendants since 1750. He found the family to be 30 times more likely to be criminal than the general population. Of the 709, 128 had been prostitutes and over 200 had been on relief. Over 76 had been convicted criminals. In addition 11–25 per cent of the sample suffered from syphilis, which, in Dugdale's view, was clearly correlated with social and behavioural conditions.[12] I will return to the connections between social pauperism and syphilis later.

At around the same time as Dugdale's influential family history had become common knowledge, people began to notice the arrival of unemployed and homeless men in major cities around the country. For the first time they were being called tramps. Many philanthropists and charity workers began to think of these men (and, to some extent, women) as the bottom of an hereditary hierarchy permitted to survive because of over-generous and indiscriminate giving by well-meaning individuals. The depression of 1873, for instance, saw the arrival, for the first time, of people classed as tramps in New York. One observer, Charles Loring Brace, a worker with the poor boys of the city, warned against indiscriminate giving to the poor. Charity, he argued, would only encourage the arrival of more tramps, who would lose any industrious habits they may have had and replace them with a spirit of pauperism. If not prevented, Brace warned, a community of tramps would develop, transmitting pauperism to their children.[13] His observations preceded full-blown eugenics by a decade or so. Nevertheless, his warnings against the propagation of a generation of paupers clearly point towards things to come. Delinquency and deviance was increasingly thought of as pathological, as one of a set of manifestations of inherited embodied weakness that deviated markedly from contemporary understandings of 'normality'. Pauperism, criminality, feeblemindedness and alcoholism were all seen to be largely explicable as pathological conditions. In the case of tramps there was the additional pathology of 'wanderlust' or 'dromomania'. Wanderlust became just one of a whole series of unsavoury characteristics associated with marginal groups and believed to be the product of hereditary processes.

The American eugenics movement, in its early years, was dominated by Charles Davenport.[14] Davenport had earned a PhD in biology at Harvard. After serving as an instructor at Harvard he moved to the University of Chicago in 1899 and took up the position of assistant professor. He had already developed a passion for statistical study and had introduced Pearson's statistical methods to the United States. Combining his interests in biology and statistics, Davenport persuaded the newly formed Carnegie Institution of Washington, DC to establish the Station for Experimental Evolution at Cold Spring Harbor on Long Island. He was its director. His work at the Station initially involved extensive breeding experiments in creatures ranging from snails to sheep, but it soon developed into a more sinister interest in tracing 'genetic traits' in people. By 1907 he was publishing papers on the heredity of eye, skin and hair colour in people, and his work moved towards eugenics.

As director of the Station for Experimental Evolution, Davenport became a figure of national prominence and was able to organize a vast array of committees in everything from deaf-mutism, through feeble-mindedness and criminality to immigration. Following a huge endowment he extended his Long Island centre to incorporate a new Eugenics Record Office. Again, Davenport became its director. From 1924 the Eugenics Record Office held summer schools in which young men and women were trained to be 'eugenics field workers'. The training included lectures on heredity by Davenport, methodology (the collection of family histories) and field trips to asylums, hospitals and the homes of 'defective families'. Once trained, field workers collected endless records of family histories in prisons, asylums and elsewhere.

One of Davenport's early explorations of Mandelian ratios in people was his book *The Feebly Inhibited* (1915). It included his work 'Nomadism, Or the Wandering Impulse, With Special Reference to Heredity'. Davenport believed that tramps suffered from an inbred desire to wander. In 'Nomadism' he considered a number of medico-psychological conditions related to the desire to stay on the move. He describes wanderlust as a mild form of desire for travel that we all exhibit from time to time but, for the most part, remains under control. At the other end of his spectrum lies the condition known as 'fugue', an extreme and markedly pathological inability to stop moving. In addition to, and somewhere between, these two is the condition known as 'dromomania', a form of ambulatory automatism. In preference to all these, Davenport chose to focus on 'nomadism', which he describes as a racial or tribal tendency to wander. 'On the whole', he says, 'I am inclined to use the word "nomadism" just because it has a racial connotation. From a modern point of view all hereditary characteristics are racial.'[15] He developed his thesis via a discussion of the wandering tendency as a normal characteristic of man and animals that sets them apart from plants. He traces nomadism through an evolutionary hierarchy, noting the 'wandering instinct' in anthropoid apes, in 'primitive' people, in young children and in adolescents. By tracing these connections he sought to show how nomadism was a primitive trait exhibited most frequently in those who have not fully enjoyed the benefits of civilization. Apes, 'primitive peoples', babies and adolescents all suffered from an excess of primitive urges and a lack of civilized constraints, and were thus likely to wander. He spent his greatest effort discussing so-called 'primitive' people in order to reveal how all the most primitive peoples are nomadic. At the bottom of this hierarchy are 'Fuegians, Australians, Bushmen and Hotten-tots', all of whom are nomadic. He refutes the suggestion that they are nomadic because they are hunters and instead asserts that they are forced into hunting by their nomadic traits. He continues up his hierarchy of peoples, noting the nomadism of Cossacks, Turkomans, Mongols, Poly-nesians and Gypsies. Indeed, his central contention is that non-nomadic lifestyles are a very recent phenomenon in human history. Nomadism, to Davenport, indicated a racial tendency to wander that, somewhat bizarrely, but in keeping with American ideology about mobility, he saw as an expression of Americanness. Quoting Lowell's *Fireside Travels*, he pointed out that 'The American is nomadic in religion, in ideas, in morals, and leaves his faith and opinions with as much indifference as the house in which he lives.'[16] Americans, he argued, were descendants of those restless elements of other, mainly European, nations, who chose to leave their ancestral homes, and so it was surely no surprise that many American families would show nomadic traits.

Like social reformers and sociologists of the time, Davenport was concerned with the classification and categorization of 'nomadism', and he looked to France for models. At the time the French were extremely concerned with vagrancy and vagabondage, and a number of people in medical and pseudo-medical fields were producing explanations for, and classifications of, vagrancy. Of particular significance was the French diagnosis of 'fugue', a diagnostic relation of hysteria that was sweeping through psychiatric circles at that time. Fugue, defined as a pathological urge to wander, was restricted mainly to men. The diagnosis of fugue in France linked many of the traits that Davenport linked through his eugenicist perspective. Mental confusion, alcohol and drug dependency and sexual deviancy are all part of a nexus of traits embodied in the wanderer.

Ian Hacking has shown how the diagnosis of fugue as a medical entity was linked in France to social concern over vagrancy.[17] Fugue (literally flight) refers to a medical disorder characterized by sudden and inexplicable travel. Someone who suffered from fugue was referred to as a fuguer. Sufferers were almost always male, could not recall their travels and often adopted startling new identities. What interested Hacking was the observation that fugue became a medical pathology around 1887 and ceased to be a topic of much concern by 1909. Hacking suggests that fugue provided a diagnosis for men that closely mirrored the feminized diagnosis of multiple personality disorder:

> Fugue was commonly run alongside multiple personality. Nine out of ten people recently diagnosed as multiple personalities are women. In the past, as now, the prototypical multiple was a woman. The prototypical fuguer was a man, and for good reason. It was very much more easy for a man to take off with little money and perhaps no papers than for a woman to do so. A woman who wants to lead another life better do it at home. She must dissociate and fragment. A man can become another person by hitting the road.[18]

Clearly, medical diagnoses, like social ones, have their gendered geographies!

One question raised by Hacking is why fugue never took off as a medical diagnosis in the United States. His answer revolves around the socio-historical conditions that differentiated France from other countries. 'There are some obvious reasons why fugue should not be an American preoccupation', he says. 'Go West, young man: the fuguer never came back. America was full of young men in flight, but fugue was never medicalized.'[19] The story of the 'tramp scare' makes this explanation somewhat suspect. Many migrants in the United States did follow circular paths and frequently returned to old haunts – particularly in major cities, such as Chicago. On top of that, all manner of medical diagnoses were made of tramps, including Davenport's eugenic explanations which, in turn, were informed by, and responded to, French discussions of fugue and vagrancy.

In many ways the French diagnosis of fugue contrasted with Davenport's eugenicist orientation. A fugue could be caused by anything from a bump on the head to an epileptic fit. Davenport's nomadism was a deeply engrained family and racial trait. But as Hacking points out, the French explanations of all forms of hysteria were based on a foundation of heredity and degeneracy. A weak organic stock could lead to first alcoholism, then hysteria, then epilepsy and eventually fugue. In Davenport's discussion of nomadism, the urge to wander was associated with a whole litany of psychoses, including suicide, temper, migraine, epilepsy, hysteria, 'sprees' and 'sexual outbreaks'. All of these could lead to a paralysis of the inhibitions that are normally relied on to prevent nomadism in civilized people. These 'nomadics' were, in Davenport's view, a product of their genetic makeup and thus were members of a special nomadic race.

Davenport came to the conclusion that nomadism was the result of a simple recessive sex-linked gene associated with these psychoses. His workers discovered 168 male nomadics and only 15 female. In the extreme case of tramps and vagabonds, Davenport suggested, 'the inhibitory mechanism is so poorly developed that the nomadic tendency shows itself without waiting, as it were, for the paralysis of the inhibitions'.[20] In other words, people who led a nomadic life were in the same category as babies, 'primitive people' and others who had none of the inhibitions typical of intelligent adults and 'civilized' people. It is revealing, although not surprising, that the pathology of nomadism is said to reside only in the minds and bodies of men. Just as the law had defined the tramp as male, so eugenics defined nomadic instincts as caused by genes linked to masculinity.

Davenport, of course, was not a lone figure in this mapping of pathologies. Other academics in various disciplines made similar assumptions, even if their diagnoses were somewhat less rigorous. Peter Alexander Speek in the *Annals of the American Academy of Political and Social Sciences* roots the mobility of the tramp in psychology. Tramping, he argued, is caused when 'a passion for wandering is increased almost to madness'. This passion is inevitably followed by a 'profound aversion to work', 'a liking for drink', 'a childlike perspective that he might strike rich' and a loss of 'ability to concentrate'. 'Wonderful human nature', he writes, 'invents other, one might say in common parlance, "artificial" substitutes for "natural" enjoyment appearing in ambition and hope. By changing environment – scenes – by constant wandering, he keeps up some sort of interest in life.'[21]

The suggestion that the mobility of tramps, vagrants and hobos was linked to 'instincts' was not, however, limited to the halls of academia.

Indeed, the logic of wandering as a pathology percolated down from specialist knowledge into the realms of common, popular awareness. A similar logic was used, for instance, in 1917 by a Chicago investigative journalist, Harvey Beardsley, who gives us an admirable insight into the politics of mobility in the following quotation:

> Part of hobos belongs to the class of wanderlust. They will see the world, they will learn, and it is a very strong impulse. But the world respects the rich man who turned to be a globe trotter and uses first class cabins and Pullman cars, but has inclinations to look over his shoulder at the hobo who, to satisfy this so strong impulse, is compelled to use box-cars, slip the board under the Pullman or in other ways whistle on the safety of his life and the integrity of his bones.[22]

In a similar vein, the well-known tramp turned railroad detective Josiah Flynt postulated that young boys became victims of a 'railroad fever' that gripped them at a young age and doomed them to a life on the rails. Allan Pinkerton, possibly the most famous of all railroad detectives, had a soft spot for a warm and romantic image of tramps. But even this seemed to be built on a foundation of universal instinct only variably controlled:

> No person can ever get a taste of the genuine pleasure of the road and not feel in some reckless way, but yet certainly feel, that he would like to become some sort of a tramp. He might rebel against any kind of compromise with his own manhood that would make him a tramp in the offensive sense in which the word is employed . . . but there would, and there does still come an irrepressible impulse to go a-tramping.[23]

Most social reformers (figures who, for the most part, inhabited a border zone between academia and practical politics) produced intricate lists of causes for trampdom. In almost all cases the vague cause of wanderlust, or a disposition to roam, featured high on the list. W. L. Bull, for example, in a report to the Organization of Charities in 1886 reported that his survey of assumed causes of trampery found a 'roving disposition' to be the fourth most popular cause alongside depravity and worthlessness.[24] Nels Anderson, in his book on the hobo, cites wanderlust as one of the five main reasons for taking to the road.

In a thesis of 1916 on the causes of vagrancy, Frank Laubach links wanderlust to the conditions of modern industry and, like Harvey Beardsley, points out the differentiating politics of mobility. In this case, though, he also connects the wanderings to the ideologies of American identity dating back to Jefferson.

> Without doubt many men begin their wandering life in revolt against the monotony of modern industry. It can hardly be expected that the descendants of the most daring and adventurous of the nations of the earth should all be willing to submit to hum-drum, unchanging toil. It is unfortunate also that the desire for adventure should so often find no better satisfaction in these times than that obtained by the tramps. The rich man may travel all he will, but the poor man, who has neither aptitude nor persistence of purpose enough to enter occupations which would give him adventure along with his work must be satisfied with a limited horizon, unless he 'tramps it', or rides by freight.[25]

So wandering was described, in differing ways, as a pathology in terms of vague diagnoses of wanderlust and roving dispositions. The root causes of mobility in tramps, in other words, were located in the tramps' own bodies and minds. This pathological form of mobility was connected to other forms of deviance, such as poverty, insanity and intemperance. Every problem calls for solutions, and the logic of embodied pathology, and particularly of eugenics, pointed in only one direction – the prevention of reproduction.

We have already seen how Davenport and other anxious observers of the tramp were influenced by European thinking on vagrancy. Another influence were the European schools of 'criminal anthropology'. Both Morel, who worked on 'hereditary degeneration', and Lombroso, an Italian specializing in anthropomorphic studies, had their fans in the United States.[26] Criminal anthropology insisted that criminality was both hereditary and connected to visible bodily attributes. Crooked feet, for instance, could be seen as a sure sign of potential criminality. David Horn, in his discussions of Italian criminal anthropology, notes how criminologists such as Lombroso simultaneously constructed Italian society as a body threatened by the activities of criminals and the body of the criminal as an embodiment of social pathology and deviance. In American discussions of the tramp a similar process emerges.

Such beliefs held out no prospect of reform for the criminal. Henry Boies, an expert on penology for the Pennsylvania State Board of Public Charities, suggested that criminals and other defectives be castrated, while lesser pests, including tramps, be forbidden to marry.[27] This line of thought reached its extreme in the work of W. Duncan McKim, who claimed in *Heredity and Human Progress* that anything from drug addiction to cancer to idiocy was the result of heredity, and that the best solution to the problem was a 'gentle, painless death'.[28] In more general and slightly more subtle terms, the evidence of criminal anthropology led many in America to believe that some form of legislation was needed to stop undesirable types from reproducing. Connecticut was the first state to introduce regulation of marriage for breeding purposes in 1896, when it declared that epileptics, 'imbeciles' and the feeble-minded would be forbidden from marrying or having sex outside of marriage until the woman was 45 years old. By 1905, Kansas, New Jersey, Ohio, Michigan and Indiana had introduced similar eugenic marriage laws. In addition to legislative efforts, others were busy developing medical means of preventing reproduction among the 'defective classes'. Vasectomy, as a method for sterilizing men, had been developed in Europe in the 1890s. The operation was introduced to the United States in 1899 by Dr Harry Sharp, a physician at the Indiana Reformatory in Jeffersonville. He performed the operation on a nineteen-year-old inmate who allegedly asked Dr Sharp to help him break a severe masturbation habit by castration. Dr Sharp tried vasectomy instead, and three weeks later the boy had ceased masturbating and improved in his school work.[29]

Tramps frequently came up as examples of people who might be subjected to sterilization or segregation from society. W. H. Brewer in the *New Englander* in 1878 made the eugenics argument quite succinctly in 'What Shall We Do With the Tramps?' This 'dangerous class,' he argued, 'is a tribe. It has its origin and natural constitution of a tribe, with its own instincts, tastes, traditions and codes. Its mental characteristics are curiously like a tribe of savages in many respects and its acts as cruel and atrocious, and like all tribes it has its foundation in heredity.'[30]

Brewer cited Dugdale's work on the Jukes family as evidence for his argument, suggesting that the only solution to the tramp evil was confinement and the separation of the sexes in order to prevent further breeding. In addition, it was certain that tramps were either foreign or weak-willed Americans, and that their personal deficiencies and moral indulgence would lead to the eventual extinction of their families.

Similar arguments were prominent at the Fourth Annual Session of the National Conference of Charities and Corrections in 1877, where there was a special session devoted to the tramp evil.[31] Professor Francis Weyland of Yale gave the key address, in which he suggested that tramps were impossible to detect due to their mobility – their lack of home and stability. 'He is simply a tramp', Weyland declared. 'In other words, he belongs to that vast horde of idle and unprincipled vagrants, who, by the fatal indulgence or apathy of our criminal legislation are permitted to roam, unchecked, throughout the length and breadth of our land.'[32] Weyland suggested that the evil could be prevented by providing necessities, by compelling tramps to work, by preventing them from committing crime, and by rendering it impossible for them to propagate paupers. One enthusiastic female participant suggested that tramps should be disenfranchised and forbidden from marriage. It is clear, then, that the combination of the tramp's mobility with other characteristics – pauperism, alcoholism and mental illness – were considered to be pathological in the sense that they were assumed to reside within the make-up of the individual, perhaps linked to family and national origin, which led to the state of tramphood. Like Lombroso's criminals, there was little hope of reform for tramps, and it was therefore necessary to stop them breeding or interacting with 'normal' society. A particular construction of tramphood and vagrancy led logically to calls for new regimes of governmental practice focused on the prevention of propagation. So while simple punishment, according to the tramp laws, was fine in itself, it could not solve the problem of pathological wandering. This could only be prevented by isolating male tramps from the rest of society – particularly from women.

SYPHILIS, MOBILITY AND DEMOCRACY

Eugenics, as a systematic body of knowledge, focused on pathological bodily characteristics and behaviours believed to be inherited. Social reformers were also concerned with another form of pathology – disease. One way in which tramps and hobos were defined as dangerous was the association of the tramp's mobility with syphilis and its spread. Diseases and plagues throughout history have implied a number of disturbing social characteristics that combine to suggest a radical out-of-placeness. Some of the characteristics of plagues that are relevant to the association between disease and tramps include a disregard for spatial boundaries, a capacity for rapid spread, a threat to 'normal' function and the possibility of foreign origin. Threat to 'normal function' included the threat to democratic government posed by the corruption of political machinery by potentially syphilitic tramps.

Throughout history, syphilis has been explicitly connected to mobility. Plagues of the pox that swept through Europe in the sixteenth century have long been thought to be the result of Christopher Columbus and his crew bringing it back to Spain from the New World. The success of a mercenary army headed by the French king Charles VIII led to the eventual capture of Naples in 1496. While in Naples the mercenary army of Swiss, Flemings, Italians and Spaniards made merry to such a degree that they were forced to leave by the Italian princes whose original enthusiasm for the invasion had been transformed into hostility. A Spanish army was also on its way to recapture Naples. On retreat the mercenary army took with them a new and strange disease. The French called it the Neapolitan disease while the Italians called it the French sickness.[33] When the disease arrived in Bristol in 1497 it was known as the Bordeaux sickness. Everywhere the disease arrived, it was named after some other place. Muscovites called it the Polish sickness, the Poles the German disease. In Holland it was known as the Spanish disease and the Japanese called it the Portuguese sickness. Systematic attempts to locate the origins of syphilis pointed towards a number of travelling groups ranging from the Moors to the Beggards – a mystic-erotic cult who roamed Europe. Later, the idea that Columbus's men had imported it with their slaves became common knowledge.

Early researchers into syphilis quickly made a connection between the threat of syphilis and new technologies of mobility. In Russia during the 1860s, for instance, Dr Eduard Shperk blamed the spread of syphilis on the material life of modernity. In particular he pointed towards the deleterious effect of railroads in weakening traditional (and implicitly moral) community bonds. Syphilis, he argued, was least rampant in agricultural peasant villages, where traditional ties remained strong between people and between people and land. 'As the railroad enters a given locality', wrote Shperk, 'it increases the number of rented apartments, rented carriages . . . and rented women.'[34]

Syphilis was also explicitly connected to America's migrant workers and played an important rôle in the tramp scares that haunted the nation after the completion of the first trans-continental railroad. Clearly, the non-address of 'no fixed abode' insinuated a looseness of morals and disconnection from normality. It was mobile people such as sailors, soldiers and tramps that were seen as the spreaders and even the causes of the disease. Of these it was hobos and tramps who were believed to have the highest incidence. Nels Anderson, for instance, claimed that hobos in Chicago exhibited a 10 per cent infection rate, twice that of servicemen. Ben Reitman was keen to have hobos tested for the disease. He pointed out that 'the majority of them are between 18 and 45. They are unmarried and they take on all kinds of sex partners. Outside of the South Side groups, they have more syphilis and gonorrhoea than any other group in the city.'[35]

In another letter to the Chicago medical authorities, Reitman made his case for a venereal disease clinic in the hobo district by suggesting that 'transients are coming and going, bringing syphilis to Chicago and carrying gonorrhoea to some other state. And nothing has been done about it.'[36] In Connecticut, another, less radical but still liberal, social reformer, John J. McCook, was also dealing with the connection between tramp mobility and the spread of syphilis.

McCook wrote to doctors all over the country to assess the prevalence of syphilis among tramp populations. He reported his findings in 'Some New Phases of the Tramp Problem'[37] in the *Charities Review*, announcing that 9.8 per cent of 1,200 tramps surveyed had syphilis and postulating a connection between physical health and political health. Even so, he recounted a letter from R. W. Taylor MD, Professor of Venereal Diseases at the College of Physicians and Surgeons, New York, that insists

> I think you are under the mark in assuming a percentage of 9.8 per cent of these revolvers, as we call them, who are infected with some loathsome disease ... I think a large number certainly are diseased. I have no doubt that the widespread existence of itch in this county – it was a rare disease here twenty years ago – is largely due to tramps. As to their spreading syphilis there can be no doubt and I am sure gonorrhoea is spread broadcast by these wretches.[38]

Another letter included in McCook's paper, from Dr C. I. Fisher, Super-intendent of the State Almshouse in Tewkesbury, Massachusetts, reads:

> During the year ending March 1890 there were admitted to the hospital 1,058 men. Of these 551, or more than 52 per cent, were syphilites . . . next to intemperance I hold that syphilis is the most · important factor in the development and perpetuation of the dependent classes. It is ever present as a factor of depression, weakening the will, lessening the vigor and lowering the sense of responsibility.[39]

Once again connecting syphilis with wider political and social health, McCook related a meeting with a tramp in Worcester, Massachusetts, who had voted in California within the past year. Using his extensive notes on tramps he had met, he picked out another example:

> #2 is a laborer; last worked at anything 'a long time ago,' 'doesn't know when he is going to work again': health 'good,' 'but has had syphilis'; has been in the almshouse; generally sleeps 'anywhere';

secures his food by 'begging', is intemperate and has been convicted of drunkenness ... He ... votes in Hartford. And what type of votes are they apt to be? Men who pass nearly half their time in jail, and never draw a sober breath when they can help it, would hardly have much intelligence or conscience to go by; but such as it is would they use it? Or would they sell themselves readily to the highest bidder?[40]

McCook was in many ways sympathetic to tramps and their way of life. He kept in constant touch with one tramp, Roving Bob Aspinwell, and obviously slipped into romantic notions of the life on the open road. Here, though, McCook makes quite clear the litany of pathologies associated with trampdom. Here in #2 we have a body that refuses to be disciplined.

A few months later McCook published a paper in the popular magazine *Forum*. In it he discussed the alarming proportion of venal voters, suggesting that as many as 25,000 out of 166,000 votes in a recent election had been bought and paid for. Of this 25,000, he suggested, the majority were tramps, who often voted more than once. McCook was certainly not the only person to note the threat to democracy the tramp posed. Reitman in Chicago noted how whole wards in Chicago were easily fixed by buying hobo votes. 'The vote buyers', he said, 'can always be depended upon to buy the hobo ward'. Election day in 'Hoboland', he went on:

> is always a gay day. The men look forward to it with great pleasure. They are always sure of a fee for voting and around election time drinks are plentiful, panhandling is profitable and it is comparatively easy to get a drink or a night's lodging on the cuff. Probably no other form of social behaviour is so demoralizing to the individual and the community as this nefarious business of buying and selling votes.[41]

Nels Anderson, too, noted that hobos travelled as far as 1,000 miles to cast a vote and would occasionally accept money for it. During the tramp scare the equation mobility equals democracy that is central to mainstream American historiography was reversed and the mobility of the tramp became a symbol for corruption. The solution demanded was disenfranchisement and confinement.

Again, Reitman provided a useful alternative to mainstream discourse concerning tramps. One arena in which he played an active, if marginal, rôle was in Chicago's anti-syphilis campaign of 1937.[42] Reitman had witnessed for years the effects of syphilis among the hobos who made up his social network. His very first job was at the Cook Remedy Company who made Syphelene, a syphilis medicine. Later he heard the hobos on the boxcars discussing the pox, and as an assistant at Chicago's Polyclinic he witnessed experiments on venereal disease. Later still he taught syphilis pathology at the College of Physicians and Surgeons. In his own clinic he treated people from all levels of society with the new drug Salversan, an arsenic compound pioneered in Paris. In 1917 he established the first municipal VD clinic in Chicago, and clinics in Cook County jail and the Chicago House of Corrections. As a prisoner himself (in relation to birth-control activism) he started a clinic in the Cleveland House of Corrections, one of the first syphilis clinics in an American prison.

Official campaigns against syphilis, sponsored by President Roosevelt, focused on providing blood tests and treatment rather than prevention and prophylaxis, a decision made largely on moral grounds.[43] On Friday 13 August 1937, a day proclaimed by official propaganda as 'unlucky for syphilis', Chicago was plastered with posters picturing stylized syphilis spirochaetes. Some 5,000 physicians were conscripted to provide tests and treatments. A play called *Spirochete* was put on in a theatre whose lobby was full of doctors with syringes. Planes circled overhead with the message 'Chicago Fight Syphilis'. Over the next two years over 1,000,000 blood tests were given in Chicago and 42,000 cases of the disease were discovered.

Reitman was impressed, but believed the whole campaign was mis-directed, as the disease would re-emerge when it was over unless people were told how to keep themselves clean and use condoms. In his own campaigns Reitman always stepped beyond the bounds of widely accepted decency. The syphilis question was no exception. Reitman's basic message was that the best treatment for syphilis was prevention, and all that was needed were condoms, soap and water.

Despite disagreements, Reitman was hired by the Chicago Syphilis Project as a special investigator earning $150 per month. His job description included lecturing to 'underworld, hobo and other groups', speaking on the issue at 'open air soap-box settings' and investigating conditions and preparing statistics on VD in the world of the prostitute, transient and homeless.[44] In the next two years he frequented the marginal areas of the city, talking to prostitutes, drug addicts, strippers, pimps and hobos – all invisible to the medico-disciplinary gaze of the establishment.[45] One of Reitman's rôles was to lead tours of the 'underworld' for medical adminis-trators and practitioners. The establishment had very little idea about what went on in Chicago's marginal areas. Reitman, on the other hand, was very familiar with, and comfortable in, this world.

On 5 August 1937 he escorted four public health researchers along North Clark Street, talking to members of organized crime syndicates, con men and exhibition dancers. He took them to Washington Square, where they mounted soapboxes to talk about the syphilis project. They met an abortionist on North State Street and later visited a pornographer by the name of Hard-On Slim, where they were shown movies of two men and a woman engaged in hetero- and homosexual pursuits. Reitman suggested that similar movies might be used to promote an early version of 'safe sex'. Later they went to the South Side and visited the Cabin Inn, a place for female impersonators, and Wentworth Avenue, where black prostitutes worked in a host of places showing live sex shows. Such tours were standard for Reitman but (apparently) entirely novel for the officials he guided. In Reitman's eyes it was only by taking such people out of the world of science and medicine and onto the streets that the dimensions of the syphilis problem might be revealed.[46]

In his reports Reitman frequently urged the Project to set up clinics in areas frequented by hobos. But his interventions were no simple extension of medical discipline to formally unreachable groups. Reitman was unusually sensitive to the perspective of the hobos, having been one himself. Another one of his projects was a 'Hobo College' in Chicago, where the syphilis campaigns were discussed in great depth. After urging the hobos present to be tested he was met with considerable anger, the hobos informing him of their experiences with formal medicine. One of the crowd said 'It is a graft of the AMA (American Medical Association) ... They take the blood test from the poor stiffs, but they never bother the rich or the Society Folks. The Health Dept. is part of the Capitalistic system who want to exploit and make life hard for the poor and the Hobos.'[47] Reitman carefully reported these views to the Project and warned them to take the feelings of the hobos seriously.

Another group Reitman was hired to work with was the black population of Chicago's South Side. There was a widespread belief at the time that Blacks were sexually overactive and prone to syphilis.[48] He was concerned to show that syphilis was not a problem connected genetically to being black but was the result of poverty and ignorance. In one of his reports he wrote 'it is significant that of the 33 positive darkfields, 23 were in the colored race and one Mexican, and only nine white. Something is radically wrong, and humiliating if nothing is done to wipe out the blot that a certain group of our citizens are allowed to have 50 times as much primary chancres as their neighbouring group.'[49] Rather than seeing the incidence of syphilis among black people as pathological, he understood it as indicative of an economic system that privileged Chicago's wealthy Whites:

> And if syphilis is more common in one neighbourhood or race than it is in another, it is because they are more ignorant – not more 'sinful' or because of the texture of their skin. Wherever any race has learned the value of personal hygiene and prophylaxis, wherever they have good homes with bathtubs, wherever they understand venereal disease, wherever they have money to purchase soap and prophylactics, there they have a low syphilis incidence.[50]

So, unlike the predominant and sanctioned knowledge of the time that often described such things as the incidence of syphilis in terms of pathology, Reitman was quite willing to point the finger at the forces he felt were responsible. At the same time as he was working for the Chicago Syphilis Project, he was also heading his own one-man organization, the Chicago Society for the Prevention of Venereal Disease. His job with the Chicago Syphilis Project forbade him from mentioning prophylaxis, and his own Society was set up explicitly to provide a platform from which the use of condoms could be promoted. Needless to say, the line between the two rôles was a blurred one and Reitman was eventually fired from his post with the Chicago Syphilis Project for promoting prophylaxis. So while he shared the belief that hobos and other marginalized groups were vectors for syphilis, he did not pathologize them for it. The problem of syphilis, for Reitman, was one located in society, not in the individual.

PATHOLOGY AND THE SOCIAL BODY

Syphilis and venal voting both played a part in the labelling of the nomadic tramp as pathological, and both helped lay the ground for repressive actions by the medical establishment and the state. The mobile body of the tramp, a body assumed to be male, was inscribed with signifiers of pathological deviance from an inbred disposition to take to the road to an economically driven desire to sell votes. In using disease in the description of transgressive people and actions, society is often compared with the human body. In the tramp example, hegemonic society is the social body that is threatened by the actions of the mobile workers. In 1877 Francis Weyland concluded that 'The evil, as we have seen, is one of enormous magnitude, and unless speedily arrested, threatens the very life of society.'[51] The idea of society having a life is of course one that goes back to Hobbes's *Leviathan* and beyond – the idea of the social body. I suggest that the connection of tramps with syphilis simultaneously drew correlations between the physical body of the infected tramp and the metaphorical body of American democracy. In the notes of social reformers and others, tramps are blamed for the spread of syphilis and for practices of multiple voting for money. In some cases the two are connected, and it is suggested that mobile people suffering from syphilis are a threat to democracy and the social body – the tramp becomes the equivalent of a disease.

Susan Sontag has argued that disease and treatment are thought of, and acted on, as war.[52] In wars, extreme measures are called for and the normal legal process is suspended. The conceptual metaphor *society as human body* makes possible the metaphor of transgression as disease and legitimates the remedy. Returning to the nexus linking the mobile body of the tramp, the disease of syphilis and the threat to the social and political body, we can see how the idea of tramps as diseased and as a disease was metaphorically linked to treatments, which, in line with Sontag's logic, were often expressed in military terms. The various methods of dealing with tramps – from the tramp laws, to hard labour, to imprisonment to the whipping-post – were all metaphorically justified by the threat, both literal and metaphorical, of disease. These were justified by the need to restore health and normality.

There is also, of course, a connection to my earlier discussion of the part played by gender in this moral panic. The threat of syphilis was most alarming, not because it made tramps sick, for that would have been welcome news, but because of the so-called innocent syphilite, i.e., the person, usually a woman, who caught syphilis innocently through her lover or husband, who in turn would have slept with a prostitute, who may have slept with a tramp. So once again the threat to society – the social body – was more explicitly a threat to a sanctified female body.

In the process of pathologization, social reform, medicine and eugenics were all implicated in the construction of American society as a body threatened by the pathology of tramphood, just as the body of the tramp – one with suspect heredity and racked with disease – was made up as an embodied sign of danger and deviance.

# 6 Laughter and the Tramp

For *Kid Auto Races at Venice* (1914), his second film for Mack Sennett's Keystone Company, Charlie Chaplin was asked by Sennett to find a comedy costume and act the rôle of a buffoon getting in the way of a crew filming the car race. When Chaplin returned from the dressing-room he was costumed as a tramp. Chaplin recalls the moment he adopted the now-familiar clothes of the 'Little Tramp' as a transformative one: 'The moment I was dressed, the clothes and make-up made me feel the character. By the time I walked on stage "The Tramp" was fully born.'[1] He explained to Sennett the key features of his new character:

> You know this fellow is many-sided, a tramp, a gentleman, a poet, a dreamer, a lonely fellow, always hopeful of romance and adventure. He would have you believe he is a scientist, a musician, a duke, a polo player. However he is not above picking up cigarette butts or robbing a baby of its candy.[2]

His five minute 'solo' was a rare opportunity, and Sennett was impressed. From that point up to his classic feature film *Modern Times* (1936), Chaplin was to keep the costume that was to make him one of the most widely recognized popular culture icons in cinema.

The marketing extravaganza that accompanied Chaplin's films pre-figures the blanket promotion of more recent figures, such as Elvis Presley or Michael Jackson. Dolls were made. Children were given Chaplin toys for Christmas. Soldiers sang songs about him as they marched towards the front in World War One. Much later Chaplin's tramp became a marketing symbol for computer giants IBM. We are still conscious of the figure today. Of all the images of the tramp produced in the United States in the period 1869–1940, the most recognizable one worldwide is that of Chaplin as the 'Little Tramp'. It seems odd that the tramp, so despised by so many, should become so celebrated.

Whereas the focus in previous chapters has been on negative views of the tramp, in this chapter it is quite the opposite. Chaplin's tramp character became a weapon directed against authority and discipline, and for many his tramp was therefore a hero. Despite this the character fed off many of the same themes used by sociologists, doctors and the like. As ever, mobility, work and the body are at the centre of the tramp's comic world, and these themes connect Chaplin's tramp to the tramps discussed in previous chapters. A further link between this chapter and others is the way in which comic constructions of the tramp were rooted in long histories of their representation both in Europe and America. Chaplin's tramp was far from the first such comic figure. Tramp-like figures had been central to forms of comic acting since the fifteenth century in Europe, with its origins in Italian *commedia dell'arte* and North European vaudeville, music-hall and pantomime. Later, tramps began appearing as cartoon-strip figures in both Britain and America.

## CHAPLIN'S TRAMP AND HIS PRECURSORS

But where exactly did Chaplin's tramp come from? One, literal, answer concerns a meeting Chaplin had with a tramp in San Francisco. Chaplin offered the man food and drink and listened to stories of his life. These revolved around the tramp's attempts to acquire the basic necessities of life – food and drink. 'Why, if I am hungry enough, I can eat grass', the tramp told Chaplin. 'But what am I going to do with this thirst of mine? You know what water does to iron? Well, try to think what it will do for your insides.'[3] Chaplin evidently enjoyed the stories of tramp life and the irresponsibilities that went with it.

The character that emerged from the dressing-room in 1914 also owed much to the history of comedy (illus. 24). The trousers are too big and the coat too tight, the shoes too big and the hat too small. Chaplin remarked that he deliberately wanted to create a character of contradictions expressed through the ill-fitting clothing.[4] While he undoubtedly made this character his own, it is clear that bits of it were borrowed from the world of clowning. The baggy trousers held up by a pin had been used by Dan Leno, a colleague of Chaplin's in the Karno pantomime troupe where Chaplin learned stage comedy. An overtight coat had been worn by Little Tich, a famous music-hall dwarf, who also wore outsize shoes. Chaplin claimed that he learned his famous walk from a drunk in London. The situations he was to get himself into were similar to those endured by the cartoon tramp 'Happy Hooligan' in Randolph Hearst's newspapers.

24 Charlie Chaplin as the 'Little Tramp'.

Chaplin's tramp was a creative hybrid, gleanings from other performers and traditions.

Chaplin's professional career started in 1898 when he joined an English company, the 'Eight Lancashire Lads', which toured music-halls in major English cities.[5] In 1907 Chaplin was recruited into the well-reputed Karno Pantomime Troupe. His star rôle was in a piece called *Mumming Birds*, which became *A Night in the English Music Hall* when performed in America. His part was a stock music-hall character, the rich drunk who can never express himself because of the effects of his chronic drinking. The rich drunk interrupts the performance with slurred nonsense, awkward acrobatics and out-of-tune singing. Chaplin toured with the Karno troupe on the Continent in 1909 and in the United States between 1910 and 1912. It was while in America that Chaplin was spotted performing his drunk rôle by talent spotter Adam Kessel and signed up to the already famous Keystone film company run by Sennett.

Keystone slapstick was heavily influenced by the vaudeville shows popular in America at the turn of the century. The term 'vaudeville' comes from the Caux de Vire area of Normandy. It was there, in the fifteenth century, that a local miller, Olivier Basselin, composed a series of cider-drinking songs that became popular throughout France. These later developed into a series of ballads accompanied by spoken dialogue, which by the seventeenth century were performed at fairs across northern Europe.

American vaudeville appears to have emerged in the period following the Civil War, at the same time as the tramp scare. Saloons encouraged buskers and performers to entertain customers to keep them happy and drinking. In some establishments, stages were built expressly for the travelling vaudevilles. By the 1880s the vaudeville tradition was firmly established in the United States, with two networks merging to produce national touring possibilities for the troupes. Vaudeville was a travelling phenomenon, unlike the similar entertainment known as 'variety', which was locally rooted and usually based in a single theatre. Vaudeville shows had much in common with carnival. The most notable similarity was the breakdown of formal barriers between performers and audience. As Nicole Vigouroux-Frey explains it:

> The audience was always willing to be entertained, to celebrate the king of the day, thus unexpectedly modifying the course of the performance. By definition the vaude had no rigid pattern of development; it always allowed for the possibility of a dialogue between those who were in the house and those who were on the stage.[6]

Late in the century vaudeville was changing from an entirely informal and masculine form of entertainment, which included elements of burlesque and freakshow, to a respectable mainstream show for the whole family. Benjamin Keith, an associate of P. T. Barnum, the showman and promoter, formed The Keith Theatre in Boston, which became a vaudeville institution of some repute, though the shows there were stripped of most of their potentially disruptive elements. By 1909 there were around 1,200 vaudeville troupes performing across the United States.[7] Karno's Pantomime Troupe appeared on vaudeville programmes throughout the country during their tours.

American vaudeville was hugely reliant on British music-hall for its material. Up to 25 per cent of the songs featured came directly from Britain, and many of the performers were recruited from the British music-hall and pantomime traditions.[8] Tramps were a stock character in vaudeville performances. One of the stars of American vaudeville was Nat Wills, who took the persona of a tramp:

> he was a bum with a red nose, a slit mouth, a battered hat and baggy pants which he held together with a string; from this waist-string hung a tomato can, the most sacred of his possessions. His boots were cracked, and his immense toes resembled bell-hammers … His specialty was a tramp monolog, recounting his glorious thirsts, his joy in lying.[9]

One element of vaudeville, alongside dance, song, circus tricks and freak shows, was the 'Dumb Show', based on largely speechless characters. A number of Dumb Show performers were Europeans who had been brought up in the traditions of pantomime. The most famous American Dumb Show performer was W. C. Fields, who had a deep influence on Chaplin. From 1902 Fields performed the rôle of the 'tramp-juggler', which, according to Vigouroux-Frey, informed the creation of Chaplin's tramp. Indeed Chaplin's cane appears to be directly borrowed from Fields's character (illus. 25).[10]

More structured vaudeville sketches frequently revolved around the ineptitude of tramps. The 1909 vaudeville sketch *The Tramp and the Actress* by Charles Ulrich[11] is typical of their structure and themes. This 20-minute sketch plays on the fears surrounding women alone at home in country houses discussed in chapter Four. It features a tramp, Jim, attempting to rob the house of a wealthy actress, Maud, who specializes in playing insane women. She sees him stealing the silver and simulates madness in order to recover her valuables. After several improvized song and dance routines she drives him away by threatening to marry him. Although there is a script to follow, it frequently allows the two principal actors to interject song and dance. When Maud asks Jim to marry her, for instance, Jim is given the line 'Not on your life – I'm not in the market'; the text then offers 'Specialty if desired. Song and Dance'.[12] At another point in the sketch Maud asks Jim to sing and dance and say something funny to amuse her.

In *The Tramps' Convention*[13] – a more substantial sketch – the directions indicate that 'The more disreputable the costumes the better, patched, torn, ragged, dirty, too large, too small clothes of a nondescript character. HAPPY HOOLIGAN should have a very small hat which keeps falling off.'[14] Further notes specify that actors should use slang expressions wherever possible and that the players should 'sprawl and lounge in lazy, ungainly attitudes, in fact *be* tramps for the time being'.[15] The dialogue is written in a curious imitation of an Irish-American accent, and the jokes consistently

25 W. C. Fields.

revolve around the gathered tramps' reluctance to work and their inability
to deal with authority. The first joke concerns the correct way to deal with
vicious dogs and incorporates a number of references to laziness. Happy
Hooligan (described in parentheses as a 'very fat Irishman') has the task of
suggesting the correct response to canine confrontation. The following is
typical of the dialogue:

> (All sprawl in chairs in slouching attitudes as if too lazy to sit up)
> DUSTY BOB (in spread eagle style). Gentlemen uv our most noble per-
> fushion, we are met here to-day ter talk over some uv de difficulties
> uv dat same perfushion and ter devise ways and means by which
> our work – excuse me, gentlemen, work is a word de bare mention
> uv which we must avoid as much ez possible – ter devise ways and
> means, I say, by which our callin' may hev a still more honored
> standin' in de community and more and more members be
> attracted ter it ...[16]

Dusty Bob introduces the first issue 'How Ter Deal Wid de Dorg' and
hands the floor over to Happy Hooligan. Happy expounds at length on an
attempt to tame a wild dog with eye contact and concludes that the best

way to deal with guard dogs is to kill them: 'De only good dorg is a ded dorg.' Dusty Bob thanks Happy and proposes a vote of thanks, which is seconded by a group of other tramps:

> DUSTY BOB. It hes been moved and seconded data vote uv tanks be given our brudder fur his noble act. All dose in favor rise.
>
> HEALTHY TIM. Aw, wot yer guvin us? Dat's axin too much.
>
> CHORUS. Well, I guess. Axin' us ter git up! Tink we're goin' ter do all dat work? Not on yer life, etc.[17]

As well as jokes about laziness the sketch features repeated references to the tramps' lack of personal hygiene based on their fear of soap and water. The laughter that such a sketch provoked must have rested on mostly negative characteristics of the tramp identity – slovenly appearance, work-shy habits and poor hygiene combined with vaguely Irish accents. There is little in *The Tramp and the Actress* or *The Tramps' Convention* to suggest a sympathetic reading of the tramp's comic stature. Perhaps the laughter that accompanied such performances was amusement rooted in the presumed superiority the audience felt it enjoyed over the bums. The tramps' transgression of the rules of property, decorum and work may have been subversively seductive, but only from a position of implied social superiority.[18]

In its heyday (1890–1910), American vaudeville existed alongside early film comedy and the emergence of comic strips in newspapers. It is possible to see in these nascent forms a departure from earlier American humour. Nineteenth-century humour had been dominated by images of Yankees and Southerners, tricksters and con-men. In the last decade of the century the figure of the 'little man' became popular.[19] A typical 'little man' type was the tramp – a man crushed by the weight of those above him, but who, none the less, fights back through cunning and trickery. Other features of American humour, however, were not transformed. Ethnicity and race had always been comic subjects. Vaudeville, while a central part of a new comedy, was rooted in older traditions of jokes involving ethnic stereotypes. Mark Winokur has argued that American laughter has always involved supposed ethnic distinctions between immigrants and Europeans or between West Coast frontier types and East Coast establishment types.[20] In vaudeville, ethnic humour based on more or less two-dimensional stereotypes played a central rôle in monologues and sketches such as *The Tramps' Convention*. And since vaudeville tramps were frequently Irish, the humour was often based on Irish stereotypes. Stupidity and belligerence were characteristics of Irish stereotypes inher-

26 Harlequin.

ited by the tramp figure along with laziness and poor hygiene. In the early days of American tramp comedy, the more positive image of the 'little man' struggling to succeed is outweighed by the more negative laughter directed against ethnic groups of one kind or another.

Then there is *commedia dell'arte*, improvised comedy that emerged in the sixteenth century featuring lovers, servants and professionals in a series of perplexing love triangles.[21] Chaplin's tramp plays rôles that clearly resemble those of the comic servant (*zanni*) Arclecchine, or Harlequin (illus. 26). Harlequin was a simple, greedy, lovelorn character who was constantly beaten and kicked around despite his cunning and agility. *Commedia dell'arte* involved a vast number of scenarios improvised in ways that, like vaudeville, involved the audience. It was also well known for the athleticism and grace of the characters. *Commedia* actors had to wear fairly cumbersome masks that covered half the face. This made it difficult for audiences to hear their words. It was, therefore, extremely important for the actors to be able to express themselves using their whole bodies – an attribute equally important to silent film actors.

Another feature of *Commedia* that runs right though American vaudeville, music-hall and slapstick was vulgarity. Much of the comedy in all these forms is rooted in sex, references to the lower parts of the body and

acts normally thought to be disgusting or obscene. The buttocks and anus were consistent sources of humour. The appearance of a huge enema syringe, for instance, always went down well with the audience. As vaudeville and music-hall evolved into silent film, the tramp's body, one that was already understood to be grotesque, was central to this vulgarity.

## CARTOONS

As well as appearances on stage, the tramp also featured in the 'funnies' – the cartoon strips that appeared with increasing frequency in American newspapers around the turn of the century. America's first continuously

running comic-strip began in 1895 in the *New York World* with Richard Felton Outcault's 'At the Circus in Hogan's Alley'. The cartoon featured a bunch of kids playing in the alleys of New York's slum district. The cartoon, at its inception, was a representation of the low and marginal. Following hard on its heels came a whole series of slapstick cartoons, including 'The Katzenjammer Kids' (1897), 'Buster Brown' (1902) and 'Little Nemo' (1905). In the formative years of the comic-strip the tramp emerged as a favourite comic character. Tramps had already been extensively lampooned in *Puck*, *Life* and other popular magazines and were the object of fun and ridicule in vaudeville and burlesque across the country (illus. 27–29). In England, Tom Browne's 'Weary Willie and Tired Tim' had appeared in 1896 and in 1900 Frederick Burr Opper's Irish tramp 'Happy Hooligan' began in American papers (illus. 30).[22]

William Randolph Hearst selected Opper as a feature cartoonist for the *New York Journal* in 1899 after Opper had already worked for a considerable time as an artist for the humour magazine *Puck*. 'Happy Hooligan' began

29  Tom Browne's 'Weary Willie and Tired Tim', from *Illustrated Chips*.

30 Frederick Burr Opper,
Happy Hooligan, 1904.

in 1900 and was to become his most popular strip (he was also the creator of 'Maud the Mule' and 'Alphonse and Gaston'). The strip ran until 1932, when Opper retired with bad eyesight. The themes of 'Happy Hooligan' were straightforward and repeated endlessly. Happy plays the rôle of a good-natured but bumbling tramp who, along with his brothers, Montmorency and Gloomy Gus, is consistently the victim of the norms of society that surround him. Everywhere he goes he meets with extraordinarily bad luck.

Opper's cartoons match the situations and themes of Chaplin's tramp character who emerged on film in 1914. Happy, like Charlie, is endlessly trying to get and hold a job, but failing miserably through his own clumsiness, bad luck and misinterpretations of his actions. Happy's tramphood is obvious from his dress: his shoes have holes; his trousers have patches; he wears an old tin can on his head. What hair he has is untidy and his features are crude. He moves clumsily. More often than not, Happy's body thwarts his intentions, producing violent and comic effects in the best slapstick tradition.

In 'Did Happy Hooligan Get Another Job? Sure He Did! This Time He is Hired as a Bill Poster'[23] (illus. 31), we see Happy trying to stop two children from fighting. As he does so he manages to hit the man in the window and the policeman with his pasting-brush. On being taken to the magistrate he continues to hit everyone in authority with the brush, resulting, as ever, in his downfall. Happy's mishaps often revolve around his attempts to find work or help other people. In another strip, for instance, he is hired as a waiter and manages to spill hot coffee over a customer while trying to help him with his coat. The misadventures of Happy Hooligan are clear precursors for Chaplin's tramp, centred, as they are, on the tramp's two defining characteristics, bodily mobility and work. Another element they share is that Happy's and Charlie's problems invariably result from their attempts to help others. The comic world of the tramp is one in which kindness and honesty are invariably not the best policy.

It is suggested by his language that Happy is an Irish-American tramp. We have already seen how vaudeville tramps were frequently represented as Irish. The link between trampdom and Irishness is commonly encountered.

31 Detail from F. B. Opper, 'Did Happy Hooligan Get Another Job? Sure He Did!'

Social reformers and media commentators supposed that tramps were mostly foreign despite the fact that most investigations into tramp origins revealed that the vast majority were 'native'.[24] Nevertheless, by using an Irish accent the cartoonists were able to mix jokes specific to tramps with more general ethnic humour.

Happy was representative of a more widespread use of the tramp as a character in early cartoons. James Montgomery Flagg, a cartoonist for the comic magazine *Judge*, developed the character of Nervy Nat between 1903 and 1907. Nat was a rascal tramp continually involved in escapades with railroad police, rich bankers and flirtatious women. There is at least some suggestion that W. C. Fields's 'tramp-juggler' act was based on Nat. His bulbous nose, in particular, was suggestive of Nat's glowing round nose.[25] In 1907 Flagg moved from *Judge* to *Life* and Nat was continued by Arthur Lewis (illus. 32). In 1916 Nat became a star in an animated feature by Pat Sullivan. Other celebrity tramp figures of the cartoon world included Mopey Dick and The Duke, created by Denys Wortman.

32 James Montgomery Flagg, Nervy Nat, from *The Judge*.

By the time Chaplin picked out the clothes that were to make him a tramp for much of his career, there was clearly an established history of tramp characters in American humour. These characters differed from one another in a number of ways, yet there was much that united them. The comic tramp was marked by particular appearances in terms of both the clothing he wore and the kinds of facial characteristics that were adopted. Unshaven faces, hats, bulbous noses, ill-fitting clothes and odd-sized shoes were all part of the tramp identity. Silly walks, behaviour that tended to act against the intended outcome of an action and general clumsiness were part of the act. On the whole these representations added up to a comic figure who was laughed *at* from a position of social superiority. The laughter was mocking laughter that, as Henri Bergson has suggested, tries to harness the socially low into society – a laughter aimed at correction and humiliation.[26]

In chapter Three I discussed the rôle of academic categorization in making up the tramp. Vaudeville and cartoon comedy were implicated in categorization too. Both the ethnic stereotypes and more specific tramp stereotypes were forms of category. Stereotyping, in general, involves an extreme and crude form of the reductionism needed to produce categories. James Dormon sums up social-psychological literature of stereotyping thus:

> there is general agreement among the specialists that perceived phenomena (and specifically, such human phenomena as immigrant populations) are, by normal cognitive processes functioning among their observers, reduced to sets of qualities, physical and/or characterological, that are accepted as definitive of a category or phenomena. Stereotyping is thus a cognitive process whereby complex phenomena are simplified and made intelligible.[27]

In the case of the tramp, as with ethnic groups, the comic stereotype is a massively simplified category of a social group. As with other forms of category, the comic stereotype produces as much as it describes. The ascribed characteristics of the tramp – uncleanliness, laziness, drunkenness, strange bodily pathologies – are isolated and magnified to form a caricature in order to make the stereotype comical. In vaudeville and the funnies, more often than not the tramp figures were caricatures – crude comic stereotypes whose only obvious function was to underline expressions of superiority. Again, like ethnic stereotypes, the tramp characters mentioned so far confirm the more negative interpretations of comedy and laughter that claim that humour 'is one of the most effective and vicious weapons in the repertory of the human mind'.[28]

Laughter, however, need not be such a negative force. It also has a subversive and regenerative rôle. I shall return to these ideas later. For now it is only necessary to point out that the Little Tramp that Chaplin created in 1914 was quite different from earlier tramp characters, although they shared many identifying traits. Chaplin's tramp was marked by considerable pathos. He took the critical force of comedy and deflected it away from himself and towards the society in which the tramp struggled to exist.

## SILENT FILM COMEDY

The tradition of silent film comedy was the most immediate context for Chaplin's tramp, one that he was to become the leading exponent of. By the time popular film entered the American cultural world, vaudeville had become a relatively tame affair, with its lewd and lascivious content cut for the benefit of 'respectable families'. According to Robert Sklar the movies came to the rescue of genuinely subversive comedy, for 'they provided visual techniques ideally suited to a new and expanded expression of the old comic violence, exaggeration and grotesque imagination.'[29]

Aspects of *commedia*, pantomime, music-hall and vaudeville had traditionally involved the ridicule of pomposity and authority. These had gradually been dispersed through self-censorship or official interference. The Keith Theatre in Boston, for instance, was extremely successful at transforming vaudeville into a mainstream, respectable spectacle. The price of this success, however, had been the removal of vaudeville's potentially subversive contents. New policies deliberately excluded dirty language and suggestive sexuality.

In silent comedies chaos and subversion made a comeback. The early silent comedies were particularly noted for the way they ridiculed wealth, power and authority, thus undermining authority and control. In this regard they continued the tradition of music-hall and early forms of vaudeville. Many of the situations in Keystone comedies are repeats of running gags in Karno's pantomime and music-hall sketches. Authority, pomposity, conventional morality and extravagant wealth were considered fair game for ridicule.

Early silent film in America was dominated by comedy. Nearly a third of pre-1912 films were comedies, with much of the remainder being newsreels. The most notable early film director, D. W. Griffith, did not successfully marry film to serious drama until 1908. Even his output at Biograph was dominated by comedy in its early years. One of his protégés was Mack Sennett, who worked as an actor and as a director of Biograph comedies until 1912, when he left to form the Keystone studio and launch the golden age of American silent film comedy.[30]

Sennett and the Keystone company immediately set about using comedy to ridicule propriety. His comedies were known as 'slapstick', and they consisted of two reels of gags loosely strung together in a rapid sequence escalating from comic misunderstandings to physical rough-housing. They almost always included an extended chase sequence, in which the famous Keystone Kops pursued wrongdoers off piers and into waste heaps and a vast array of other unlikely situations. The comedy was extremely physical (the term 'slapstick' derives from the sticks used by clowns to strike each other in English pantomime).

Sennett's first batch of four films for Keystone featured films about incompetent cops, sexual competition, inappropriate dress and the ridiculously wealthy. These were just a foretaste of the barrage of films to come that directed laughter at the prevailing mores and codes of the day. The films were shot at a frantic pace. Griffith taught Sennett the art of cutting pictures in order to produce pace and keep the audience's attention. Griffith was known for cutting between two or more lines of action repeatedly – never allowing the audience to focus for too long on one piece of a story line. Sennett accelerated this process still further, aware perhaps that the power of the acting or the story line was not going to hold that much attention. As Robert Sklar explains it:

> In some comedies he cut the shots twice as swiftly as even his earlier fast tempo and with his cameraman cranking slowly in order to increase the speed of movement on the screen, Keystone comedies are sometimes little more than a blur of frantic action.[31]

The Keystone Kops were surreal expansions of Burlesque and earlier figures of authority.[32] It was obligatory in British stage comedy to have scenes in which a clown outwits the police. Almost as soon as the 'Peelers' were formed in 1829 to police London they became the butt of jokes. The police were most often in direct conflict with the clown or Harlequin in pantomime stage comedy. Usually the police were corrupt thieves and bullies. Later stage policemen were simply stupid and slow.

> Reel after reel, week after week, year after year, Sennett's audiences were privileged to observe a society in total disorder. The vast

majority in Sennett's world were motivated by greed and lust; they cheated, lied, stole and committed casual acts of violence against others ... Authority always arrived, more or less promptly, in the persons of the Keystone Kops, but proved to be, if anything, more disordered than the world that whirled around outside the precinct station's door.[33]

Initial reactions to Keystone slapstick were highly ambivalent. While many reviewers commented on the amount of laughter the films provoked, they were uneasy about the cause of that laughter. They could not come to terms with the fact that vulgarity and violence might be funny. The following extract from a 1915 review in *Photoplay* illustrates this well:

> There are very few people who don't like these Keystones; they are thoroughly vulgar and touch the homely strings of our own vulgarity ... some of the funniest things in this picture are too vulgar to describe ... There is some brutality in this picture and we can't help feeling that this is reprehensible. What human being can see an old man kicked in the face and count it fun.[34]

Once Chaplin was well known, he too became the object of high-minded scorn and censure. In an article in *Variety* magazine, one reviewer commented that 'never anything dirtier was placed upon the screen than Chaplin's Tramp'.[35] Chaplin became Sennett's lead man at Keystone following his success as the tramp figure. In February 1916 Chaplin moved to Mutual for $670,000 a year and attracted a substantial amount of criticism for such a salary while he was notably absent from the fields of Europe in World War One. In October 1917 he moved once more to First National, where he was paid $1,000,000 for eight movies in eighteen months, all produced by himself. Chaplin was in complete control as star, as director and even as composer of the film music.

CHAPLIN'S COMIC TECHNIQUE

Chaplin developed a unique and revolutionary comedy style that marked a dramatic break from the Keystone slapstick tradition and from earlier representations of tramps in comedy. In the slapstick tradition that held sway in silent comedy before Chaplin, order was subverted by presenting total chaos – society falling apart at the seams. Chaplin never really took to the constant frantic nature of slapstick and persuaded Sennett that the camera needed to spend more time on longer scenes in which a character

33 Chaplin eating his shoelaces in *The Gold Rush* (1925).

could be developed. While Sennett's comedies were based on frenetic movement Chaplin was more interested in developing personality. His scenes were often cut up into small segments by Sennett and would appear throughout a film. Chaplin's early films for Sennett were put together in little more than a week. In contrast, Chaplin's two-reel films at Mutual took up to six weeks to make, and later, when Chaplin made feature films such as *Modern Times*, he would use masses of film to reach his desired scene. For one scene he is said to have used 50,000 feet of film when only 75 feet were necessary.

As Chaplin gained control of the production process he began to subvert the social order not through chaos but through the magic of trans-formation. His actions were far slower and more graceful than those dominant in slapstick. While the camera focused on Chaplin, he would perform subtle and startling transformations without the aid of trick photography, speeding up and slowing down. Filmic fantasy was lifted from the realm of tricks in the production process to the ingenuity of human movement and imagination. Objects were magically transformed in Chaplin's hands (illus. 33).

> Material objects and even living things become magically adaptable in his hands. The technique was first demonstrated in *His Night Out*,

when Charlie, a drunk, tries to get water out of a telephone receiver and shines his shoes with his toothbrush and paste ... In *A Woman*, impersonating a woman, he sits down on a feather hat, the hat pins stick in his pants and he jumps around looking like a rooster; in *Work* he turns a lampshade into a skirt for a nude statuette and sets it dancing; and in his famous scene in *The Gold Rush*, he cooks and eats his boots, devouring the shoelaces as if they were spaghetti.[36]

This comedy of transformation often centred on the comic inappropriate use of objects. In *The Floor Walker* he waters some flowers neatly arrayed on a hat in a department store. In *Caught in the Rain* he tries to open a door with a cigarette and pours whisky on his hair rather than oil. Such comedy is anarchic, but in ways very different from slapstick anarchy. It is an anarchy based on the confusion of categories, the dislocation of time and disorientation of cause and effect. Things are always out of time and place. This constant but subtle overthrow and inversion of the taken-for-granted order of things imaginatively, and often touchingly, liberates us from the way things are. As Raoul Sobel and David Francis have argued, much of Chaplin's comedy is derived from basic incongruity – 'the situation when two planes of reality not normally associated with each other are suddenly brought together'.[37] This incongruity is disturbing because it makes the divisions we have become used to seem absurd, no longer rooted in necessity. Anything becomes possible.

The other key to Chaplin's comedy is, of course, bodily movement. Following in the traditions of *commedia* and pantomime, silent movies – particularly comic ones – relied heavily on bodily movement and gestures for their effect. In the late twentieth century we are not well prepared to make sense of silent film because we have become used to the power of the spoken word and the abstraction from bodily lived experience that the spoken word involves. Indeed, as we look back from our present position, it is hard to understand the levels of laughter that were common at the time of Chaplin's films. While we clearly use our bodies in a myriad of ways in everyday life and are able to read the bodily movements of others, we have been stripped of our ability to understand visual culture without sound. Our vocabulary for thinking about and through the body is impoverished. It is a characteristic of a culture of abstraction that we constantly talk of films and other visual arts by separating the form of expression from the content. It is much easier to think of films as though they were literature, and it is, therefore, no surprise that we live in an age dominated by the metaphor of text. Thinking through, and writing about, the elusive visual qualities of film has become a difficult task. Yet to ignore the visual qualities of Chaplin's tramp would be foolhardy, for it is in the physicality of his bodily movements that his comic appeal lies.[38]

> There is always such an abundance of detail in a Chaplin performance that his acting might well be described as rococo. Yet Chaplin's every gesture, every facial expression is so economical that he always seems to make a necessity of unnecessary movement, transforming his whole body into the expression of one emotion … every emotion he feels finds an external expression in his body.[39]

Chaplin's most astonishing ability was that of mime. He was able to use his body so expressively that words were made to seem cumbersome and foolish in comparison.

> This was Chaplin's supreme gift. No amount of intelligence, perception, emotion and ideas could have taken its place, for without the ability to translate them into gesture and movement, the 'Little fellow' would have remained a dead letter, a character Chaplin might have dreamed about but never have realized … Chaplin's grace of movement and variety of expression made his colleagues appear a gang of bumpkins.[40]

There are a number of scales at which Chaplin's movements produce a comic effect, but it is at the scale of the body and its interrelations with the surrounding environment that Chaplin's comedy is produced. Most obviously, perhaps, the constant movement of his body breaks with the constant hum of expectation. Many of his best-known bodygags involve stylized mechanical forms of movement that suited silent film particularly well. Chaplin's body seems more organized and therefore more funny than everyday human movement. When Chaplin lifts his hat he does so in a straight line – vertically. His legs often appear to stick straight out to the side as he walks away from the camera. When he shrugs his shoulders it is as though he has been wound up and some arrangement of cogs has whirred into action to produce the comic movement that follows. In Henri Bergson's thesis on laughter, one of his primary laws of laughter revolves around mechanical movements: 'The attitudes, gestures and movements of the human body are laughable in exact proportion as that body reminds us of a mere machine.'[41] The comic effect generated by the cyborg-like merging of the mechanical and the living 'makes us incline towards the vaguer image of *some rigidity or other* applied to the mobility of life, in an awkward attempt to follow its lines and counterfeit its suppleness'.[42] This machine/body merging also reminds us of the body's more general materiality (a theme of carnival par excellence) as we fixate on the trouble it gets into by not moving in a way that conforms to expectations and thus goes unnoticed.

The mechanical movements of Chaplin's tramp are well-suited to the medium of silent film. The comedy associated with Sennett's Keystone company was based around the frantic speed of the chase. Many of Chaplin's jokes were impossible actions made possible on screen by the use of speeding up and reversing techniques:

> Chaplin's movement was uniquely attuned to motion picture conventions in the silent era such as undercranking, black and white photography, and silence. The modulation of film speed, for example ... served to make Chaplin's mechanical movements look even more mechanical and precise. Chaplin became masterful at matching the mood of a scene with its speed ...[43]

Chaplin plays with mobility and rhythm in extraordinary ways. In *The Great Dictator* he pours a drink from his canteen and watches the water go up rather than down. He had failed to realize that he was flying upside down. In *The Floorwalker* he spends much of his time trying to go up down-escalators and thus remains trapped in the same place while frantically running. Rhythm and momentum are also used to great effect. In *Modern Times* he becomes so used to tightening bolts that his body continues to perform the action after the work is over. His jerking body hilariously goes around 'tightening' any object that looks like it might need it. Chaplin's tramp is always at play with the fundamental forces of the world. He manages to engage with the fundamental kinaesthetic and tactile senses of the film viewer through his play with motion and rhythm.[44]

Another source of laughter, for Bergson, is a certain incongruence of actions and objects that leads to unexpected outcomes. The man who sits on a chair and finds himself sprawling on the floor because his chair has been tampered with, or the woman who picks up a glass of milk, starts to drink and discovers she is swallowing white paint. These are examples of comic incongruities in everyday life. The comedy lies in momentum. The man who sat down did not stop moving but continued all the way to the floor. So much of the meaning of Chaplin's comedy jokes depends on out-of-placeness against expectations – doing things at the wrong time and in the wrong place. The basic elements of slapstick bodily humour involve the transgression of expectations – *faux pas*, falling over, wearing the wrong clothes, not noticing there is spinach between one's teeth, walking into walls, getting custard pies in the face, speaking words that are meant to remain hidden.

Umberto Eco has examined the relationship between 'the comic and the rule'. His argument is that laughter arises when everyday and unspoken rules are broken:

> What are the scenarios that the comic violates without having to repeat them? First of all, the common scenarios, the pragmatic rules of symbolic interaction that society takes for granted. The custard pie in the face makes us laugh because we normally assume that, at a party, pies are eaten and not thrown at other people.[45]

The kind of slapstick body jokes Eco refers to here assume a deeply understood, embodied set of expectations that are 'overwhelmingly present at the moment of violation'.[46] Jokes that have to be explained are not good jokes.

## MOBILITY, WORK AND THE BODY IN *THE TRAMP* AND *MODERN TIMES*

Chaplin clearly took the bodily humour of slapstick into new realms of expressiveness. While he continued to use fairly violent and often vulgar actions to create chaotic laughter, he also paid far more attention to the context that surrounded the joke. So while he produced comedy through the movements of the body, he also produced comic effects in the tension between the movement of the tramp character and the mobility going on around him. The best-known example of this is the classic late film *Modern Times* (1936), which has become a canonic text of cinematic modernity. The film, the last in which Chaplin played the Little Tramp, features this character job-seeking in the city during a time of mass unemployment and worker activism.

The first scenes of the film feature the Little Tramp struggling with life in a factory. They are an account of the marginal, bemused individual caught up in the impersonal machinery of modern society. Chaplin made it clear he intended to produce a critical representation of the new Fordist production system:

> I remembered an interview I had had with a bright young reporter on the New York *World*. Hearing that I was visiting Detroit, he had told me of the factory-belt system there – a harrowing tale of big

34  Chaplin practising with the Feeding Machine while rehearsing for *Modern Times* (1936).

industry luring healthy young men off the farms who, after four or
five years at the belt system, became nervous wrecks.[47]

The mobility of the factory is the structured and disciplinary motion of
Taylorism. Frederick Taylor, in his 1911 book, *The Principles of Scientific
Management*, had broken down the totality of factory labour into minutely
observable, precise repetitive motions in a way that enabled the transformation of labour organization. The invention of the assembly line became
the event that brought the modern production process now known as
'Fordism' into being. This invention allowed the factory manager to
control the pace of production and the labour processes that went into
it in minute detail. Both Lenin and Ford became great fans of Taylorist
principles. As Lenin wrote:

> The Taylor system, the last word of capitalism in this respect, like
> all capitalist progress, is a combination of the subtle brutality of
> bourgeois exploitation and a number of its great scientific achieve-
> ments in the fields of analysing mechanical motions during work,
> the elimination of superfluous and awkward motions, the working
> out of correct methods of work, the introduction of the best
> system of accounting and control, etc.[48]

Key to Taylorist principles were the mechanization of the human body and the production of mobile bodies. Important here, though, is the specificity of the mobility allowed. 'Superfluous and awkward motions' were to be eliminated.

Workers become alienated from their labour as they are increasingly dominated by technology. Machines and the human body become interchangeable. In one classic sequence, the Little Tramp is force-fed by a feeding machine that has been developed to reduce the time workers need to spend away from their work (illus. 34). In another scene the Little Tramp retreats to the bathroom, where he is observed by the boss through a prophetic CCTV system. The industrial process becomes internalized in the body of the tramp as he is forced to work ever faster and faster. Finally, the Little Tramp enters the body of the machine itself, playing out his comic transgressions among the cogs of modernity (illus. 35, 36).[49]

The Little Tramp brings an element of play into the carefully ordered motion of Taylorist production. Almost everything Chaplin does in the factory constitutes 'superfluous motion' – motion that acts against the intended outcome of the factory system. The Tramp's playful mobility thus challenges the ordering principle of the new modern world that Chaplin sought to critique. His hysterical infusion of playfulness into the mechanized world of modernity produces a moment that is both comic and potentially revolutionary.

35 Chaplin tightens bolts superfluously in *Modern Times* (1936).

36 Chaplin caught in the cogs of modernity in *Modern Times* (1936).

> The factory creates an atmosphere in which all significant action must be movement of one kind or another. In the factory, one cannot choose how to move, and one can barely choose whether to move with the machine or in opposition to it. The greatest transgression possible is stillness.[50]

If the machinery of production is representative of a repressive state of being, then the Tramp is its sworn enemy. Chaplin's tramp is unemployable and undisciplined. But he has fun. His movements are those of gay abandon. He likes pleasure for the sake of it. The Tramp presents his body as a force for pleasure – a carnivalesque riot of gestures and motions played for laughs.[51] Indeed, in the Tramp's final job in *Modern Times*, work and play are joined in the singing-and-dancing waiter who delivers a song about lewd sexuality to an encouraging audience. In this job, at least, the Little Tramp appears to be at home.

Much of the humour in *Modern Times*, as in many of Chaplin's movies, is derived from the attempt to provide the essentials of life – food, work and shelter. There are many scenes of people trying to get food in a plethora of illegal ways. Chaplin connects work to hunger. Honesty is constantly punished and dishonesty rewarded. The Little Tramp is arrested for trying to return a red flag to the truck it had fallen from. Seen carrying the red flag by the police, he is mistaken for a strike leader and apprehended. Official ways of making-do are constantly seen as soul-destroying and doomed to fail, while unofficial making-do is often rewarded with the ownership of the means of survival – food. The ethical universe of 'honesty is the best policy' is turned on its head. Honesty is obviously the worst policy for Chaplin's tramp, for it invariably gets him in trouble. There is considerable irony in the way in which the central institutions of normal life in the United States – those providing not only the essentials of life but the deeper feelings of satisfaction and belonging – are the greatest sources of frustration and alienation for Chaplin's tramp. We have seen how lack of work forms a central part of the definition of tramps in a number of different forms of knowledge. In early tramp comedy this lack had been coded as laziness and exaggerated for comic effect. In Chaplin this lack is seen as an effect of the systems surrounding the Little Tramp – which he is simply unable to conform to.

The other central part of the tramp's definition involves mobility. In negative portrayals, he is seen as excessively mobile and thus threateningly untraceable. Chaplin used mobility (alongside work) to produce different forms of laughter in *Modern Times*. The various mobilities of *Modern Times* grind against one another and the friction produces laughter. The Fordist factory seeks to inscribe a uniform sense of bodily mobility; stillness is punished. The commands that emanate from the factory boss are to work faster and faster, but Chaplin's body cannot be controlled in this way. He either moves inappropriately or he is inappropriately static. There are moments of stillness in the film, but they invariably revolve around punishment and incarceration. Stillness has its appropriate setting – not the factory but the prison. In the factory, transgression takes the form of stillness or movement not directed to production. In the tramp's first job, work is a finely regulated activity that produces bodies moving in particular ways. Work is the limiting of the self to one particular task that involves parts of the body in one kind of repeated movement while the rest of the body remains motionless. The Tramp's body is simultaneously not moving enough (insofar as it does not meet the aims of production) and moving too much (insofar as the Tramp's movements jam up the cogs and wheels of modernity).

*Modern Times* ends with the oft-repeated scene of Chaplin, this time with his female companion, walking down a road into the distance. This, of course, is another form of mobility. Viewers of this scene at the time would have been aware of its customary appearance at the end (and sometimes the beginning) of Chaplin movies, and may have thought of it as a join between films, suggesting the Tramp's progress towards whatever is to happen in the next film. In the sense that the Tramp always returns to

37 Chaplin on the road in *The Tramp* (1915).

the road, the road serves as a replacement for the home (illus. 37). Earlier in the film, the Little Tramp and the 'Gamine', his female companion, had made a pathetic attempt to construct an ideal home in a little wooden shack. Other than that, though, the couple are never located in a rooted place. This is linked to the lack of work, as it is work which is supposed to provide the means to construct a home and start a family. Ironically then, movement is made to be homelike – a point of return where the Tramp is joined by his female partner. In this final scene, Chaplin reasserts the paradoxical freedom of forced mobility and the humanity of his character freed from the mobilities of work. The apparently negative fact of failure at work and expulsion from the geographies of normality becomes a positive affirmation of alternative geographies of home and movement.

Another comedy of mobilities in friction occurs in the much earlier film *The Tramp* (1915), reckoned by many to be Chaplin's first classic film, which also begins and ends with the figure on the road. It was in *The Tramp* that Chaplin explicitly developed the character of the Little Tramp who was to travel through all his films up to *Modern Times*. *The Tramp* is a short-length film made with the film company Essenay when Chaplin was reaching the height of his popularity. It concerns a good tramp (played by Chaplin), a farming family and three 'bad tramps'.

The film opens with Chaplin's tramp walking down a country road. A car speeds past and knocks him over. He gets up, but is soon knocked down by a car coming the other way. He sits down by a tree to eat. While cleaning his fingernails, another tramp steals his lunch. Meanwhile, at the farm, we see three tramps (looking much more dishevelled than Chaplin's) watching the farmer give his daughter a roll of banknotes. One of the tramps steals the banknotes from the girl, but Chaplin intervenes, knocks the tramp over and returns the money to the girl. This is followed by a series of incidents in which the tramps take turns to steal the money, but each is repelled by Chaplin. The girl takes Chaplin back to the farmhouse for some food and Chaplin agrees to work on the farm. The following scenes involve him failing to get anything accomplished, while the other farmhands badly suffer from his incompetence. Meanwhile, Chaplin is becoming infatuated with the farmer's daughter and the three malicious tramps are plotting to seize the money from the farmer. They ask Chaplin to join them, which he pretends to agree to. He repels their attempt to enter the farmhouse through an upstairs window and accidentally gets shot by the farmer. The girl looks after him until he recovers; meanwhile her boyfriend enters the scene. On seeing this Chaplin writes a note declaring his love and noting 'I can offer you nothing'. Finally, we see Chaplin walking away from us down the road, first slowly and pathetically and then jauntily. The film ends where it began: on the road.

*The Tramp*, like most of Chaplin's tramp movies, revolves around the necessities of life – food, shelter, work, money and love. While *Modern Times* is set in the urban world of Fordist time–space routines, *The Tramp* is set in the bucolic world of American rurality. While these settings occupy opposite ends of a familiar urban–rural continuum, they share the characteristic of established patterns of stillness and movement. While the urban movements of *Modern Times* are those of Taylorist modernity, those of the farm are of a sedimented routine world rooted in the pre-modern. Just as the structures of the factory are incapable of disciplining the Tramp's constant motion, so the routines of the farm are incapable of assimilating him. Much of the laughter the film provokes arises from the disjuncture between the routine of the farm and Chaplin's frantic mobility.

The farm's routine is one that has the appearance of being rooted in nature. While the monstrous machines of the factory are the supreme symbols of artificiality against which the Tramp's body rebels, the time–space routines of the farm revolve around a combined natural/economic/social cycle of sunrises, sunsets, harvesting, animal feeding, milking, bedtimes and dinners that have been coded over time to represent authenticity. The mobility of the Tramp cannot fit the requirement of either artificiality or authenticity. The modernity of *Modern Times* and the pre-modernity of *The Tramp* are linked by the opening scene of *The Tramp*, where Chaplin is seen walking down a rural road and hit by speeding cars, not once but twice. These reminders of urban life are too fast for the Little Tramp. He cannot keep up. Dazed, he sits down by a tree to have a picnic, and thus his adventure begins.

Just as he does in the factory, the Little Tramp attempts to conform to the work routines of his new context. Much of the film shows Chaplin working alongside a farmhand. In one scene Chaplin is asked to milk a cow and, not knowing how, pulls the animal's tail up and down like a pump-handle, hoping to produce milk. In another scene he is given a pitchfork by the grateful farmer and asked to help the farmhand in the barn. Chaplin, looking for all the world like he knows what he is doing, promptly stabs the farmer in the foot. Once instructed on how to carry the pitchfork over his shoulder, he turns around and knocks the hapless farmer on the head. After a series of pitchfork incidents the farmer ends up with a sack of grain falling on his head from a great height after Chaplin has prodded the farmhand carrying it. Chaplin's constant mobility is a hazard to him and to all around him. He is always tripping over things and leaving objects for others to trip over. Chaplin is moving, but his actions work against their intended outcome. One period of enforced stillness follows a scene in which the Little Tramp is accidentally shot by the farmer as he moves (too hurriedly) into the line of fire while chasing the marauding tramps out of the farmyard. His leg wound immobilizes him, and he is forced to sit down and be nursed by the farmer's daughter.

The Little Tramp is simply out of step with the embedded and routinized activities of farm life. While Chaplin's mobilities are playful, laughter-provoking and expansive, the mobilities of the farm are sedimented, circular and routine – connected to social ritual, the demands of nature and economic necessity.

Clearly the laughter that *The Tramp* generates is slightly different from that of *Modern Times*. In *Modern Times* Chaplin asks us to laugh at the factory system. The surrounding structures are objects of criticism, and thus they are ridiculed. In *The Tramp* our laughter is not against the farm. The farm is not shown to be exploitative or repressive. It is simply a time and space that cannot accommodate the Little Tramp. Our laughter is sympathetic, both for Chaplin and for those on the farm. Chaplin has lost his love; the farm has lost a source of fun and vitality.

What binds these two films together, along with many of Chaplin's tramp films, is the consistent, inventive play on the themes of the body, work and motion. Chaplin's supreme achievement was to create a kind of comic relational ontology from these three themes. They are, of course, themes that run through all forms of knowledge about tramps. By 1914 the tramp had already been made-up as a marginal and troubling figure marked by a pathologized body that refused to work and was excessively mobile. Chaplin reconstituted this triad to create a new figure who actively subverted the environments in which he was immersed and yet attracted sympathy rather than loathing. In Chaplin's hand the lack of work, the strange bodily appearance and the excessive mobility are animated and reconfigured with the help of much laughter to produce a new tramp whose transgressions are applauded.

## THE TRAMP AND THE SUBVERSIVE GEOGRAPHY OF LAUGHTER

Clearly, understanding the Little Tramp involves thinking through the familiar matrix of embodiment, work and mobility in new ways. Chaplin's comedy has been described as one of transformation, and among the things he transformed was the tramp. Although he drew on a rich history of comic tramp characters and used many of the characteristics ascribed to tramps, he did not make the tramp into a caricature. In Chaplin's hands the tramp became a rich, many-sided, often contradictory character with whom the audience is evidently supposed to identify.

Some have argued that Chaplin's character was not, in fact, a tramp at all apart from in the films explicitly titled as such. Raoul Sobel and David Francis, for instance, claim that Chaplin's character (they call it the 'Little Fellow') looks nothing like a picture of a British tramp from London's Embankment. Sobel and Francis are British, and assumed that Chaplin, an emigrant to America, would have modelled his tramp on originals seen in England:

> His character is aggressive, resourceful, jaunty. He is always clean-shaven and washed. There is no suggestion of dirty fingernails, grubby underwear, rotting teeth, bad breath or rheumy eyes; his clothes never hang in tatters, his boots never gape open. Although he is a wanderer in *The Vagabond* and *The Tramp* ... nevertheless the fundamental rootlessness of the vagrant is as foreign to Chaplin's conception of the 'Little Fellow' as building a house is to a Bedouin.[52]

Sobel and Francis miss several important points. First, a more appropriate context for thinking about Chaplin's character in the films from 1915 onwards is the American context of the ongoing moral panic about tramps who, because of the different class structure and transportation potential in the United States, were quite different from tramps in England. Second, Chaplin's intended audience was, in the initial stages at least, American. Finally, their interpretation is far too rooted in a mimetic understanding of film. Chaplin's films are not simple reflections of actuality. Clearly it would be absurd to suggest that the activities that went into Chaplin's films were in any way likely to occur in reality. Indeed, it was the distance between the films and any notion of reality that made Chaplin a favourite among European intellectuals. Rudolf Arnheim, for instance, pointed out that

> In a Chaplin film no face, no motion of the hand is true to nature, and it is indeed a shameful thing for the apostles of 'Objectivity', who always preach that the mission of cinema is unvarnished realism, that the first blossoming of the young art of film presented itself as so made-up, and in such unnatural colors.[53]

Arnheim delighted in the moments when Chaplin's humour derives from the disjuncture between his actions and our expectations of them:

> This happens when Chaplin, hanging over a ship's railing, wiggles his hind quarters to the audience; everyone thinks he's fallen to his death because of seasickness, when suddenly he turns around, having caught a fish. This is the first step toward the emancipation of the filmstrip from the real spatial conditions of the represented object.[54]

Chaplin's character is not incidental to the comedies of mobility he is so central to. Clearly, the tramp is a figure who embodies mobility in an array of pathologized and romanticized ways. In addition, the tramp is an outsider, a figure on the margins, whose marginal position allows a novel perspective on the workings of normality.[55]

As a marginal figure the tramp has constantly to make do with the flotsam and jetsam of normal life. He eats the leftovers of society in his Mulligan Stew, he wears clothes passed on and handed down, he (mis)uses the spaces of home, work and travel in novel and transformative ways. The tramp, in short, is a master of appropriation and tactical transgression.[56] His life necessitates the kinds of activities proposed by Situationists and Surrealists in their attempts to recapture everyday life. Kristin Ross has written of the unique appropriations of everyday objects in the Paris Commune in order to delineate a new lived social space. She uses the term *bricolage* to describe 'the wrenching of everyday objects from their habitual context to be used in a radically different way' as barricades.[57] In a more general sense, the activities of both actual tramps and Chaplin's comic tramp are examples of the Situationist *detournement*, in which the terrain of the dominant is used to new ends in order to transform a landscape of propriety into something more useful or interesting.[58] Having no place of their own, tramps have to make do with the spaces and places that are already there, belonging to others – the barn in the country or the jungle by the railroad lines in cities. *Bricolage* and *detournement* are often thought of as key tactics of resistance, transgression and reappropriation, but not often as comic devices. It is exactly these tactics that the Little Tramp uses to such comic effect.

In *City Lights* (1931), the first Chaplin film to tentatively use sound, the opening scene is a perfect example of tramp comedy, involving, as it does, misuse, trespass, transformation and *detournement*. The film starts with a ceremony, held in the depths of the Depression, unveiling a group of statues dedicated to 'peace and prosperity' in a city centre. As the statues are unveiled and the National Anthem is played, the crowd that has gathered see the 'Little Tramp' sleeping on one statue. He awakens, discovers the crowd and attempts an escape, only to sit accidently on the face of one statue and become impaled on the sword of another. He uses a stone hand to thumb his nose at the onlookers and proceeds to make his getaway

38 A picture taken during the filming of *City Lights* (1931): Chaplin awakens in the arms of a statue (see also illus. 39, 40).

39 Chaplin sits on the face of another statue.

(illus. 38–40). It is clear here that the fact that Chaplin is a tramp is important. The absurd, comical and critical juxtaposition of a marginal and impoverished citizen with a monumental space of authority and pomposity could hardly be less subtle. The comparison between the bombast and authority of excessive pretension and the needs of a homeless man who uses the monument's covers to protect him from the elements is a clear and critical one. The Little Tramp is the marginalized outsider, one of the weak, the oppressed and the vulnerable, who is able to fight against the system on its own turf using what Michel de Certeau has called the weapon of the weak – the tactic:

> It operates in isolated actions, blow by blow. It takes advantages of 'opportunities' and depends on them, being without any base where it could stockpile its winnings, build up its own position, and plan raids. What it wins it cannot keep. This nowhere gives a tactic mobility, to be sure, but a mobility that must accept the chance offerings of the moment, and seize on the wing the possibilities that offer themselves at any given moment.[59]

The tramp as a creature of marginality plays on the unknown underground of modern life. In films such as *City Lights* and *Modern Times* the tramp is a Simmelesque character who is attempting to create himself on the stage of the city. As Chaplin noted in his autobiography, the tramp character could play any number of rôles. This playfulness with appearance is, of course, a key to our understanding of both urbanity and modernity. The tramp is a con-man and trickster. Chaplin rolls together the classic stage harlequin/clown and the alleged wily attributes of the 'real' tramp to produce an archetypally protean modern character. Living on the go, full of invention, the tramp makes up his own identity as he goes along.

The tramp's actions have a magic effect on the city. Chaplin's city is not just hard and impersonal but soft and magic, like the 'soft city' described by Jonathan Raban.[60] In *Soft City* Raban emphasizes the individual, the magical, the ephemeral (the illusory array of endless possibilities the city offers), the city as a theatrical space quite distinct from the hard city of money and power. In Raban's soft city the basic fact of urbanity is the requirement to act – to put on a disguise. People experience themselves as actors, and they put on performances. City life is thus subject to 'intrinsic theatricality', in which people perform a fresh ironic sense of self:

> To a very large degree, people can create their cosmologies at will, liberating themselves from the deterministic schemes which ought to have led them into a wholly different style of life. To have a platonic conception of oneself, and to make it spring forth, fully

40 Chaplin uses a third statue to thumb his nose at the audience.

clothed, out of one's head, is one of the most dangerous and essential city freedoms.[61]

Raban's own preferred city 'is one where hobos and loners are thoroughly representative of the place, where superstition thrives, and where people often have to live by reading the signs and surfaces of their environment and interpreting them in terms of private near-magical codes'.[62]

Thus Chaplin's tramp is a Rabanesque character. As a perennial outsider the tramp enters 'normal society' in a variety of disguises, sometimes gracefully, sometimes clumsily, making vain attempts at appropriate behaviour with predictably comic results. Magically, the seemingly hard and uncompromising world is transformed through his actions into a world of play and comic energy. A monument to prosperity in the midst of a depression becomes part of a joke. It is transformed by the tramp into both a place to sleep and a place to make fun. As Dan Kamin has observed, for the tramp 'objects become what he needs them to be, and his comic energy transforms the world to match his own imaginative flexibility'.[63]

Chaplin uses the tramp to make jokes that are, simultaneously, critiques of the structures within which the tramp has to survive. This is how Chaplin's tramp differs from earlier slapstick, vaudeville and cartoon tramps. Although we laugh at the improprieties of the tramp character we also laugh at the ridiculousness of the structures that make his actions improper – the factory, the farm, the monument, and the rules, laws, norms and manners that constitute the acceptable. The laughter that came to engulf the tramp is, of course, highly ambivalent. It is not unusual for society's 'others' to get laughed at. It happens all the time. What is less common is the way the tramp became someone audiences laughed with at the expense of the normal and expected way of being.

A number of people have commented, in passing, on the ambivalence surrounding tramp comedy in general. The cartoonist Al Capp, for instance, thought that the use of a comic figure who was well below 'us' (the audience) on the social ladder made it easier to laugh both at and with him/her:

> No matter how badly off any of us was, we were all in better shape than that bum. The fact that we had enough spare cash to buy a ticket to that movie made us superior to him. That was the first thing that made us feel good. Next we saw him starving. That wasn't going to happen to us – another reason for feeling superior, better off at least than one person.[64]

In addition to the feeling of superiority gained by watching the comic plight of someone worse off than ourselves there is the more subtle vicariousness of a pleasure produced by seeing someone transgress the expectations of the everyday and on occasion remain immune from the consequences. Umberto Eco suggests that

> in the violation of the rule on the part of a character so different from us we not only feel the security of our own impunity but also enjoy the savor of transgression by an intermediary. Since he is paying for us, we can allow ourselves the vicarious pleasure of a transgression that offends a rule we have secretly wanted to violate, but without risk.[65]

Not only do we laugh *at* a figure more pathetic than ourselves but we also laugh *with* a character who takes risks on our behalf and shows the structures of authority – both visible and invisible – to be foolish, possibly even transformable. By the time Chaplin's movies had become popular, the majority of his audience was working-class and he was their hero. Robert Sklar believes that Chaplin's popularity derived from a sense of empathy between the audience and Chaplin's tramp in contrast to Capp's belief that the laughter was rooted in feelings of social superiority.

> No wonder working-class audiences found movies so much to their liking – among all the other good reasons, movies gave palpable expression to their feelings of hostility and resentment against those who brought misery into their lives. Order was invariably restored, of course, but not before authority and respectability had had their pretences unmasked.[66]

Invariably it is the idiocies of law, order and convention that get laughed at in Chaplin's films. Early on in his career Chaplin was clearly aware of the critical power his comedy potentially had. In 'What People Laugh At', an article published in 1918, he wrote 'Here were men representing the dignity of the law [policemen in his early comedies], often very pompous themselves, being made ridiculous and undignified', and he noted 'the delight the average person takes in seeing wealth and luxury in trouble'.[67]

What Chaplin did with the figure of the tramp was to make it into a subversive comic figure. To understand this construction of the tramp we need to understand the nature of both subversion and laughter. It is because of its potential subversiveness that laughter is important in a social sense. As Walter Benjamin explained it,

Chaplin has directed himself toward both the most international and most revolutionary affect of the masses – laughter. 'Certainly,' says Soupault, 'Chaplin only makes us laugh. But apart from the fact that this is the most difficult thing to achieve, it is also the most important in the social sense.'[68]

Probably the best-known account of laughter is that provided by the Russian anti-Formalist critic Mikhail Bakhtin in his work on medieval popular culture, *Rabelais and his World*.[69] Bakhtin was intrigued by the world of the marketplace, the fair and the carnival – the unofficial world of the popular that exists alongside the official, the formal and the polished. To Bakhtin the carnival was a time and place of apparent disorder, a deliberate break from normal life and established forms of behaviour. Typically, carnival took place just before the formal religious observances of Lent and was marked by excess, not least of food, drink, sex, dance and laughter. Actors and spectators mixed; everyone was involved. Separation and hierarchy were ignored or inverted. Spatial boundaries – particularly those distinguishing public from private – were ignored. The carnival flooded into people's homes, and normally private activities, such as sex and use of the latrine, were brought out into the open.

The body was a particular site of symbolic inversion in carnival. Whereas official society celebrated the head above all else, the carnival emphasized the lower body, the genitals and buttocks, the orifices that pointed to the process and incompleteness of life rather than the cerebral and closed classical body of high art. Through its constant sense of inversion and transgression, carnival appears to question the dominant official order, showing people the arbitrary nature of conventional socio-spatial boundaries.

The *processes* of carnival are not limited to actual carnivals, however. The term 'carnivalesque' describes a generalized sense of the type of things that go on in carnival – a pervasive sense of anti-order, a movement against coherence that is rooted in the everyday, the popular, the mobile and the profane. The carnivalesque is also marked by an embrace of the grotesque – the glorious imperfect body and its profane functions that poke fun at the smooth symmetry of the classical body. The carnivalesque is more about the features of everyday life than it is about discrete events in the calendar.

Central to all of this is the rôle of laughter. Laughter is seen to mock and deride formality and is thus a tool with the power to erase domination and revive and re-energize the spirit. Laughter is excluded from the seriousness and pretension of formal space and routine. In medieval Europe, Church and Court were sites of pomposity and reverence, while the market and fair were places of laughter. Official culture marginalized laughter, as Bakhtin recognized:

> Laughter was eliminated from religious cult, from feudal and state ceremonials, etiquette, and from all the genres of high speculation. An intolerant, one-sided tone of seriousness was characteristic of official medieval culture. The very contents of medieval ideology – asceticism, sombre providentialism, sin, atonement, suffering, as well as the character of the feudal regime, with its oppression and intimidation – all these elements determined this tone of icy petrified seriousness.[70]

Laughter did, however, become an important part of any number of feast days that stood outside the official calendar of seriousness:

> laughter, which had been eliminated in the Middle Ages from official cult and ideology, made its unofficial but almost legal nest under the shelter of almost every feast. Therefore, every feast in addition to its official, ecclesiastical part had yet another folk carnival part whose organizing principles were laughter and the material bodily lower stratum.[71]

This laughing chorus of the popular included elements of Roman Saturnalia and more local imagery. Part of the laughter revolved around the long tradition of mime that Chaplin inherited. Laughter, for Bakhtin, belongs to the people: 'The truth of laughter embraced and carried away everyone; nobody could resist it.'[72]

Bahktin provides a useful tool for thinking about Chaplin's tramp. Much of what Bahktin has to say makes sense in relation to Chaplin's character. His tramp, for instance, often becomes someone else, someone well above the social position of a tramp, for a day or two. In *City Lights*, for example, he is mistaken for the friend of a wealthy drunk. Chaplin's body jokes often involve copious amounts of violence and crudity. Buttocks are frequently the objects of laughter. The tramp never understands or conforms to the rules of official etiquette. Most important, though, his comedy reveals the absurdity and arbitrariness of the normal world, whether it is the world of factory work or farm routine. What could be more carnivalesque than the first scene of *City Lights*, with Chaplin debunking the pomposity and hypocrisy of the unveiled monument to prosperity and official mumbo-jumbo that accompanied it? The tramp as a symbol of the low and the marginal is able to magically transform the high into the ridiculous. Key to this is the juxtaposition of the smooth monumentality of classical bodies with the marginal figure of the tramp dressed in poorly fitting clothes and performing unusual bodily movements. There is Chaplin lying in the arms of a statue. Waking up he notices that he is in front of a huge crowd. He comically raises his hat to the watching police and then to the statues. Quickly he becomes impaled through a hole in his trousers on one statue's sword – just one of many references to the lower body Chaplin employs in this carnivalesque scene. As if to reinforce the upper body/lower body comparison, he proceeds to sit on the face of the sword-bearing statue and then to use the thumb of another statue to thumb his nose at the watching crowd and police. Here we have the monumental being debunked. He uses his body, in need of shelter and sleep, to deflate the seriousness of the occasion. Not only is there a juxtaposition of bodies – classical and profane – but a juxtaposition of needs. The value of the monument as a monument is made serviceable and everyday by the simple needs of the tramp.

The classical completeness of the statues is, of course, saturated with seriousness. Their unveiling is accompanied by local dignitaries, and by the first instance of Chaplin using the sounds of speech to signify power, authority and formality. Later, in both Modern Times and The Great Dictator, he opposed the silence of his Little Tramp with the pomposity of voices associated with mind-numbing authority. In Modern Times the boss speaks through the public-address system saying little else than 'speed up' to his machine-like workers. In The Great Dictator the tramp has disappeared, but the chief character, an obvious caricature of Adolf Hitler, talks endless nonsense. Once more, speech is associated with power and misguided authority. In the case of City Lights the speeches of the dignitaries involved in unveiling the statues are completely unintelligible whines and grunts.[73] While it is obvious from the actions of the speakers that what they are saying is authoritative, the sounds they produce undermine them and only serve to make the silent tramp more eloquent as he undermines seriousness. Allon White has remarked how seriousness is based on the exclusion of laughter, and as such is more about control and power than it is about anything intrinsically important: 'The social reproduction of seriousness is a fundamental – perhaps the fundamental – hegemonic manoeuvre. Once the high language has attained the commanding position of being able to specify what is and is not to be taken seriously, its control over the language of its society is virtually assured.'[74]

The insertion of laughter into the dignified proceedings of the unveiling is, therefore, highly subversive. The audiences for this film were trapped in the depths of the Great Depression. The need to find food and shelter would have been familiar experiences. It is not hard to imagine the sympathy many would have had for the tramp and the contempt they would have had for the functionaries at the unveiling.

In addition to undermining the hegemony of seriousness, jokes and laughter often serve the purpose of revealing the invisible and making the normal seem strange. Barry Sanders has pointed out that

> Most laughter springs from ... the unexpected, the momentary surprise, prompted by a sudden slip of the body, or the tongue, which delights us for a whole range of reasons. First, a person who stumbles or stutters surprises us by re-presenting the mundane in an absolutely fresh way. The stumbler permits us to see the grammar of walking, just as the stammerer allows us to hear the grammar of speech. In a sense, both take back what we take for granted in the everyday.[75]

Laughter, then, is a result of the transgression of normality. By breaking from the continuity and rhythm of life, it can prise open the powerful grip of civilised, 'proper' behaviour. Laughter's power lies in its ability to mark the transformation from the unspoken, unquestioned and invisible to that which is asserted, in a visible way, to be correct, right, true and enforceable. This is a dangerous power, for it can provoke the full force of official malevolence:

> The peasant knew he could laugh at some stupid regulation and wipe the slate clean. He could deflate the word, by letting his own air out. From the point of view of the marginalized and the disenfranchised, if they cannot participate in the writing of history, they can at least try to erase it. To pull this off, however, one must realise that while a laugh can turn the subtleties of power inside out, making them suddenly visible, it can also turn power into pure brutality, for power, finally, has nothing to say to laughter – it remains dumb in the silent sense, dumbfounded in the weakest way. When it responds, it can only resort to mere physicality – torture, imprisonment, or even death.[76]

There is no simple reading of the tramp as a product of comic knowledge. Theorists of laughter range from those who see it as a nasty means of domination and ridicule to those who believe that laughter is the re-energizing tool of the down-trodden, who use it to debunk society's pretensions. Both ends of the spectrum, and most positions in-between, can be applied to tramp comedy. In this chapter I have shown how the tramp was constructed in a number of ways in American humour between 1869 and 1940. Clearly, many vaudeville sketches involving tramps combined stereotypes of ethnicity with stereotypes of tramps to produce caricatures that magnified many of the negative characteristics discussed by sociologists, social reformers, eugenicists and others. The ramshackle body of the tramp is every bit as pathological in vaudeville as it is in the notes of Charles Davenport.

Chaplin's Little Tramp, however, was something quite different. While clearly using the ascribed characteristics of worklessness and mobility, Chaplin made up a tramp who was far more complex than a two-dimensional caricature. His tramp's activities are marked by considerable pathos, a critical capacity to highlight the tyrannies of 'normal life' and a startling range of transformative energies. Chaplin played with the established knowledge of the tramp and transformed it into a positive, sympathetic and critical force. His critique of capitalism in *Modern Times*, not least the 'red flag' scene, proved to be deeply troubling to Government agents, who kept a thick dossier on him and eventually expelled him in 1952, having accused him of Communist sympathies. He spent the rest of his life in exile in Switzerland.

# 7 Picturing the Tramp

Like other visual forms with inscribed narratives, from carved burial urns to stained glass windows, comic strips, and movies, photographs seem to make do without an overt narrator: their fiction is that the world tells or writes about itself through images, that in photographs we see not the view of a 'narrator' but the world itself – people, rocks, fences, clouds. No teller tells (or writes) these stories; they happen by themselves.[1]

In addition to being counted, interviewed, satirized and imitated, tramps, from the moment they were labelled as such, were photographed. In this chapter I consider photographic representations of tramps by Jacob Riis, John J. McCook and Dorothea Lange. In each case I suggest that the images produced of tramps and migrants can be understood in association with particular forms of knowledge production and dissemination that provided a context for the photographs. As with the other forms of knowledge discussed earlier there is a marked symbiotic relationship between the production of knowledge, in this case documentary photographic knowledge, and the production of the tramp as a figure on the margins.

## DOCUMENTING THE OTHER, DEFINING THE SELF

Documentary photography blossomed following the development of technology that made photography significantly more mobile. By the 1880s cameras had shrunk drastically and were easier to carry around. Wet plates had given way to dry plates and roll films were introduced. Photographers started to travel far afield to capture the life of people in places previously uninterrupted by the gaze of the photographer. One side of this was the picturing of foreign lands and peoples. John Thomson, a Scottish photographer, had published *The Antiques of Cambodia* in 1867 and *Illustrations of China and its People* in four volumes in 1873. These collections sought to present a picture of Chinese life for consumption in Britain. Thomson's next project was a volume on *Street Life in London*, published in eleven parts between 1876 and 1877. *Street Life* featured 'outcast London', including pictures of beggars, boot-cleaners and swagmen. The pictures were immediately seen as invaluable resources for sanitarians and philanthropists, who declared that pictures could not lie and that actions needed to be taken to alleviate the conditions of these outcasts. Early in its history documentary photography was intimately tied to the origins of the social sciences. Indeed, the exploits of Thomson and others were implicated in the construction of the very concept of the 'social' as both an object and a problem that demanded solutions.

The interest in the inhabitants of London's East End was hardly new though. Thomson's photography was just part of a long-standing middle-class curiosity concerning the conditions of the capital's poor.[2] Books such as Chadwick's *Report . . . on an Inquiry into the Sanitary Conditions of the Labouring Population of Great Britain* (1842) had been bestsellers.

> In Chadwick, in Mayhew, in countless Victorian reformers, the slum, the labouring poor, the prostitute, the sewer, were recreated for the bourgeois study and drawing-room as much as for the urban council chamber. Indeed, the reformers were central in the construction of the urban geography of the bourgeois imaginary. As the bourgeoisie produced new forms of regulation and prohibition governing their own bodies, they wrote even more loquaciously of the body of the Other – of the city's 'scum'.[3]

The body of the 'Other' produced both loathing and desire in the bourgeoisie. On the one hand, the books of Chadwick and others acted as *surveys* – as disciplinary views from 'some high window' that sought to make the hitherto invisible visible. On the other hand, the books reveal an obsessive fascination with the horrors of the city – an eroticized interest in the low and the marginal. In classifying and describing the urban poor in great detail the bourgeois observer produced his own antithesis and in doing so helped define the bourgeois self. The so-called wandering tribes of Mayhew's London, for instance, were marked by a reluctance to labour, an excessive consumption of alcohol and drugs, a love of libidinous dances, a lack of religion and a low level of respect for property. The inverse of this description is no less than the ideal of a proper bourgeois body.

Returning to Thomson, it is clear that photography added a new - dimension to the bourgeois desire to survey the poor. The fact that

Thomson moved from images of far away countries to the East End of London is no surprise. The far reaches of the world shared some of the same space in the bourgeois imaginary as that inhabited by the domestic poor. Parts of London were often described in ways that matched descriptions of empire. In Mayhew's work, for instance, the wandering tribes of London are compared to people elsewhere: 'In their continual warfare with the force, they resemble many savage nations, for the cunning and treachery they use ... Their love of revenge too, is extreme – their hatred being in no way mitigated by time ...'[4] The slums of London were linked to Africa and Asia by reference to 'Darkest London' and 'wandering tribes'.[5]

In the United States the best known early documentary photographer was also directing attention towards the socially marginal. Edward Curtis began his survey of Native American life in 1896. It was published in twenty volumes between 1907 and 1930. Curtis took over 40,000 negatives. He aimed to record the lives of a people he considered were disappearing.[6] His photographs, many of them doctored so as to make them appear more authentic, were clearly an example of a particular way of seeing, which saw the native American from the point of view of an affluent and metropolitan white audience who could afford to buy the books. Curtis felt compelled to airbrush out any tell-tale signs of modernity from his photographs (especially early on), so that an image of untouched and unchanging aboriginality was produced.

A decade or so earlier Jacob Riis had undertaken a similar task among the tenement dwellers of New York for his book *How the Other Half Lives*.[7] Like Thomson in London, Riis sought to picture the poor of the city in order that the middle classes might appreciate the conditions under which the poor had to live and even do something to change them. Riis was instrumental in penetrating the tenements and allowing people to explore the underside of the city from their own armchairs. His photographs, many of them harrowing, were often deliberately manipulated to make the poor look especially degenerate and helpless. Riis's photographs engaged the public consciousness and introduced a visual element to the idea and image of the Victorian slum in New York.[8] We shall return to Riis's exploits later.

The history of documentary photography is one that makes marginality central. Just as Mayhew, Chadwick and others had provided an endless source of fascinating detail about London's down-and-outs, photographers, such as Thomson in London and Riis in New York, had focused on the abject poor to tell their stories. This links documentary photography to other forms of knowledge and representation that we have explored, including sociology, social reform and eugenics. The socially marginal was paradoxically central to all of these.

## DECEIT AND DOCUMENTARY

The word 'documentary' is full of ambiguity. It seems irrevocably tied to issues of truth, identity and authority. To document is to prove, to provide evidence. To be asked for your documents is to be asked for proof of who you are – usually a picture and some text on a passport or driving-licence. 'Documentary' as a noun is most often associated with non-fiction TV films – accounts of 'how it really is'. And yet we know that the history of the word 'documentary' is one shot through with forgery and deceit. When combined with photography, 'documentary' becomes ever more entangled with issues of truth and authenticity.

As social reform became more specialized and 'scientific' in its outlook, it incorporated photography as a valuable weapon in its arsenal. Photography appeared to be ideal for the purposes of persuading because of its naturalizing character in addition to its reproducibility. Black and white photography marked by informal lighting and composition was useful in communicating the world-view of liberal social reformers who were keen to stress their own expertise and organization in addition to the worlds they were seeking to illuminate.[9]

Photographs produced by reforming documentarians have to be understood in relation to the knowledge system within which their images were produced. This system includes the presenting agency (either the individual or society or Government agency), the text that surrounds the images (from captions to whole books) and the way in which the photos are disseminated to a wider audience. Both for the institutions that encouraged such photography and for the audience that saw it, the photographs took on powerful meanings within a framework of knowledge created by the picture's interaction with text and agency, even when the photographers and their subjects may have had wholly different intentions. As Maren Stange has asserted:

> Editorial and exhibition practices, relying on photography's presumed immediacy and transparency to help legitimize the ideological underpinnings of the reformist vision, often distorted or obscured the social and esthetic significance that the photographs held for their makers or (more conjecturally) for their subjects.[10]

The power of photography as a documentary tool relied on the exact opposite assumption: that the photographs were an uncontaminated window on reality with no message other than that which was self-evidently in the image. Reformers relied on the presumption that the photographs were mimetic devices with an indexical relation to their subject-matter. It was this claim to realism that provided the central motif for early photographers. The camera, it was claimed, captured and illuminated reality and presented the subject as it was. If something was there in the photograph it was undeniably there in reality. Assumptions such as this were behind the explicit use of Thomson's photographs to promote philanthropy. They were accompanied by a text that pointed out that while readers may have doubted textual descriptions of outcast London they could not deny the unquestionable accuracy of photographs. The quest for reality also famously informed the photography of Dorothea Lange, who displayed the following words of Sir Francis Bacon over the door of her studio:

> The contemplation of things as they are,
> without substitution or imposture,
> without error or confusion,
> is in itself a nobler thing than a whole harvest of invention.[11]

Despite such claims, it is clear that documentary photography was a long way from being a neutral representation of reality. Any engagement with documentary knowledge has to start from the acknowledgement that documentary *constructs* a particular vision of the real, of truth and of identity. Occasionally this involved lies. Probably the most notable early documentary film, Robert Flaherty's *Nanook of the North* (1922), continued in the tradition of constructing documentary knowledge through the representation of the socially peripheral. In this case Flaherty produced an acclaimed film about the life of an Inuit man, Nanook. The film allegedly represented the gripping life of people close to nature. One scene showed Nanook fighting heroically with a seal before killing it. We now know the seal was dead all along. The film was funded by a French fur-trading company and the Inuit men were wearing the best furs while out hunting. After successfully defeating the dead seal Nanook embraced his wife and children, who, it turns out, were unrelated either to him or each other.[12]

The issue of documentary's relationship to the real occasionally gave rise to heated exchanges between photographers about what constituted the documentary. Two photographers of the Farm Security Administration (FSA) who had been sent to photograph the South during the Great

Depression had quite a falling out. Walker Evans discovered that his colleague, Arthur Rothstein, had moved a steer's skull from one location to another in order to illustrate the impact of overgrazing. Evans was outraged: 'That's where the word "documentary" holds; you don't touch a *thing*. You "manipulate," if you like, when you frame a picture one foot one way or one foot another. But you're not sticking anything in.'[13] Despite Evans's protestations, documentary photography involved as much construction of its subject as any other form of representation. Even Evans, when working with James Agee on *Let Us Now Praise Famous Men* (1941), frequently rearranged the domestic interiors of sharecroppers' homes in order to reveal the order and beauty that he saw, and wanted to show, below the surface appearance of poverty.[14] Regardless of the implications of the quotation from Bacon, Dorothea Lange was no documentary purist either. Her most famous photograph – *Migrant Mother* – was far from spontaneous. After arriving at the California pea-pickers camp where the photo was taken in 1936 she was careful to rearrange the children, exclude a teenage daughter and pose Florence Thompson (the principal subject of the image) is such a way that she expressed a combination of fatigue and determination. Such stories lead to the recognition that, as with any other form of knowledge, it is necessary to ask what its claims are, how these claims are made, who is making them and who they are about.

With these questions in mind let us turn to a brief history of images of tramps. The photographs taken by Riis, Lange and others are all understandable as small parts of much wider contexts of knowledge production and dissemination. They cannot simply be seen as reflections of the tramp/migrant, as part of reality. Rather, they go hand in hand with social science, medicine, law, comedy and a plethora of other forms of knowledge in the process of making up, and then ushering out, the tramp.

## JACOB RIIS

One of the earliest photographs of the tramp was Riis's *The Tramp in Mulberry Street Yard* taken in 1887 (illus. 41). The image formed part of a lecture he gave in a number of forms in New York, beginning in 1888. It also features in Riis's classic account of poverty in the city, *How the Other Half Lives* (1890). In the lectures the tramp was referred to as a 'tramp and a thief', and Riis told the story of how he offered the man ten cents to pose for the picture. The man, perhaps aware of the kind of image the photographers wanted, took the pipe out of his mouth and 'struck', demanding 25 cents to pose with the pipe in his mouth. Thus he became a 'thief' as

41 Jacob A. Riis, *Tramp in Mulberry Street Yard*, 1887.

well as a 'tramp'.[15] This kind of posing created images that fit into precon-
ceived categories and types. This was standard strategy for Riis. In another
instance he asked some street boys to feign sleep in a secret and picturesque corner to match earlier drawings of street children curled up
under steps.

The image, however, illustrates more than the rôle of posing in
Riis's photography. The caption *Tramp in Mulberry Street Yard* turns this,

obviously active, participant into a mere object of knowledge. He is labelled as a tramp, a representative of a broad social classification – one that evidently involves smoking a pipe. As Miles Orvell has pointed out: 'Riis gives us, with the often willing and knowing collaboration of his subjects, a metonymic typology of urban slums, representing for us "the poor," "the miserable," "the other half." He is after the general truth of a general category, and inner truths of individuals necessarily escape him.'[16]

There is little attempt to get at the individuality of the subject. Riis invariably told stories about his picture-taking exploits but said relatively little about the context of those being photographed. There is clearly a surveilling, voyeuristic and objectifying gaze at work here. This photograph, like his others, is not remarkable for its creativity or even its ability to convey the context of the tramp in New York, but for its 'documentary' nature – its capacity to provide an inventory and evidence. Despite the man's attempts to impose his own monetary agenda on the photographic event, he is ultimately denied his dignity and ceases to be an active subject in the act of being pictured and then displayed, complete with amusing anecdote.

This picture needs to be understood in the broader context of Riis's pioneering social journalism and philanthropic work. Riis was born in Denmark in 1849. In 1870 he emigrated to America and lived in poverty and isolation before starting his career in journalism. Like many people at the time he was on the road through the 1870s in the period of rising tensions leading to the railroad strike of 1877. He had little sympathy for the strikers, seeing them as an unruly mob. He developed a very liberal, middle-class, individualistic world-view that he carried with him into his reforming photographic projects.[17] In 1877 The New York Tribune assigned him to the city's police headquarters. In this rôle he quickly became acquainted with the notorious tenement districts of the city and with the reform organizations seeking to provide model houses in order to produce model citizens.[18] In the early 1880s Riis learned of the Blitzlichtpulver, a dangerous magnesium flash recently developed for taking photographs in the dark and realized it could be put to effective use.

> We used to go in the small hours of the morning to the worst tenements . . . and the sights I saw there gripped my heart until I felt that I must tell of them, or burst, or turn anarchist, or something . . . I wrote, but it seemed to make no impression. One morning, scanning my newspaper at the breakfast table, I put it down with an outcry that startled my wife, sitting opposite. There it was, the thing I had been looking for all those years. A four-line dispatch

from somewhere in Germany, if I remember right, had it all. A way had been discovered, it ran, to take pictures by flashlight. The darkest corner might be photographed that way.[19]

One of the central motifs of philanthropic work in the city had been penetrating the shadows with light – making the invisible visible. Two decades earlier Matthew Hale Smith's *Sunshine and Shadows in New York* (1868) contrasted the ordered and bright life of respectable New York with the shadows of the notorious area surrounding Five Points. Poverty was metaphorically darkness. Needless to say, the darkness needed the light of missionary zeal. Photography helped in this respect. In 1887 Riis began to use photography to dramatize the situations he encountered in his journalistic expeditions. He was particularly fond of roaming the streets of the slums at night, surprising the residents with loud, bright magnesium flashes. On two occasions he set fire to the place he was photographing and on another he set fire to himself.[20]

By 1888 Riis was giving illustrated lectures on New York's tenement areas. His first lecture, 'The Other Half, How It Lives and Dies in New York', featured more than 100 slides, including his image of the tramp. These performances were known as stereopticon lectures. Riis used two projectors together to produce a ten-foot-square image showing slides in sequence illuminated by a mixture of oxygen and hydrogen gases burned against a pellet of lime. In this period, before the era of movies, such shows were extremely popular and had a history of moral evangelizing about the conditions of the poor. Far from being dull lectures, these shows were full of anecdotes and entertainment. Sometimes music (such as *Where is my Wandering Boy Tonight?*) would accompany the presentation.

These presentations enabled Riis to embed his photographs in stories and ideologies that resonated with familiar popular attitudes.[21] By telling stories and playing music he imposed his own order on the images, constructing a master narrative that foreclosed the possibility that the photographs might offer other, oppositional, meanings to their own. The outline of this narrative seems fairly clear. Riis used the familiar philanthropic trope of comparing the slum to countries of the developing world. He described himself as a kind of excursionist who could mediate the horrors of the essentially foreign to respectable audiences through his slides and stories. Maren Stange has described how this touristic way of seeing offered a reassuring gloss of respectability on the photographs while assuring the audience that they were the 'half' designated to colonize, dominate and administer:

He or she deserves both the information needed to transform or control the slums, and the security and privilege of distance that obviates the 'vulgar, odious and repulsive' experiences that the actual slums would inevitably present. By conflating the language and perspective of geographical inventory and settlement with that of social surveillance and control, Riis was able to imply as well that his audience's mobile and 'colonial' position in relation to the slums it 'visited' was a natural one.[22]

An important part of this excursionary vision was surveillance. Riis's career in investigation had its roots in his rôle as police reporter for *The Tribune*, where he developed an understanding of surveillance techniques. When he came to give his talks he mixed his own slides with mugshots from police files without distinguishing between the two. Both were images of the 'other half' and both needed to be kept at a safe distance from the respectable audience. This combination of images made possible by photography and the flash pan, in Riis's view, spared the audience 'the vulgar sounds and odious scents and repulsive exhibitions attendant upon such personal examination'.[23] His presentations suggested that the liberal, middle-class audience had a right to a dominating, if philanthropic, gaze.

Riis's illustrated lectures were very popular and quickly led to illustrated articles in magazines and popular books. His most famous undertaking, *How the Other Half Lives*, was addressed directly to the philanthropic middle class. Riis was against fundamental changes in the law and opposed to further forms of Government intervention concerning the poor. Instead he favoured the wise use of private capital to reform the conditions of the slums. He proposed the solution of 'philanthropy at five per cent' – the idea that private capital could be used to produce model housing with the aim of achieving a return of only five per cent on the investment through rent. Such an idea was not radical, but one affirming the centrality and social worth of traditional entrepreneurial middle-class values.

Riis's photography was implicated in the moment when the 'social' and 'society' as concepts and as sets of problems were being invented.[24] Just as the 'social' as a problem was being constructed, so a middle-class perspective in poverty was being formed and maintained. Riis's *Tramp in Mulberry Street Yard* cannot simply be understood as a straightforward image of a tramp. When the photograph is interpreted in the context of his wider project it takes on an array of meanings in an extended field of reference.

*Tramp in Mulberry Street Yard* was part and parcel of the construction of the social as a field of enquiry and, simultaneously, the construction of a distinctive liberal middle-class perspective on the poor.

## JOHN J. MCCOOK

Today, Riis's work is seen as central to the development of documentary photography. Less well known is the work of John J. McCook and his assistants.[25] McCook was born in 1843 in Ohio, the grandson of an Irish immigrant. He served as a Union soldier in the Civil War and rose to the

42 John McCook in his classroom.

Illustrate moral + physical traits (1) bad; (2) weak; (3) Un- 76
fortunate.
Institution *Central police Station* Number 8 A.D. 1891
Place *Milwaukee Wis.* (4) bad + unfortunate
— or even good + do

## CASUAL LODGERS OR TRAMPS. [SC6]

1. Occupation. *Reporter for papers*
2. When did you last work at it *Jan 1872*
    at anything? *Feb. 1872*
3. When did you take to the road? *March 1872*
4. Why? *To lazy to work + a drunkard*
5. When are you going to work again? *never*
6. Have you tried to get work to-day?
7. Health. *Poor on account of old age*
8. Ever had Syphilis? *Yes*
    Itch? *Yes*
9. How often in Hospital? *6 times*
    At whose charge? *County*
10. When last in Alms House?
11. Married? *yes*
    Children.— Number, *3.* { Males, *1* Ages, —
                             { Females, *2* Ages, —
12. Where are Wife and Children? *New Jersey*
13. Where do you generally sleep? *any place*
14. How do you generally secure your food? *beg*
15. Age. *70*
16. Color. *White*
17. Nativity. *Germ.*
18. Can you read and write? *yes*
19. When and where did you last vote? *New Jersey 1871*
20. Temperate, intemperate, or abstainer? *Intemperate*
21. Ever convicted of crime? *no*
    of drunkenness? *about 150 times*
22. Religion? *Catholic*
23. Name? *Aug. Steinhauser*
    Real Name?
24. Remarks, including corrections of statements known to be incorrect
    and impressions as to the person's mental and physical vigor.
    *Steinhauser was a journalist*
    *of some note in his days.*

*Note.— Use a separate blank for each individual.*

Particulars, as above, are desired for 150 unselected cases occurring in the month of December. To
this please add the total number entertained for one night during the entire month.

*Please return by January 1, A.D. 1892, to*
PROF. J. J. McCOOK,
Trinity College,    HARTFORD, CONN.

43 Questionnaire
sent by McCook
to police chiefs
in 1891.

rank of Second Lieutenant. He then enrolled at Trinity College in
Hartford, Connecticut, graduating in 1863. In 1866 he was ordained as a
deacon of the Episcopal Church. After a brief spell in Detroit he returned
to East Hartford, became editor of the *Church Weekly* and gradually established a regional, even national profile in Church affairs. In 1883 he joined
the faculty of Trinity College as a Latin instructor. Later he was appointed
Professor of Modern Languages, teaching French, German, Italian and
Spanish (illus. 42). When asked to provide biographical data by Trinity
College he explained his occupation as '1. Clergyman; 2. Teacher; 3. Investigator of so-called sociological phenomena and writer concerning them;
4. Beggar General for Trinity College.'[26]

McCook's investigations of 'sociological phenomena' were wide-ranging and included research into aid for paupers (which he considered excessive), problems associated with drink and the practice of venal voting. All of these involved tramps in one way or another. His study of tramps became by far his most extensive enquiry. It began in 1891 when he was asked to speak on the tramp problem to a local religious group. McCook turned down the opportunity as he felt uninformed about the problem. He spent the next year trying to find out about the nature and extent of the 'tramp problem'. On 18 November 1891 he sent out letters and 150 questionnaires each to the mayors of 40 cities asking for their assistance in constructing a tramp survey. He wanted the questionnaires given to authorities wherever tramps were given shelter. He received 1,346 replies from 14 cities and proceeded to publish the results in a number of articles and lectures.[27] This survey was followed by another, this time of police chiefs throughout the country (illus. 43). McCook was evidently fascinated by the life of the tramp. He interviewed tramps on the streets of Hartford and visited almshouses, wayfarers' lodges, public baths and police stations in order to understand their world better. His investigations even went as far as sampling the various forms of liquor they consumed. In addition, McCook and a colleague conducted a survey of laws concerning tramps and vagrants in several states.

In order to support his documentary and survey research McCook commissioned over 100 photographs of tramps between April 1893 and May 1895. As with his tramp research in general, this photography took a variety of forms. Many of his pictures are posed in a studio while others are *in situ*. In addition McCook asked tramps to pose as if involved in characteristic tramp behaviour. In one instance they showed McCook how to ride the rails and on another occasion he staged and photographed a tramps' picnic. Finally, McCook and his associates, reflecting Riis's excursions, would accompany the police on raids of tramps' sleeping places.

McCook's photographs of tramps in the studio stand out from the work of Riis and the later FSA. Most obviously, these photos do not provide any form of context for those pictured. The environment is anonymous. McCook has no status as a photographer. His photographs, and those he commissioned, have never been used as objects that are interesting as photographs. Unlike Riis and Lange, McCook does not appear in histories of documentary photography. Little has been written about McCook's photographs. There is no evidence of McCook having anything approaching Riis's interest in the development of photographic technology. McCook was a proto-sociological investigator and social reformer. His photographs are nothing more than evidence for his investigations. It

44 *A Common Shovel*
*Bum. Property man in*
*Buffalo Bill's show . . .*
*'Lost my place . . . by*
*getting in a boose'.*
*May 1, 1893.*

doesn't matter who took them.[28] These pictures of tramps are the photo-graphic equivalents of biological samples of species. We see each example framed by the space of the studio. Sometimes a tramp's eyes are fixed firmly on the camera. On other occasions they have obviously been instructed to look at some space to the left of the camera. There is a remarkable similarity in their dress. They all seem to have a hat, a waist-coat, a jacket. They look for all the world like run-down versions of the well-to-do gentlemen of the road. Each is accompanied by a short piece of text that tells a small story: Dan the Dodger and the other fellow drink but manage to get by; Michael Keefe is incorruptible (illus. 44–6).

These tramps are pictured from head to toe. We see the whole body. This is quite distinct from the standard portrait of the time. A portrait of someone as respectable as McCook no doubt would be surrounded by darkness and feature only the upper half of his body. We are all familiar

45 *Dan the Dodger (left) and other fellow. They are a little unsteady, but by bracing against one another get through and are paid. April 25, 1893.*

with those notable Victorians looking out at us from the darkness. The completeness of the tramps underlines their status as specimens rather than as historical actors – as subjects of knowledge rather than masters of it. The lower half of the body was allegedly of no interest to respectability – it signified the lower orders of society, animality, the mundane and everyday in opposition to the cerebral and evidently important. These tramps were bodies, not just heads.[29]

The status of the tramp as specimen, as type, is further underlined by the photographs of tramps in their 'natural environment'. McCook was dogged in his determination to provide a complete picture of their world. He accompanied the police to Lodging Houses in Boston and he had pictures taken of tramps on trains and in the 'jungle'. The Lodging House pictures are similar to Riis's. Both went into the marginal spaces where tramps slept and photographed the conditions there.

46 *Michael Keefe. Ain't never going to vote again; the politicians think that a poor laboring man is always for sale. He isn't. May 6, 1893.*

Like the studio pictures, these are clearly forms of 'evidence' for McCook's wider investigations. Unlike with Riis, there is no sense that McCook or his photographers were attempting to make poverty picturesque. There is little that is deliberately aesthetic about these photographs. You can tell that the photographer has no pretensions to art. The photographs are not obviously posed. There are too many backs turned towards us. Again the closest equivalent to these photos would be natural history. Here are tramps at work. Here are tramps eating. Here are tramps bathing. The naked body of the Lodge resident and line of men in baths is indicative of their social standing. And what are the clothed men doing? Are they tramps waiting their turn? Why is one man standing on a raised ledge looking down on the baths? My best guess is that these are charity workers making sure the tramps are clean. These are pictures of tramps in their habitat. A record of the times, spaces and activities that McCook deemed significant in the day of the Wayfarer's Lodge (illus. 47–49).[30]

McCook's explorations of tramping also took him out into the world. He wanted to show how tramps went about their everyday business outside of the lodges and boarding-houses. Providence Bob and Philadelphia Shorty are shown riding the rails in the most dramatic, and least attempted, manner possible – using the tramp's ticket to ride on the rods under the train (illus. 50–51). The train is obviously not moving and the tramps seem unworried by their circumstance. One stares at the camera. Both were demonstrating tramp techniques for the sociologist.

> I took two veterans out with me to pose for train-jumping photographs. An early snow storm had covered everything, and after several hours of wading, uncomfortable enough with Arctic shoes and great coat, they, with their ragged shoes, made no complaint of wet feet: and on my offering, at parting, to take them to a restaurant for a square meal, they preferred to 'take its price in money and get supper at their own boarding house.' I deferred to their wishes and

47  *Wayfarer's Lodge: Dressing, 5:40 A.M., Boston, January, 1895.*

48 *Wayfarer's Lodge: Breakfast, 6:45 A.M. Boston, January, 1895.*

then followed them at a distance to their 'boarding house' – which turned out to be a saloon, where, as the friendly bartender told me next morning, they had two rounds of ale apiece.[31]

Bob and Shorty went through the complete range of trainriding techniques for McCook. They even acted out a confrontation with the police. According to McCook, they had both been drunk as children, both had run away from home, both had contracted diseases, been in jail, and sold their votes repeatedly. One of them, a 'sorry liar and a desperate drunk', eventually died in a fit.[32]

The photos of a 'jungle' picnic were taken by McCook and his son Philip on 5 May 1895. It was the result of a completely staged picnic complete with soup pot for the Mulligan Stew.[33] Unlike the photographs of the lodging houses, the tramps are obviously a part of the proceedings. To a man they face the camera (illus. 52). Photographs of tramps riding the rods and 'jungling' are, like the studio photos, 'scientific' evidence of tramp life. They are representative moments that stand for the rest of authentic tramp existence. They say 'look, this is what it is to be a tramp'. With his 100 or so

49 *Wayfarer's Lodge: The Bath, 1895.*

photographs, McCook tried to produce as complete a picture as possible of the tramp's world in the interest of social inquiry and reform. The photos accompanied the questionnaire returns and police reports to provide a remarkably detailed account of tramping in the Eastern states during the 1890s. These photos appeared in McCook's publications and especially in his account of the travels of one tramp – Roving Bill Aspinwall.

In many ways McCook's photographs reflect his liberal use of research methods. While the studio pictures with captions are used as support for his survey research of types and causes of tramphood, this image of William Aspinwall accompanies an extensive set of letters and postcards from a single man, Roving Bill, sent to McCook over a twenty-year period (illus. 53). This photo was actually taken by M. E. Watson in Vermont on 8 June 1893 and sent to McCook.

It is unlike any of the photos McCook was directly responsible for. The backdrop depicting rural New England places the tramp within an idyll. The box Aspinwall carries under his arm apparently holds the tools for his trade – fixing umbrellas. The image is more than a little amusing. McCook went to great lengths to get this photograph.

50 *Providence Bob and Shorty Riding the Rods*, 1894.

51 *Providence Bob and Shorty On the Pilot*, 1894.

I had greatly desired to have my friend's portrait, but since I remained true to my first resolve to have no question of dollars and cents cloud or complicate our relations, it was matter of some difficulty to know how to get it and be sure of its genuineness. At length I wrote to him to go to the best artist in Bennington and tell him that if he would take his picture and send me one copy with the negative, I would forward my check for a dollar and half, and that my letter might be exhibited as evidence of my good faith. It was further stipulated that there must be no fixing up, no shaving or polishing, but that everything must be taken as if on the road. Would any photographer assume the risk?[34]

McCook was evidently satisfied with the results. It is the only photograph he comments on in artistic terms:

With true artistic feeling the operator has arranged a hillside background, with attractive cottage in the distance, embowered in trees, and in the foreground rocks, weeds and wild flowers. Against this stands a man rather under the middle size with mustache and stubby beard, smallish eyes, and nose slightly *retrousse,* a long, straight mouth, with lips braced to sustain the weight of a long stemmed corncob pipe. The chin is not strong nor notably weak. The throat is bare, save for a little patch of dark woolen shirt with white cording. Jacket, waistcoat and trousers are of dark check, of uniform pattern. The trousers are turned up, and the shoes, an important item in the diagnosis of these cases, are muddy and worn. The hat is a derby and looks in fair condition.[35]

What makes this photograph stand out from all the others is the amount of information we have about the individual it portrays.

McCook had met a tramp called Connecticut Fatty in May 1893 and given him six postage-paid postcards so that he could provide accounts of his travels (illus. 54). Evidently the postcards were passed on to William Aspinwall, who enthusiastically wrote to McCook about tramp life. The first postcard was sent on 18 May 1893 and the correspondence continued until 1917, by which time Roving Bill was in the care of a war veterans' home. The correspondence formed the basis of a series of nine publications in 1901–2 in *The Independent* called 'Leaves from the Diary of a Tramp'. McCook also discussed Aspinwall's correspondence in a lecture called 'Tramping: Roving Bill' given to different audiences between April 1904 and May 1906. McCook never met Aspinwall; the photo is the closest

52 *Presently a four-gallon kettle with the materials for the stew, beef, potatoes, carrots, water, is bourn on a pole on the shoulders of the cook and his assistant. May 5, 1895.*

he got. Aspinwall's letters provide a rare insider's view of tramp life. Aspinwall managed, to some extent, to go beyond the meanings of the category.

Aspinwall was a loner who made his way by fixing umbrellas, clocks and sewing-machines as well as accepting any money or food offered him. He preferred to walk and rarely travelled by train. He attempted to give up tramping at least once in 1893 when he set up a repair shop in Pittsburgh. This only lasted a few months and he was soon back on the road. He had a certain amount of pride in his tramp identity and had little time for those who put him down. He had a problem with drink. He blamed immigrants for the tramp problem and was 'disgusted' by homosexuality among the tramp community. Some of his letters eloquently expressed the feelings of freedom he associated with life on the road: 'How well I enjoy this lovely Sabbath morning and how Happy I feel with Nature adorned in her lovely Summer Robes all around me; everything so quite [sic] except the

Rusling of the Breeze through the Butiful foliage and the sweet singing and the warbling of Birds.'[36] He even saw fit to lecture McCook:

> I think this nomadic life is a healthy life. I think if some of you Professors, students, etc., would live more of a nomadic life and feel the enjoyment of the fresh air more and make more good whole-some outdoor exercise and live more of a rough and tumble life you would enjoy better health and live longer.[37]

McCook invested a considerable amount of trust in Aspinwall and frequently adjusted his general view of tramps in order to accommodate the sympathies he felt for Aspinwall's way of life. It was important to McCook that Aspinwall was essentially a good person. He looked at his photograph and interpreted goodness:

> The photograph reveals the garments as being fairly neat and tidy. And this shows that 'Roving Bill' is not a vulgar shovel or city bum. They are prone to be very ragged and slatternly – tho even they never look like the comic newspaper type. It also exhibits the parts as belonging to the same original suit. This is fair evidence that the owner has been reasonably sober and well to do during his immedi-ate past. Otherwise the pawn shop would have introduced variety.[39]

Thus the body of the tramp is once more subject to the most strained interpretation. The trousers match the jacket, so he must be sober. Good-ness, sobriety, propriety and normality are all embodied in McCook's photograph of Aspinwall. While his other photographs were all forensic, diagnostic and illustrative of a marginal and deviant lifestyle, the photo of Aspinwall is one of redemption. This ambiguity is present in McCook's general diagnoses of the tramp problem, which range from the severe to the sentimental. When he originally became involved in the study of tramps his aims were almost entirely disciplinary. He was a firm believer that alms were too generous and encouraged tramping. He was equally convinced that tramps represented decay in the democratic system due to the practice of venal voting. He believed that tramps should be forced to work and forbidden from drinking – a view with foundations in his religious calling and in his understanding of social science. The problems of the tramp were, to McCook, a moral problem rooted in personal weaknesses of licentiousness and idleness. McCook's views, in other words, were little different from those of his contemporaries involved in social reform movements. All these views, however, were placed in the realm of the general, confirmed by general analysis of questionnaires and

returns from the police as well as by the majority of McCook's photo-graphs.

The ambiguity in McCook's views derive from his personal contact with tramps such as Aspinwall. Put simply, he was often charmed by the life that Aspinwall and others led, and found tramps to be charming. So while he was suggesting work, prohibition and reformation on the one hand, he was pleading for sympathy on the other. His accounts of Aspinwall – *Leaves from the Diary of a Tramp* – are full of passages of rural bliss and nostalgia for a simpler life. McCook wrote in 1895 'Give the tramp a chance! I know him very well. I have generally found him a pleasant, approachable fellow and I should rather take my chances of reforming him, with purely civil and secular measures, than the ordinary felon.'[39] Behind all the social science, the statistics and photography was a magnetic fascination with the life of the tramp and the alternatives it presented to 'normality'.

'The average man grows up to live a regular life and to work as a part of it', he wrote.

We are taught to believe that there is a necessary relation between doing our daily tasks, eating our regular meals, going to bed in a fixed place, rising at a pre-arranged hour, wearing a certain kind of clothes, that there is between all this and being 'good' an unalterable relationship: as also between being good and being happy. Religion gives its aweful sanction to this theory, habit fortifies it; successive generations of what we call civilization even create an instinct which even makes us think, or at least say, we like it: When suddenly to one of us comes the discovery that we can stop all this and yet live – nay, grow fat, perhaps and vigorous and strong; drop worry and responsibility . . . go everywhere, see everything . . . and when that discovery comes, it is apt to be fatal.[40]

54 'Connecticut Fatty'.

Dorothea Lange's *Migrant Worker on California Highway June 1935* (illus. 55) shows a single man walking down a road with a heavy backpack. This is an image of a passing generation of 'bindle-stiffs' – single men who travelled from job to job with blanket rolls and a few possessions tied to their backs. These were the 'fruit tramps' who worked up and down the West coast. These were the migrant workers whom the 'Wobblies' (the International Workers of the World, or IWW) recruited semi-successfully. This image and a number of others of the same man were taken by Dorothea Lange as part of a nationwide project to document the nation during the years of the Great Depression and the New Deal. The vast majority of her photographs were not of single men but whole families, or women or women with children. It is notable that this man is labelled a 'migrant worker' and not a 'tramp' or a 'hobo.' It is important, when considering the making up of the tramp, to ask why such a picture is not of 'a tramp'. His singularity, his hat and boots, his seemingly endless wandering along the road all point towards tramphood. Lange's photography marks a transformation in definitions from tramp/hobo to migrant.

If the tramp came into being around the construction of the transcontinental railroad in 1869 and the depression of 1873, then the tramp's end was marked by the wide availability of the mass-produced automobile and the Great Depression of the early 1930s. Following World War One and the invention of mass production, the car became affordable, even to poor tenant farmers. As early as 1919 an historian of the Wobblies, Paul Brissenden, noted how the IWW, who had successfully recruited single male migrants before the War, suddenly found it hard to recruit:

> The Ford 'flivver' was already working its wonders among the migratory harvest hands. Where once migratory workers had been mostly unattached men who beat their way from job to job on 'side-door coaches' they were fast becoming more and more family units that traveled as far and as often as their battered cars carried them.[41]

The IWW's problems stemmed from the fact that tramps no longer needed to travel by train (IWW members carried a red card that often allowed them protection while on the trains). Automobiles were not so easily policed. In addition, tramps now travelled with families. By the 1930s hundreds of thousands of people made homeless sought to make a better life elsewhere, principally in California. Unlike the earlier generations of migrants these Arkies, Okies and others were family groups travelling in

55  Dorothea Lange, *Migrant Worker on California Highway, June 1935.*

cars laden with their belongings. The sudden and massive appearance of
people on the road became a new national panic and the tramp was transformed into the migrant.

## THE FARM SECURITY ADMINISTRATION

The migration was documented by a remarkable group of people
employed by the Farm Security Administration (FSA) and directed by Roy

Stryker. Some of their images of tramps and migrants almost equal Chaplin's tramp in terms of their fame and recognition. Indeed, some of the best-known images in the history of photography were taken by FSA staff in the 1930s. They took tens of thousands of photos that, together, form a remarkable record of life and land in 1930s America. Of all these images, it is those of migrant workers and families that stand out. The images are very different from the scenes of 30 or 40 years earlier. Rather than featuring single men in the city, in the 'jungle' or on the train, they are predominantly of groups of migrants on the road, either in or around cars. Women and children are centre stage. The image of the single 'bindle-stiff' is a picture of a dying world. What the FSA photos have in common with those by Riis and McCook, however, is the need to understand them in terms of the institutional contexts of production and consumption.

FSA photography was an important propaganda tool that served to legitimate the New Deal, a paradigmatic example of high modernism in action, the nearest the United States has come to social engineering on a national scale. FSA photographs were a literal example of what James Scott has called 'seeing like a state'.[42] This is true insofar as they were part of a national attempt to order society and nature through the application of rational and scientific principles during a chronic depression. The photos were an element in a larger project to make society more *legible*. The images of migrants were a way of saying that things need to be made better for these people leading disordered lives. They needed migrant camps – nicely ordered, geometric simulations of 'normal life', which the FSA also photographed. FSA photographers differed from those like Riis and McCook in that they were part of a much bigger, national, project that was centrally planned. The intentions of the FSA photographers were also more radical than those of their predecessors. What they had in common, however, was the desire to use the subjects as a way of illustrating a bigger story and as a way of constructing a particular form of knowledge.

The origins of the FSA were partly the result of the imagination and intellect of the liberal economist Rexford Tugwell. Tugwell was made a member of President Roosevelt's Brain Trust in 1932. He was to become a central contributor to the development of New Deal legislation. In 1933 he left his position at Columbia University and became Roosevelt's assistant secretary of agriculture. While at Columbia, Tugwell had a postgraduate, Roy Stryker, collect photographic images for his textbook *American Economic Life*. Tugwell believed that students would benefit from visual contact with what they studied. In the course of compiling the photographs Stryker got to know Lewis Hine, the pioneering documentary photographer, and used many of his pictures. In the summer of 1934 Tugwell hired Stryker again, in the Information Division of the Agricultural Adjustment Administration. By 1935 Tugwell became the administrator of the newly formed Resettlement Administration, which became the Farm Security Administration in 1937. Stryker became the director of the 'Historical Section – Photographic' of the Resettlement Administration's Information Division.[43]

The Resettlement Administration was created by executive order and funded by the Emergency Relief Act of 1935. Its principal purpose was the provision of rural relief and land-use administration. Government aid to farmers in the United States already had an established history but had been largely ineffective. In 1933 – with Roosevelt's New Deal – the Federal Emergency Relief Organization, Farm Credit Administration and Agricultural Adjustment Administration made loans, manipulated markets and resettled farmers. Early policy focussed on farm owners and not the tenant farmers who were most often displaced by rural distress. One strategy, used many times since, was to raise prices by paying farmers to reduce production. This only made things worse for the landless.

Part of the Resettlement Administration's rôle was to focus policy on the very poorest of the rural displaced. It was controversial from the outset. It provided for the resettlement of the landless, established rural cooperatives, constructed model towns, and administered grants and loans to the poorest farmers. Its projects were seen as dangerous by critics, and Tugwell was labelled a socialist by conservatives who questioned the constitutional legitimacy of his undertakings. In December 1936 the Resettlement Administration was transferred to the Department of Agriculture. Tugwell resigned and was replaced by the less controversial Will Alexander.

It was thought necessary to provide justification for the Resettlement Administration / FSA's activities to both the public and Congress through publicity, and so the Photography File was established for all publicity pertaining to them. The File was to be directed by Stryker until 1943 and eventually included 270,000 prints and negatives (of which 170,000 are now in the Library of Congress). The photographs served the twin purposes of publicizing rural distress and promoting the Government's ameliorative efforts. While the original intentions of the File appear to have been quite modest, Stryker soon developed the idea of an encyclopaedic file of American life. This idea was apparently influenced by conversations with the sociologist, and author of *Middletown*, Robert Lynd, who not only encouraged it but came up with specific suggestions for individual photo-shoots.[44]

Stryker's office in Washington, DC, was responsible for the printing, filing and distribution of images taken by up to thirteen photographers who travelled around the country under Stryker's direction. Starting in the spring and summer of 1935, he hired, among others, Walker Evans, Arthur Rothstein, Carl Mydans, Ben Shahn, Dorothea Lange and Russel Lee. That year he distributed 965 pictures for publication in just five months. By the end of 1936, FSA photos had appeared in *Time*, *Fortune*, *Today*, and *Literary Digest* and in 23 exhibitions, including one at New York's Museum of Modern Art.

The production of the photographs was a massive, labour-intensive undertaking involving making over 70 prints a day. But this was just one part of the process. Stryker had divided the US into eleven administrative districts, each of which was covered by a photographer. He insisted on the photographers being well informed about the areas they were working in. He asked each to carry a copy of Columbia geographer J. Russell Smith's *North America* – a thorough socioeconomic regional geography text that informed them of the major crops and industries of each locale.[45] In addition to the information available in Smith's book, photographers in the field were directed, sometimes quite explicitly, by Stryker and were guided to their subjects by local government officials. All the photographers were required to send their negatives to the Washington office for editorial selection, captioning and distribution.[46] Each photograph, then, is the end product of a considerable amount of direction. The photographers were being asked to contribute to a story being composed in Stryker's office.

## STRYKER, REALISM AND THE RÔLE OF PHOTOSCRIPTS

Stryker was the mastermind for the FSA photographers. He had firm views about the value of documentary photography. He distinguished the work of documentary photographers from pictorial photographers by their 'love for life':

> They insist that life as it is being lived daily everywhere in the streets, in the fields, in the skyscrapers, the tenements, the hotels and huts, is so exciting that it needs no embellishment. The best of a man's ability to see, to understand, and to appreciate is required for their job: interpretation by selection.[47]

For Stryker, documentary photographers were both recorders of reality and people with a burden of responsibility to society:

> It hardly seems necessary for anyone today to emphasize the importance of visual aids as a media for imparting information and instruction. Not only are they time savers but often they furnish more lasting and accurate impressions than may be gained from the printed page. The camera alone enables us to reproduce with great exactness the image of men, places, buildings and landscapes.[48]

Stryker, in other words, was firmly tied into an ideology of the photograph as a window on reality and it is in this fact of realism that photography could serve to persuade and convince. In Stryker's own mind the photography of the FSA was connected to science and social science. He relied on Lynd, Tugwell and others to produce an objective plan of what kinds of subject his photographers should concentrate on. 'By the precision of their instrument', he wrote, 'by the very mechanical limitations of shutter, lens, and film, they are invested with credibility; simple honesty will render to their pictures the dignity of fact; feeling and insight will give their fraction of a second exposure the integrity of truth.'[49] He was firmly convinced that well-trained documentary photographers had a unique angle on the real. He saw photography as a positivist enterprise, arguing that the photographer 'had as his purpose the recording of something actual . . . something which was verifiably a true detail of the real world'. 'The urge to accuracy and verification', he continued, 'created the camera'.[50] He compared the photograph to the painting:

> Unlike the painting, which was suspect as a part of organic life and had, in those days, to invoke the science of optics for public verification of some of its statements, the photograph while dealing with the promiscuous data of experience was itself a part of the neutral and sovereign world of fact.[51]

Photography was seen by Stryker as a guarantee of factuality and, more than that, as a weapon for democracy. It was only in a democracy, he believed, that documentary photography could exist, and by its existence, by its ability to record reality, it fended off the threat of totalitarianism.

Stryker's faith in the realism of photography is in tension with the actual process through which the photographs were produced. The images of migrants taken by Dorothea Lange are but one part of a process of production and presentation that centred on Stryker. His rôle was to direct photographers towards appropriate subject-matter, to select images for publication and then to archive them in such a manner as to be available to the wider public. In undertaking these tasks Stryker was constructing a particular narrative that placed these photographs in overarching contexts of meaning.

By tracing the moments that led to, and followed from, the taking of these images we can see how Lange's photographs of migrants were not just accidents of chance. In their general intent they were the product of a much bigger story being worked on by Stryker and his superiors. The first such moment was his development of 'photoscripts'. Many of the photographs were prompted by him through the use of these 'photoscripts' or 'shooting scripts'. After having met the sociologist Robert Lynd in 1936, Lynd had produced a 'photoscript' suggesting a series of photographs to illustrate life in a small town:

HOME IN THE EVENING
Photographs showing the various ways that different income groups spend their evenings, for example:
    Informal clothes
    Listening to the radio
    Bridge
    More precise dress
    Guests[52]

This simple idea of producing a short, almost poetic, list of subjects for photographers to locate and shoot formed the basis of Stryker's practice as a grand conductor of his photographers around the country. By producing photoscripts and sending them out to his regional photographers he effectively inscribed a master narrative in the process of documenting before the pictures were even shot.

By 1939 Stryker had elaborated on Lynd's original short list of suggestive shots and was producing detailed shooting scripts that ran to several pages. The following is just a small section of a script sent to all photographers in 1939:

SMALL TOWNS
Stores
    *outside views*
    front views
    cars and horses and buggies (hitching racks)
    *inside views*
    goods on shelves

people buying
people coming out of store with purchases
farm machinery displays

Churches
On Sunday, if possible
'Court Day'
Children at play (dogs)
Movies
Men loafing under trees

Local baseball games
players
spectators

'The Vacant Lot'

Main Street.[53]

By reading a photoscript such as this it is possible to read a narrative of decaying rural culture, the marginality of uprootedness and the quest for roots and place. A sedentarist metaphysics is clearly at work. This list encapsulates a kind of Normal Rockwell vision of the small town, down to the detail of men loafing under trees while the baseball match gets into full swing and children playing happily with dogs. It is possible to think of the FSA images as representations of a simultaneously longed for and disappearing cultural geography of place-bound rurality. The migrants are thus symptoms of a disappearance, visible evidence of something that is not in the photographs – the material manifestation of *Gameinschaft*. FSA photographs are replete with symbols, often deeply ironic, of modernity's intrusion into the rural. Billboards were a favourite example. Forms of transportation were another. In Lange's *On the Road Towards Los Angeles*, for instance, we see two men walking away from the camera down the highway. Lange juxtaposes the men and their obvious burdens with the billboard for the luxuries of the Southern Pacific Railroad (illus. 56). The FSA photographers in general and Lange in particular frequently used billboards to ironically point out the situation of the poor and dispossessed. Here the billboard underlines the politics of mobility with the relaxed, obviously wealthy, train passenger lying back and closing his eyes to the plight of the two migrants. The image also points towards the contrast between the technology of the railroad and an older, more traditional, rural life.

Some photoscripts were general ones sent out to all photographers. Migrants were a recurring theme:

56 Dorothea Lange, *On the Road Toward Los Angeles, California, March 1937.*

To: All photographers
From: R.E.S.
Some Suggestions for Pictures of Migrants
Health
    Sanitary Facilities
    Sickness
    Medical attention (or absence of)
Recreation
    What do the migrants do for amusement?
    What do youngsters do?
'Help Wanted' signs
Farmer 'hunting' help in the towns

Washing clothes
Eating
Cooking
Do the youngsters work in the fields?
Get ages of those you take if possible
'Air views' of camps (from as high a spot as possible)[54]

The photoscripts are clear evidence of Stryker's desire to see in a particular way. From his office in Washington he would send out these scripts on a weekly basis, specifying in some detail the kinds of images that would best serve his office. Imagine the noted photographers receiving these notes asking them to find old men talking under a tree and take a photograph of them. These notes remind us, if any reminder is needed, that the

57 Dorothea Lange, *Napa Valley, California. More than twenty-five years a bindle-stiff. Walks from the mines to the lumber camps to the farms. The type that formed the backbone of the Industrial Workers of the World in California before the war. December 1938.*

practice of documentary photography is not the capture of 'reality' but its construction. It could hardly be plainer that the photographs Lange and others took were stories based on a loose plot sent from Washington. The ability to see these photographs as nostalgic versions of the past can, as Alan Trachtenberg has put it, 'free us from the tyranny of any fixed version, permitting critical historical judgment'.[55]

## DOROTHEA LANGE'S MIGRANT IMAGES

Thus we come to the images of migrants taken by Dorothea Lange in the Western states during the mid- and late-1930s. In two images of men walking (illus. 55, 56), there is clearly a connection between these 'fruit tramps'

58 Dorothea Lange, *Migrants, family of Mexicans, on road with tire trouble. Looking for work in the peas, California, February 1936.*

59 Dorothea Lange, *Drought Refugees Following Crops, California, August 1936.*

and earlier images of tramps. They are men without women; they are
walking; they carry their belongings with them. There are more images
like these. *Napa Valley,* for instance, shows a tramp picking up his 'bindle'
to continue his long walk into the distance (illus. 57). The title frames the
image, like earlier ones, as a type – a 'bindle stiff', a single tramp looking
for work. Most of her photographs are not of a single man or even just of
men, but are of family groups or of women and children. *California Fruit
Tramp and Family, Marisville, California, June 1935* is annotated with the note
'The mother is twenty two years old.' The man is specified as a fruit tramp,
but this time we are shown the characteristic family setting, the woman
with a child in her arms and the curious mixture of mobility and domesticity signified by the lived-in vehicle behind them.

60 Dorothea Lange, *Missouri family of five, seven months from the drought area. 'Broke, baby sick, car trouble', U.S. 99 near Tracy, California.*

*Migrants, family of Mexicans . . .* is even more typical of Lange's migrant images (illus. 58). Here we see a large family and a car encumbered with the trappings of domestic life. The accompanying text tells the story of the family's movement in search of work. Images of migrants typically focussed on the fact that the migrant population frequently travelled in family groups and were therefore distinct from the single men of earlier decades. The car is also a key icon in these photographs. While tramps and hobos either walked or took rides on the trains, these families travelled in cars. The cars enabled migrant families, sometimes comprising several generations, to move from harvest to harvest, from early spring vegetables to cotton in the autumn. Lange saw the car as a new covered wagon containing social pioneers. Often they became stranded or stuck and were more symbols of imprisonment than hopeful mobility.

The car is present in many of Lange's images, often combined with the children who also feature heavily (illus. 59–61). Children, combined with the various domestic belongings attached to the car – in *Drought Refugees* (illus. 59) we see a container marked 'Mothers Oats' – have the obvious effect of promoting sympathy. The parents may well be blamed for their own condition, but the children are innocent. The children also have the effect of domesticating mobility. While earlier generations of tramps and hobos were portrayed as threats to domesticity, Lange's migrant photographs emphasize domesticity on the road even in the most difficult circumstances.

These photographs differ from earlier representations of tramps in further ways. There is a transformation in the moral light being cast on the socially marginal. Lange's migrants are objects of sympathy – not of disgust or fear. Her photographs are, as Sandra Phillips puts it, of 'hard working, good-spirited, and fair people, some of whom need a little help'.[56] Lange used many of the signifiers of deviance and displacement to create images of sympathetic characters. Foremost among these is dirt.

In all these images we are confronted with images of dust and dirt combined with mobility and domesticity. These three themes in Lange's

61 Dorothea Lange, *Oklahoma Share-cropper and Family entering California. Stalled in the Desert near Indio, California, February 1937.*

photography form a curious triad. Domesticity is, of course, predominantly a discourse of home. It is also partly constructed through highly gendered considerations of cleanliness. Lange's bringing together of domesticity, dirt and mobility transgresses several well-established sets of relationships. Frazer Ward has argued that the documentary tradition typically associates dirt with femininity and the socially low, combining gender-specific coding with a representation of class relations.[57] Dirt, as Mary Douglas has shown, is symbolically 'matter out of place' – a form of categorization familiar to many societies. 'Dirt', she writes, 'is a by-product of a systematic ordering and classification of matter, in so far as ordering involves rejecting inappropriate elements'.[58] Dirt plays the rôle of transgression, of threat and of abjection in photography and in much modern art. Dirt signifies the 'out of place' in culture – it represents displacement from familiar contexts.[59] Dirt provides a means of arranging cultures along class and gender lines, to which we might add ethnicity and sexuality.

In Lange's photographs, dust and dirt are pretty much constant. Even the captions highlight the presence of dust/dirt. Families in cars or makeshift shacks and tents combine domestic dirt with the socially low. 'Class relations displace dirt downward, so that it "naturally" represents the lower boundaries of culture.'[60] It is the association of dirt with both displacement and the socially low that gives it power to unsettle the viewer and raise questions about the ordering of society and culture. Lange's photos present us with the abject depths of culture in a way that is simultaneously loathsome and aesthetically pleasing. The beauty of her compositions aestheticizes the dirtiness of the women, children and families that feature in her pictures. They are allowed to exist as families with a simulation of conventional domesticity symbolized by beds and food canisters and the rudiments of everyday life surrounding them. Many of these images are of families and communities that have become displaced. The cars that feature alongside, behind or around these families are their homes. Children play in them, people sleep in them. Often they are clearly not working and the people are stranded. The means of mobility and of escape become traps – prisons within which the migrants are frustratingly stuck. On other occasions, though, they are determined attempts to maintain a 'home' and all the moral connotations that accompany the idea of home. Cooking and washing gets done, children can play and men sit down and smoke a pipe.

Lange, as an FSA photographer, was taking pictures in order to gather sympathy for the migrants and legitimate the Government programs designed to alleviate their poverty. She is using dirt, a symbol of displacement and transgression, to produce sympathy – to signify the conditions that need to be overcome by the people and by the Government agency employing her. These images of migrants stranded in cars need, therefore, to be compared with images of the camps set up by the FSA in California. The FSA sought to promote the construction of these camps, and photographs by Lange and others were used to convince Congress and the general public that the expenditure was justified. *Schafter* is an image of a clean, rational and ordered space (illus. 62). Nothing could contrast more with the images of migrants in their informal settings, where domestic life is mixed up with work, children's spaces are mixed up with those for adults, and mobile technologies are used as homes. In this image we see the camp arranged in characteristic blocks of living space, each of which forms a sanitary unit around its own laundry, toilet and cleaning facilities. Dirt, here, is firmly under control. *Kern County* is a close-up of one tent in

62 Dorothea Lange, *Schafter California June 1938. FSA camp for migratory agricultural workers.*

an FSA camp that reminds us of other images of women with children. In this image, unlike most of the photographs Lange took of migrants, the woman and the manager appear content. It appears that the baby is being presented for display. The manager's stance seems to be saying 'look, this is what we can do.' The woman's clothes seem clean and the space is comparatively well ordered (illus. 63).

Stryker and Lange clearly wanted to help the migrants. Many of these photographs, with their emphasis on children, domesticity and simulated ordinary life, point towards the similarities between the migrants and more settled people. Nevertheless, the images do exist in order to promote a more ordered and settled existence – a particular vision of proper existence that is made material in the migrant camps. Lange makes her feeling about migrant existence and its wider implications quite clear in some of the notes that accompany her photographs. Under one typical image of a family and their car she writes 'U.S. 101 migratory pea-pickers near Santa Monica, California, February 1936. Constant movement does not favor the

63 Dorothea Lange, *Kern County, California, November 1936. The Arvin migratory farm workers' camp of the Farm Security Administration. Tom Collins, manager of the camp with migrant mother and child.*

development of normal relationships between citizens and community, and between employer and employee for the proper functioning of democracy.'[61] Lange and her husband, the economist Paul Taylor, held on to a Jeffersonian ideal of a rural property-owning democracy with firm connections between the people and the soil. It is not surprising, therefore, that the metaphor of erosion is a dominant one in her imagery. The erosion of soil and the dust-storms of Oklahoma produced the human erosion of the migrants.[62]

Insofar as Lange's photography has such a liberal, even radical, agenda, it shares with Riis's and McCook's work the quality of deindividualizing the subject. As did earlier photographers, she uses people as representative 'types'. William Stott has noted how reductive the pictures by Lange and other FSA photographers are:

> They come to us only in images meant to break our heart. They come helpless, guiltless as children and, though helpless, yet still unvanquished by the implacable wrath of nature – flood, drought and the indifference of their society. They come, Pere Lorentz said, 'group after group of wretched human beings, starkly asking for so little, and wondering what they will get.' Never are they vicious, never depraved, never responsible for their misery. And this, of course, was intentional.[63]

Lange allowed her subjects to look determined and resolute but rarely happy. Most famously, the Migrant Mother picture was just one of a series of six that had included a dreamy-looking teenager and a smiling toddler. As she took the series these were gradually pushed out of the frame until only the mother and rather sad-looking children remained. Lawrence Levine sees this process as one that removes the dignity of those who are photographed:

> The urge, whether conscious or not, to deprive people without power of any determination over their destiny, of any pleasure in their lives, of any dignity in their existence, knows no single part of the political spectrum; it affects radicals and reactionaries, liberals and conservatives, alike. The only culture the poor are supposed to have is the culture of poverty: worn faces and torn clothing, dirty skin and dead eyes, ramshackle shelters and disorganized lives. Any forms of contentment or self-respect, even cleanliness itself, have no place in this totality.[64]

Levine may have overstated his case here. While it is true that the best publicized images of migrants rarely expressed happiness, they most certainly did appear resolute and determined, even when worn down by circumstances. What does seem to be clear, however, is that the photographs were taken in order to illustrate issues beyond the particular situation of an individual or family group. The migrants are used as examples of migrants – as social types to illustrate the need for New Deal reforms. As in the case of Riis and McCook, the people are turned into categories. What Lange and the FSA photographers present us with are 'fruit tramps', 'migrants', 'sharecroppers', 'the unemployed', 'mothers' and 'children'. Migrant Mother is a migrant and a mother. Florence Thompson is lost behind these labels.[65] It is for this reason, perhaps, that the landscape photographer Ansel Adams told Stryker that 'What you've got are not photographers. They're a bunch of sociologists with cameras.'[66]

By reducing their subjects to representatives of social types, Lange and others objectified the migrants just as surely as had earlier social reformers and sociologists. The fact that Lange was sympathetic to their plight does not change this fact. Charles Shindo has gone so far as to claim, with some justification, that the migrants of the 1930s were deliberately misrepresented as a group by the FSA, by John Steinbeck in *The Grapes of Wrath* and by the radical folk singer Woody Guthrie. All of these liberal or radical perspectives on the migrants, he argues, were far removed from the essential conservatism of the migrants themselves. Shindo sees the migrants as the ancestors of Reagan Republicans, who were religiously, politically and culturally well to the right of the well-meaning people who represented them.[67] Lange and others, in this view, were appropriating the migrant experience wholesale for their own ends.

The reduction of Florence Thompson and others to categories cannot simply be located in the photographic practice of Lange, however. The FSA photographs have to be understood as part of a wider production of knowledge that was passed down to them through photoscripts from Stryker's office, which was itself part of Roosevelt's administration. We also have to bear in mind the way they are presented to us through the archive.

THE ARCHIVE

In addition to the narrative inscribed in the photoscripts it is instructive to think through what has happened to them since they were produced. In particular, it is important to take into account the way we have inherited them in the form of a huge file of photographs at the Library of Congress catalogued some years after Lange's term with the FSA. Alan Trachtenberg has magnificently illustrated the rôle of the catalogue, in its tangible materiality, in the construction of the meaning of these photographs. He starts from the position of today's researcher walking into the Library of Congress, as I did, and trying to make sense of the collection. In my case I went in trying to find photographs of tramps. I was faced with a catalogue and row after row of filing cabinets that, in their very structure, were making sense of the photographed world for me. Just as the arrangement of spaces in modern cities or in 1930s migrant camps makes society legible, so an archive inscribes meaning on chaos and produces particular forms of knowledge.

In the summer of 1939 Stryker had begun to suggest particular groupings of pictures for the purposes of creating newspaper and magazine stories. The pictures were loosely arranged around suggestive headings such as 'crop stories' and 'place stories'. In addition, photos were kept in 'lots' of pictures taken together on particular assignments without cross-references.[68] By 1942 Stryker had been assembling a working file of photographs for seven years but had not attempted systematically to organize them. That year he hired Paul Vanderbilt, who had been working on cataloguing Navy photo archives, to arrange and catalogue the ever-expanding collection of the FSA and Office of War Information (OWI). When Vanderbilt arrived he wanted to produce a clear and rational code through which photographs could be found and interpreted. The basis for his new scheme, the one that I and an endless number of other researchers have been confronted with, was on a dual grouping of sets of photos based on assignments (the original 'lots') and groups based on similarity of subject. These two ordering principles took distinct material forms. The 'lots' were microfilmed and the new subject classifications were put into file cabinets as hard copies. Every photo had a lot that connected the two systems.

The new system of subject categories is based around a pyramid-like structure of main headings and subheadings. The major headings are these:

The Land – the background of civilization
Cities and Towns – as background
People as Such – without emphasis on their activity
Homes and Living Conditions
Transportation
Work – agriculture, commerce, manufacturing
Organized Society – for security, justice, regulation, and assistance

War
Medicine and Health
Religion
Intellectual and Creative Activity
Social and Personal Activity
Alphabetical Section.

A further rationale for organization was based on geography. All the photos under the subject headings were further divided into six regional divisions, so as to make clear where the photograph was taken. The major headings above were, and still are, simply the first point of access for the researcher. They do not reveal the 1,300 descending subheadings that were designed to give the collection intellectual coherence.

This system orders the photographs in particular ways while presenting itself as transparent and obvious. Indeed, my encounter with the catalogue was one of functional innocence. I wanted to find tramps, preferably pictures labelled as such. It did not occur to me that this means of locating, this hierarchical structure of ordering, was in itself worth pausing to think about. What researcher has not used a catalogue in such an instrumental way? Vanderbilt wanted to rebuild the file based on some obvious form of knowledge that relates the photographs to the reality they allegedly help us to know. He claimed that the basis of his classification was 'the actual literal subject matter of the picture itself, and not its connotation or association'.[69] But as Trachtenberg shows, it is far from simple to tell these things apart, and yet such a division is central to the whole edifice of the FSA file. Photos do not suggest their own category, as Vanderbilt liked to think, but require that choices be made. Do photographs get filed under 'tramps' or 'migrants'?

Vanderbilt was convinced of his success. He believed he had developed an objective and workable framework for the photos that allowed an infinite set of relationships between them that would be determined by people's future use of the system. The catalogue and the material form of the collection were, in his mind, a vast machine for storage and retrieval with no particular meaning or ideology – just regions, subjects, facts and data – all agreed, objective and uncontroversial. Only the user would release the photos from the cell-like categories they had been filed under. Despite his claims to objectivity Vanderbilt admitted that 'There is no such thing as an ideal general sequence of subject matter.' He intended an open-ended, ever-changing structure. 'The order of classes is neither a very important not very profound matter', he wrote, and while one might 'claim that work, in the class sequence comes before play, it is not in the spirit of analytical criticism, but merely to facilitate storage and have a place to keep the photograph while endless discussion goes on'.[70]

Vanderbilt's admission notwithstanding, it is clear that this great panoramic machine of memory does impose its own meanings. His classification system constructs an order that seems permanent and authoritative – representing the FSA project in a particular way. What it constructs, through its headings and subheadings, microfilms and filing cabinets, is a meta-narrative that tells the story of civilization, starting with the 'land' and proceeding to a complex human culture and society.

Vanderbilt placed the photographs of the FSA into a structure with roots in liberal ideas of progress and individualism. The catalogue he produced shapes the interpretation of the photographs. The photos are not self-evidently categorizable. They do not speak their own meanings. They have to be interpreted. Vanderbilt's classification shapes them into a system of meaning that reflects cultural mythology and seems natural.

This apparent transparency is achieved through its illusion of objectivity. Vanderbilt's original supposition – that he could split the actual contents of a picture from its connotations – was based on the presumption that it was possible to split the objective from the subjective. It was this belief that gave the meta-narrative implied by the classification scheme an ideological power that suggests more than a mere filing device. In its apparent objectivity the narrative was able to make the claim that it was not a narrative at all, but simply a neutral arrangement of the obvious put there for the convenience of people like me – researchers – who would then produce their own stories from the inert contents of the filing cabinets.

When we come across a photo of a migrant family in their stranded car, or an image of a neatly ordered migrant camp, we need to keep in mind both the photoscripts that preceded the image and the archive and catalogue that came after. Both of these place the photo in much larger stories – grander systems of knowledge – and impinge on the meanings of the photograph and reveal the lie of the images' factuality. Stryker, Vanderbilt and others were busy telling stories.

The principal tension in the photographs of Riis, McCook and Lange is the tension between the 'realism' of the photograph and their position in ideologically laden stories that reveal the images as particular ways of seeing. They are not simply evidence of what tramps looked like, and what they did, but moments in the construction of knowledge about the tramp and thus the making up of the tramps themselves. All these photographs were produced within broadly liberal frameworks. Riis wanted to alert his middle-class audience to the need to reform New York's tenements. McCook sought to document the life of the tramp in order to illustrate the effects of drink, disease and venal voting as well as overgenerous charity. Lange, as part of the FSA, was involved in a major national project to resettle the migrants and uplift the poor. Each came with an agenda and meta-narrative. Their photographs are as much about their own values and stories as they are about tramps. Documentary photography has, as Martha Rosler argued, 'come to represent the social conscience of liberal sensibility presented in visual imagery'.[71] In contrast to the quotation from Trachtenberg that opens this chapter, pictures of the tramp show us not so much 'the world outside' but the view of a narrator.

AFTERWORD  The Subject Strikes Back

In this book I have outlined some of the ways in which the tramp was made up in the years following 1869. This has not been an exhaustive account and there are certainly other potential lines of enquiry to point to. I have not, for instance, followed the more nostalgic view of the tramp that emerged around the turn of the century and continues to this day. Tramps have appeared in literature as a kind of counter-cultural hero. The works of Jack London and Jack Kerouac spring to mind.[1] More important, perhaps, I have not said much about the views of those who were called tramps. This is not entirely surprising, as few of them bothered to write down their experiences and we only get their voices through the answers to questionnaires and ethnographer's inquiries. There are so-called tramp autobiographies, but these tend to be written by middle-class drop-outs.[2] In addition, there are a huge number of tramp songs and poems that have been handed down, ranging from The Big Rock Candy Mountain to The Wabash Cannonball.[3] The lack of the tramps' own perspectives clearly means that the stories I have told are not the only stories. However thorough the process of making up the tramp was, it was never complete. I do not want to give the impression that the tramps of the 1880s were completely the product of others. The power of knowledge to make up people is never complete, it always leaves room for other stories and other knowledges.

The kind of knowledge most easily overlooked, and has been here, is the practical knowledge of tramp life.[4] Tramps clearly had a number of learned and embodied strategies for managing the life they led. Their ways of finding food, shelter and work were multiple and mostly successful. The many ways in which tramps were mobile can only be hinted at through the words of contemporary accounts. The life of the tramp adds up to more than the stories told by observers of tramps. My argument, then, is not that tramps were purely the objects of powerful knowledge; rather, it is that various powerful forms of knowledge had a considerable and material effect on the people so labelled. Tramps were not straight-forwardly on the receiving end of dominant knowledge, and their existence cannot be explained entirely by processes of 'social construction'. Indeed, an optimistic reading of the processes I have outlined here would be that the words and pictures of sociologists, lawyers, eugenicists, comedians and photographers were always reactions to events that disturbed. The existence of men, and especially women, on the road in the United States transgressed some of the most deeply held moral geographies of American life in the 1870s onwards. One thing that links the kinds of know-ledge in the earlier chapters is that they all made the existence of such people legible – intelligible – through the process of making up the tramp. Far from being agentless objects of knowledge, the tramps were con-stantly using the tactics of the weak to transgress and resist the established codes, many of them geographical, of society at the time.[5]

Perhaps the tramp should have the final say. Several times in the course of my research I was struck by a kind of knowingness on the part of those being represented. The first instance concerns the case of James Moore – the Daredevil Hobo. Moore was the hobo asked by Nels Anderson to pro-vide a classification table of tramps. The table is reproduced in chapter Three. The first section of the table, you will recall, is labelled 'Tramps of Society'. It is worth a second look.

I TRAMPS OF SOCIETY
(Those who have some graft or excuse)
1 Missionaries – organized beggars or parasites.
2 Professional beggars.
3 Tourists and autoists; these have taken the place of the old wagon tramp. Tramp families may go about in autos; gypsies, for example.
4 Vacationists.
5 Street fakers; those who work some selling game.
6 Loiterers; those who stay home but do not work – the idle rich.

These few words provide an insight into the politics of mobility in turn-of-the-century America. Here the object of knowledge – the hobo – slyly con-flates the mobility of the tramp with that of a number of other familiar characters in American society. 'Missionaries' become 'organized beggars and parasites' and, along with 'tourists' and 'vacationists', members of the tramp family. The word 'loiterers' is used to describe the 'idle rich'. Like a 'bum', only with money. Perhaps Chicago School sociologists could be added to the list.

The second moment of comic self-awareness comes from the refusal of a tramp in New York to replace a pipe in his mouth for nothing for the benefit of the photographer Jacob Riis (see chapter Seven). This is Riis's account:

> On one of my visits to 'the Bend' I came across a particularly ragged and disreputable tramp, who lay smoking his pipe on the rung of a ladder with such evident philosophic contentment in the busy labor of a score of ragpickers all about him, that I bade him sit for a picture, offering him ten cents for the job. He accepted the offer with hardly a nod, and sat patiently watching me from his perch until I got ready for work. Then he took the pipe out of his mouth and put it in his pocket, calmly declaring that it was not included in the contract, and that it was worth a quarter to have it go in the picture. The pipe, by the way, was of clay, and of the two-for-a-cent kind. But I had to give in. The man, scarce ten seconds employed at honest labor, even at sitting down, at which he was an undoubted expert, had gone on strike. He knew his rights and the value of 'work,' and was not to be cheated out of either.[6]

Here the tramp literally strikes back. There is a lot going on in this account. Riis enters the exchange loaded with moral and aesthetic expectations. The references to laziness resonate with the history of tramp categorization, from the legal definition of those without work to the comic attempts of Happy Hooligan to get a job. He clearly had more specific expectations of what a tramp should look like, and the pipe was part of it. Why was it worth a quarter to get it in the picture? Is not a pipe just a pipe? What is more interesting is that the tramp also seems to have realized the categories and expectations that were being activated here. The tramp knew that he was being made into an object and he knew that the pipe was important. He went on strike and won his extra fifteen cents. The pipe went back into his mouth. This is what differentiates social objects from their 'natural' counterparts. A glove or a tree cannot know that it is a glove or a tree and therefore cannot act accordingly. A tramp, on the other hand, can know that he or she is a tramp – and frequently does act accordingly, or otherwise.[7]

# REFERENCES

## 1 TRAMPS, KNOWLEDGE AND MOBILITY

1 The idea of a moral panic originates in Stanley Cohen, *Folk Devils and Moral Panics: The Creation of the Mods and the Rockers* (London, 1980).
2 Kenneth Allsop, *Hard Travellin': The Story of the Migrant Worker* (London, 1993).
3 *Ibid.*, pp. 110–13 for these two opinions and many more.
4 *Ibid.*, pp. 1 13–14.
5 See Tim Cresswell, 'Weeds, Plagues and Bodily Secretions: A Geographical Interpretation of Metaphors of Displacement', *Annals of the Association of American Geographers*, 87, no. 2 (1997), pp. 330–45 for an account of the material effects of metaphors of displacement.
6 *St Louis Journal* ( 27 June 1879), p. 4.
7 See Edmond Kelly, *The Elimination of the Tramp, Questions of the Day* (New York, 1908), for a plan to establish Swiss labour camps, and Allsop, *Hard Travellin'*, p. 114, recalls how the *Unitarian Review* called for the importation of the Victorian almshouse.
8 I elaborated on this point in *In Place / Out of Place: Geography, Ideology and Transgression* (Minneapolis, 1996) through the lens of 'transgression'. David Sibley makes similar arguments, in a more psychoanalytic mode, in *Geographies of Exclusion: Society and Difference in the West* (London, 1995). A book that nicely ties together the body and wider geographies around the issues of marginality and transgression is Peter Stallybrass and Allon White, *The Politics and Poetics of Transgression* (Ithaca, NY, 1986).
9 Paul Ringenbach, *Tramps and Reformers, 1873–1916* (Westport, CT, 1973). This book has been extremely helpful in developing my interest in the world of tramps. Other significant texts devoted to the history of tramps in the United States include the collection of essays in Eric H. Monkkonen, ed., *Walking to Work: Tramps in America, 1790–1935* (Lincoln, NE, 1984), and Victor Hoffman, 'The American Tramp, 1870–1900', MA thesis, University of Chicago, 1953, which provided much of the background knowledge needed for this book.
10 Ian Hacking, 'Making Up People', in *Reconstructing Individualism: Autonomy, Individuality, and the Self in Western Thought*, ed. T. Heller, M. Sosna and D. Wellbery (Stanford, CA, 1986), p. 365; Ian Hacking, *Rewriting the Soul: Multiple Personality and the Sciences of Memory* (Princeton, NJ, 1995); Ian Hacking, 'Les Alienes Voyageurs: How Fugue Became a Medical Entity', *History of Psychiatry*, 7 ( 1996), pp. 425–49.
11 Hacking, 'Making-up People', p. 227.

12 Hobbes, cited in Hacking, 'Making up People', p.228.

13 Hacking, 'Making up People', p. 228.

14 *Ibid.*, p. 231.

15 See John Searle, *The Construction of Social Reality* (London, 1995), for a similar account of the construction of social reality. Searle distinguishes between 'brute facts' (such as the mass and size of Mt Everest) and 'institutional facts' (such as the value of money) in much the same way. I differ from Searle in that he clearly retains a foundational project that suggests what he calls 'social reality' is based in biology.

16 The idea of a sedentary metaphysics comes from Liisa Malkki, 'National Geographic: The Rooting of Peoples and the Territorialization of National Identity Among Scholars and Refugees', *Cultural Anthropology*, 7, no. 1 ( 1992), pp. 24–44.

17 Any number of geographic texts load place with positive moral connotations, for instance Yi-Fu Tuan, *Morality and Imagination: Paradoxes of Progress* (Madison, WI, 1989); Yi-Fu Tuan, *Space and Place: The Perspective of Experience* (Minneapolis, 1977); R. Sack, *Homo Geographicus* (Baltimore, 1997); Edward Relph, *Place and Placelessness* (London, 1976).

18 This is particularly the case in Relph, *Place and Placelessness*.

19 This is best stated in Yi-Fu Tuan, 'A View of Geography', *Geographical Review*, 81, no. 1 (1991), pp. 99–107.

20 Tuan, *Space and Place*, p. 179.

21 *Ibid.*, p. 183.

22 The negative value of mobility is not unique to Tuan; it is a strong theme in Relph's *Place and Placelessness*, for instance.

23 See Relph, *Place and Placelessness*, for a faithful geographical implementation of Heidegger's ideas. Relph argues that places of mobility, such as drive-ins, highways, airports and housing with high turnover, are 'placeless'.

24 Relph, *Place and Placelessness*, p. 38.

25 The Marxist geographer David Harvey has recently engaged with these notions of place. He argues that place can be both a potent site for political resistance but, more often, is a reactionary and insular force in human life. See David Harvey, 'From Space to Place and Back Again: Reflections on the Condition of Postmodernity', in *Mapping the Futures: Local Cultures, Global Change*, ed. Jon Bird, *et al.* (London, 1993), pp. 3–29. A feminist take on Heideggerian notions of place and home is given in Iris Marion Young, *Intersecting Voices: Dilemmas of Gender, Political Philosophy and Policy* (Princeton, NJ, 1997), which attempts to rescue some of the positive connotations of home for feminists.

26 For a range of critiques of the place / identity relationship see James Clifford, *Routes: Travel and Translation in the Later Twentieth Century* (Cambridge, MA, 1997); Akhil Gupta and James Ferguson, 'Beyond Culture: Space, Identity and the Politics of Difference', *Cultural Anthropology*, 7, no. 1 ( 1992), pp. 6–22; Smadar Lavie and Ted Swedenburg, 'Between and Among the Boundaries of Culture: Bridging Text and Lived Experience in the Third Timespace', *Cultural Studies*, 10, no. 1 (1996), pp. 154–79; Lawrence Grossberg, 'Cultural Studies and / in New Worlds', *Critical Studies in Mass Communication*, 10 ( 1993), pp. 1–22; and Liisa Malkki, 'National Geographic'.

27 Malkki, 'National Geographic', p. 31.

28 Cited in Malkki, 'National Geographic', p. 32. Malkki looks at the perception and treatment of refugees in the light of a dominant sedentary metaphysics. She shows how refugees are frequently pathologized.

29  Zygmunt Bauman, *Life in Fragments: Essays in Postmodern Morality* (Oxford, 1995), p. 94.
30  Bauman, *Life in Fragments*, p. 94.
31  This story is told in Zygmunt Bauman, *Legislators and Interpreters* (Oxford, 1987).
32  See A. L. Beier, *Masterless Men: The Vagrancy Problem in England, 1560–1640* (London, 1985), for an account of this.
33  Ian Hacking, *Mad Travelers: Reflections on the Reality of Transient Mental Illnesses* (Charlottesville, VA, 1998).
34  Jean-Claude Beaune, cited in Hacking, *Mad Travelers*, p. 69.
35  Cited in Hacking, *Mad Travelers*, p. 69.
36  Daniel Boorstin, *The Americans: The National Experience* (London, 1966), p. 95.
37  John Kouwenhowen, *The Beer-Can by the Highway: Essays on What's American about America* (Baltimore, 1961), p. 156. There are many other statements of the centrality of mobility in American history and identity, for example G. W. Pierson, 'The M–Factor in American History', *American Quarterly*, 14 ( 1962), pp. 275–89.
38  Here I am following the lead of the 'new Western history'. See, for instance, Patricia Nelson Limerick, *The Legacy of Conquest* (New York, 1987).
39  In *The Social Construction of What?* (Cambridge, MA, 1999) Ian Hacking uses the term 'matrix' to refer to a social setting for an idea such as 'tramp' or 'vagrant.' He develops the idea of a matrix with reference to the category 'woman refugee'.

2  THE TRAMP IN CONTEXT

1  For an account of time–space compression see David Harvey, *The Condition of Postmodernity*, (Oxford, 1989). Doreen Massey has argued that this compression affects different people in different ways and produces a 'politics of mobility'. Her argument has influenced my thinking here. See Doreen Massey, 'Power-Geometry and Progressive Sense of Place', in *Mapping the Futures: Local Cultures, Global Change*, ed. Jon Bird *et al.* (London, 1993), pp. 59–69.
2  See John Agnew, *The United States in the World Economy* (Cambridge, 1987) and William G. Robbins, *Colony and Empire: The Capitalist Transformation of the American West* (Lawrence, KA, 1994) for accounts of the centrality of the railroad to American capitalism.
3  George H. Douglas, *All Aboard! The Railroad in American Life* (New York, 1992), p. xvi.
4  Cited in Patricia Hills, 'Picturing Progress in the Era of Westward Expansion', in *The West as America: Reinterpreting Images of the Frontier, 1820–1920*, ed. William H. Truettner (Washington, DC, 1991), pp. 97–149 ( p. 101).
5  Cited in Hills, *Picturing Progress*, p. 127.
6  Stephen Daniels, *Fields of Vision: Landscape Imagery and National Identity in England and the United States* (Cambridge, 1993) gives a good account of this picture.
7  Douglas, *All Aboard*, p. xiv.
8  *Ibid.*, p. xvi.
9  *Ibid.*, p. xviii.
10  Cited in Roger Bruns, *Knights of the Road: A Hobo History* (New York, 1980), p. 49.
11  Kenneth Leslie Kusmer, 'The Underclass: Tramps and Vagrants in American Society, 1865–1930', PhD thesis, University of Chicago, 1980, p. 116, citing *Railroad Age Gazette*, 46 (1909).
12  Orlando Lewis, *Vagrancy in the United States* (New York, 1907), p. 4.
13  Lewis, *Vagrancy*, p. 7.

14  Kusmer, *The Underclass*, p. 56.
15  Josiah Flynt, 'The Tramp and the Railroad', *Century Magazine*, 58 (1899), pp. 258–66; Victor Hoffman, 'The American Tramp, 1870–1900', MA thesis, University of Chicago, 1953; Clark Spence, 'Knights of the Tie and Rail – Tramps and Hoboes in the West', *Western Historical Quarterly*, 2, no. 1 (1971), pp. 5–20; James Forbes, 'The Tramp; or, Caste in the Jungle', *Outlook*, 98, no. 19 (1911), pp. 869–75. Forbes noted (p. 870) that from 1901 to 1905, inclusive, 50 railways had reported 25,236 trespassers killed, of whom between 50 and 75 per cent were tramps.
16  Jack London, *The Road* (Santa Barbara, CA, 1970), pp. 43–4.
17  Douglas, *All Aboard*, p. 224.
18  This timetable is available in the cartography archives of the Newberry Library, Chicago.
19  This article is to be found in the Ernest Burgess archive at the University of Chicago, Box 126, p. 13.
20  Bruns, *Knights of the Road*, p. 27.
21  E. Hale, 'Reports on Tramps' (paper presented at the Conference of Charities, Saratoga, November 1877), pp. 102–10.
22  Flynt, 'The Tramp and the Railroad', p. 265.
23  See Robbins, *Colony and Empire*, ch. 4 for an extended account of this process. See also William Cronon, *Nature's Metropolis: Chicago and the Great West* (New York, 1991) for a detailed narrative of the rôle of the railroad in transforming the rural landscape of the Great West.
24  Robbins, *Colony and Empire*, p. 69.
25  Don Mitchell, *The Lie of the Land: Migrant Workers and the California Landscape* (Minneapolis, 1996); Walter J. Stein, *California and the Dust Bowl Migration* (Westport, CT, 1973).
26  Eric H. Monkkonen, ed., *Walking to Work: Tramps in America 1790–1935* (Lincoln, NE, 1984), p. 8.
27  The Great Northern Railroad was owned and operated by Jay Cooke, the man whose company's failure was responsible for the panic in the first place.
28  Priscilla Ferguson-Clement, 'The Transformation of the Wandering Poor in Nineteenth Century Philadephia', in *Walking to Work*, ed. Monkkonen, pp. 56–84 (pp. 60–61).
29  Forbes, *The Tramp*, p. 870.
30  Edmond Kelly, *The Elimination of the Tramp, Questions of the Day* (New York, 1908). Kelly calculated this, somewhat bizarrely, by taking as a basis the number of tramps killed on the railroad and multiplying it by the figure representing the proportion of train men killed in the year to the total number of train men employed.
31  Monkkonen, *Walking to Work*, p. 8.
32  Kusmer, *The Underclass*, p. 177.
33  *Ibid.*, p. 176. Kusmer also suggests that there was a higher percentage of blacks among female vagrants (7.5 per cent) and that women were generally slightly younger than their male counterparts.
34  Peter Kolchin, *First Freedom: The Responses of Alabama's Blacks to Emancipation and Reconstruction* (Westport, CT, 1972), p. 23.
35  See David Delaney, *Race, Place and the Law* (Austin, TX, 1998), pp. 49–54 for a concise account of the geopolitics of black mobility in this era.
36  Kusmer, *The Underclass*, p. 181.

37  John C. Schneider, 'Tramping Workers 1890–1920: A Subcultural View', in *Walking to Work*, ed. Monkkonen, pp. 212–34, p. 216.

38  Kusmer, *The Underclass*, pp. 181–2. These figures are supported by Alice Willard Solenberger, *One Thousand Homeless Men: A Study of Original Records* (New York, 1911); James McCook, 'A Tramp Census and its Revelations', *Forum*, 15 (1893), pp. 753–61; Flynt, 'The Tramp and the Railroad'.

39  See Nels Anderson, *The Hobo* (Chicago, 1925) for the classic ethnographic account of trampdom in Chicago.

40  Schneider, *Tramping Workers*, p. 221.

41  Kusmer, *The Underclass*, pp. 129–30.

42  Anderson, *The Hobo*, pp. 104–6.

43  *Ibid.*, p. 17.

44  For a collection of these songs see George Milburn, *The Hobo's Hornbook: A Repertory for a Gutter Jongleur* (New York, 1930).

45  Stein, *California and the Dust Bowl Migration*, p. x.

46  Mike Davis, *City of Quartz: Excavating the Future in Los Angeles* (New York, 1992).

47  John Wesley Powell, *Report of the Lands of the Arid Region of the United States with a More Detailed Account of the Lands of Utah* (Washington, DC, 1879). For accounts of the politics of water and drought in the American West see also Marc Reisner, *Cadillac Desert: The American West and its Disappearing Water* (Harmondsworth, 1993) and Donald Worster, *Rivers of Empire: Water, Aridity, and the Growth of the American West* (Oxford, 1985).

48  For an excellent, insistently materialist but nuanced account of migrant workers in California see Mitchell, *The Lie of the Land*.

49  Mitchell, *The Lie of the Land*, ch. 3, discusses the potential and actual subversiveness of the tramps' mobility when organized by the IWW.

50  See Mitchell, *The Lie of the Land*, ch. 4, for a discussion of racialized migrant labour in California.

51  Stein, *California and the Dust Bowl Migration*, p. 37.

52  *Ibid.*, p. 37 (p. 44).

53  Stewart Holbrook, *The Story of the American Railroads* (New York, 1947), p. 398.

3  KNOWING THE TRAMP

1  Paul Ringenbach, *Tramps and Reformers, 1873–1916* (Westport, CT, 1973). Ringenbach discusses the emergence of the word 'tramp' as a noun. The word tramp had had a longer existence as a verb to denote both walking and a more general sense of travel. Soldiers in the Civil War, for instance, were said to tramp.

2  Ben Reitman in Roger Bruns, *The Damndest Radical:The Life and World of Ben Reitman, Chicago's Celebrated Social Reformer, Hobo King, and Whorehouse Physician* (Urbana, IL, 1987), p. 44.

3  Nels Anderson, *The Hobo* (Chicago, 1925), p. 89.

4  For accounts of tramp law and vagrancy law in the United States see Orlando Lewis, *Vagrancy in the United States* (New York, 1907); Michigan State Library, *Laws of the Various States Relating to Vagrancy* (Lansing, MI, 1916); Jeffrey S. Adler, 'A Historical Analysis of the Law of Vagrancy', *Criminology*, 27, no. 2 ( 1989), pp. 209–29; Elbert Hubbard, 'The Rights of Tramps', *Arena*, 9 (April 1894),

pp. 593–600; Victor Hoffman, 'The American Tramp, 1870–1900', MA thesis, University of Chicago, 1953.

5 See A. L. Beier, *Masterless Men: The Vagrancy Problem in England, 1560–1640* (London, 1985) for the classic account of sixteenth-century vagrancy laws in Britain.

6 Quoted in Beier, *Masterless Men*, p. 9.

7 See Leonard Leigh, 'Vagrancy and the Criminal Law', in *Vagrancy: Some New Perspectives*, ed. Tim Cook (London, 1979), pp. 95–117, and Peter Archard, 'Vagrancy – A Literature Review', in *Vagrancy: Some New Perspectives*, ed. Cook, pp. 11–28.

8 The French term *gens sans aveu* referred to people not tied to a Lord and thus unprotected under the law. The word 'place' here, as elsewhere, is both social and spatial.

9 Kristin Ross, *The Emergence of Social Space: Rimbaud and the Paris Commune* (Minneapolis, 1988), p. 58.

10 Adler, 'An Historical Analysis of the Law of Vagrancy', p. 214.

11 See Sidney Harring, 'Class Conflict and the Suppression of Tramps in Buffalo, 1892–1894', *Law and Society Review*, 11, Summer ( 1977), pp. 873–911 for an account of the events in Buffalo.

12 These Tramp Acts are subjected to greater scrutiny in my chapter Three. For accounts of the model status of New York's act see Ringenbach, *Tramps and Reformers*, and Harring, 'Class Conflict and the Suppression of Tramps'.

13 Harring, 'Class Conflict and the Suppression of Tramps', pp. 885–6.

14 The most famous of these was Coxey's Army, which left Massilon, Ohio, for Washington, DC, in March 1893.

15 Hoffman, 'The American Tramp', p. 57.

16 A tramp was defined here as an idle person without employment, a transient person who roamed from place to place, and who had no lawful occasion to wander.

17 Hoffman, 'The American Tramp', p. 58.

18 Lewis, *Vagrancy in the United States*, p. 13.

19 *Ibid.*, p. 14.

20 Quoted in Hubbard, 'The Rights of Tramps', p. 593.

21 *Ibid.*, pp. 593–4.

22 *Ibid.*, p. 594.

23 *Ibid.*, p. 595.

24 *Ibid.*, p. 598.

25 *Ibid.*, p. 599.

26 Don Mitchell, 'The Annihilation of Space by Law: The Roots and Implications of Anti-Homeless Laws in the United States', *Antipode*, 29, no. 3 ( 1997), pp. 303–35, provides an astute analysis of what he calls 'anti homeless laws' in the United States in the 1990s. Clearly the story of the war against vagrancy does not end with the tramp laws.

27 The classic essay on social construction is Peter Berger and Thomas Luckmann, *The Social Construction of Reality: A Treatise in the Sociology of Knowledge* (New York, 1966). For a recent set of essays on the issue of social construction see Irving Velody and Robin Williams, eds., *The Politics of Constructionism* (London, 1998). For discussions of legal process within a geographical context see Gordon Clark, *Judges and the Cities: Interpreting Local Autonomy* (Chicago, 1985); Nick Blomley, *Law, Space and the Geographies of Power* (New York, 1994); David Delaney, *Race, Place and the Law* (Austin, TX, 1998).

28 David Delaney, 'Geographies of Judgment: The Doctrine of Changed Conditions and

the Geopolitics of Race', *Annals of the Association of American Geographers*, 83, no. 1 (1993), pp. 48–65, p. 50.

29  See Ross, *The Emergence of Social Space*, for an account of vagabondage in France.

30  Theodore Homberg, quoted in Ross, *The Emergence of Social Space*, p. 57.

31  *Ibid.* In this sense the French vagabond and the American tramp were similar to the Los Angeles gang member of the 1980s and 1990s. See Mike Davis's *City of Quartz* (New York, 1992) for the way in which potential or alleged gang members were / are seen to be potential criminals without having committed any crime other than that of belonging to a gang.

32  Beier, *Masterless Men*, p. xxii.

33  L. Adrian, 'Introduction', in *Tales of an American Hobo*, ed. C. Fox (Iowa City, 1989), pp. xv–xxiii, p. xvi.

34  Jeff Davies's notes on tramps and hobos appear in many copies of the *Hobo News* in 1938–9. These can be found in the New York Public Library on microfilm. A few issues also turn up in Ben Reitman's archives in the special collections department of the University of Illinois, Chicago.

35  C. D'Andrade, 'Cultural Meaning Systems', in *Cultural Theory: Essays on Mind, Self and Emotion*, ed. R. Shweder and R. Levine (Cambridge, 1987), p. 91.

36  Josiah Flynt, *Tramping with Tramps* (Montclair, NJ, 1972 [ 1899]); C. Fox, *Tales of an American Hobo* (Iowa City, 1989); Harry Kemp, *Tramping on Life* (New York, 1922); A–No 1 Livingstone, *The Curse of Tramp Life* (Cambridge Springs, PA, 1912); E. Lynn, *The Adventures of a Woman Hobo* (New York, 1917); B. Starke, *Touch and Go: The Story of a Girl's Escape* (London, 1931).

37  Flynt loved alcohol and let it ruin his health. He died at the age of 38.

38  See Rolf Linder, *The Reportage of Urban Culture: Robert Park and the Chicago School*, trans. Adrian Morris (Cambridge, 1996), ch. 3, for an account of Flynt.

39  Flynt, *Tramping with Tramps*, p. ix.

40  *Ibid.*, p. 2.

41  Anderson, *The Hobo*, published in 1925.

42  For contrasting accounts of the Chicago School see Linder, *The Reportage of Urban Culture*; Carla Cappetti, *Writing Chicago: Modernism, Ethnography and the Novel* (New York, 1993); and Ulf Hannerz, *Exploring the City: Inquiries Toward an Urban Anthropology* (New York, 1980), ch. 2.

43  Cited in Hannerz, *Exploring the City*, p. 22.

44  Linder, *The Reportage of Urban Culture*, provides an excellent account of the connections between urban journalism and the new sociology.

45  Cited in Hannerz, *Exploring the City*, p. 22.

46  R. Park and E. Burgess, *The City: Suggestions for Investigation of Human Behavior in the Urban Environment*, ed. M. Janowitz (Chicago, 1925), pp. 40–41.

47  The primary critique is that the model pretends to be universal and yet is clearly specific to Chicago in the early twentieth century. Other critiques include the lack of attention paid to lines of transportation, the dominance of land rents rather than sentiment and symbolism and the overriding and deeply suspect ecological metaphors that lie behind the model.

48  Ernest Burgess, 'The Growth of the City: An Introduction to a Research Project', in *The City*, ed. Park and Burgess, pp. 47–62 (p. 54).

49  Nels Anderson, 'The Trends of Urban Sociology', p. 13. This manuscript can be found

at the University of Chicago special collections division in the Ernest Burgess papers, box 126.

50  Burgess, 'The Growth of the City', p. 58.

51  *Ibid.*, p. 59.

52  Anderson, 'Trends', p. 14.

53  Robert Park, 'The Mind of the Hobo: Reflections upon the Relation Between Mentality and Locomotion', in *The City*, ed. Park and Burgess, pp. 156–60 (p. 156).

54  *Ibid.*, p. 156.

55  *Ibid.*, p. 158.

56  *Ibid.*, p. 159.

57  Quoted in Park, 'The City', pp. 18–19.

58  David Sibley, *Geographies of Exclusion: Society and Difference in the West* (London, 1995), p. 116.

59  Ben Reitman's extensive notes and correspondence, including this map, are to be found in his archive in the Special Collections department at the University of Illinois, Chicago Circle Library. The map is found in Supplement II, folder 216.

60  See Bruns, *The Damndest Radical*, for an excellent popular biography of Reitman.

61  Chris Philo, 'Introduction, Acknowledgements and Brief Thoughts on Older Words and Older Worlds', in *New Words, New Worlds: Reconceptualising Social and Cultural Geography*, ed. Chris Philo (Aberystwyth, 1991), pp. 1–13. This is certainly true of Anglo American geography despite an older strand of social geography in France.

62  See John Wreford-Watson, 'The Sociological Aspects of Geography', in *Geography in the Twentieth Century*, ed. Griffith Taylor (London, 1951), pp. 463–9 for an account of early social geography.

63  Ben Reitman, 'The Geography of the Underworld and the Mental Topography of the Educator', Reitman papers, supplement II, folder 3, p. 2, University of Illinois, Chicago Special Collections.

64  *Ibid.*, p. 2.

65  *Ibid.*, p. 6.

66  *Ibid.*, p. 6.

67  See Capetti, *Writing Chicago*, and Tim Cresswell, 'Weeds, Plagues and Bodily Secretions: A Geographical Interpretation of Metaphors of Displacement', *Annals of the Association of American Geographers*, 87, no. 2 (1997), pp. 330–45.

68  Again, this is contrary to the majority of the Chicago School work, which either subsumed processes of exclusion/inclusion under an ecological metaphor or reduced causality to the distribution of land rents.

69  Reitman collection, supplement II, folder 15, University of Illinois, Chicago Special Collections.

70  Letter from Reitman to Taylor, 16 June 1931, Taylor archive, Newberry Library, Chicago.

71  Letter from Reitman to Taylor, 15 August 1931, Taylor archive, Newberry Library, Chicago.

72  Bruns, *The Damndest Radical*, p. 212.

73  *Ibid.*, p. 264.

74  Anderson, *The Hobo*, pp. 172–3.

75  Michel de Certeau has argued that the establishment, the powerful, those with authority, typically act in strategic ways to secure their position in society. A strategy,

he argues, 'assumes a place that can be circumscribed as proper and thus serve as a basis for generating relations with an exterior distinct from it. Political, economic and scientific rationality have been constructed on this model': *The Practice of Everyday Life*, trans. Steven Rendall (Berkeley, CA, 1984), p. xix.

76  Anderson, *The Hobo*, p. 87.
77  *Ibid.*, p. 87.
78  *Ibid.*, p. 89.
79  *Ibid.*, p. 94.
80  Alice Willard Solenberger, *One Thousand Homeless Men: A Study of Original Records* (New York, 1911), p. 209.
81  From Burgess archives, box 126, folder 11.
82  These categories and many others are to be found in Anderson, *The Hobo*, ch. 6.
83  For an account of this process see Pierre Bourdieu, 'The Practice of Reflexive Sociology', in *An Invitation to Reflexive Sociology*, ed. P. Bourdieu and L. Wacquant (Chicago, 1992), pp. 218–60.
84  Anderson, *The Hobo*, pp. xxvi–xxvii.
85  Bourdieu, 'The Practice of Reflexive Sociology', p. 238.
86  Ian Hacking, 'Making Up People', in *Reconstructing Individualism: Autonomy, Individuality, and the Self in Western Thought*, ed. T. Heller, M. Sosna and D. Wellbery (Stanford, CA, 1986), p. 365.

4  GENDERING THE TRAMP

1  See Keith Tester, ed., *The Flâneur* (London, 1994), for an insightful series of essays on the flâneur.
2  See Marshall Berman, *All That is Solid Melts into Air: The Experience of Modernity*, 2nd edn (Harmondsworth, 1988).
3  Feminist discussions of the *flâneur*/*flâneuse* include Janet Wolff, 'The Invisible Flâneuse: Women and the Literature of Modernity', in *Feminine Sentences: Essays on Women and Culture*, ed. J. Wolff (Oxford, 1990), pp. 34–50; Elizabeth Wilson, *The Sphinx in the City* (Berkeley, CA, 1991); Elizabeth Wilson, 'The Invisible *Flâneur*', in *Postmodern Cities and Spaces*, ed. Sophie Watson and Katherine Gibson (Oxford, 1995), pp. 59–79; Susan Buck-Morss, 'The Flâneur, the Sandwichman and the Whore: The politics of Loitering', *New German Critique*, 39 ( 1986), pp. 99–141.
4  Wolff, 'The Invisible Flâneuse', pp. 34–50.
5  See Gill Valentine, 'The Geography of Women's Fear', *Area*, 21, no. 4 ( 1989), pp. 385–90; R. Pain, 'Space, Sexual Violence and Social Control: Integrating Geographical and Feminist Analysis of Women's Fear of Crime', *Progress in Human Geography*, 15, no. 4 (1991), pp. 415–31, for accounts of female fear in public space.
6  See Mona Domosh, 'Those "Gorgeous Incongruities": Polite Politics and Public Space on the Streets of Nineteenth-century New York', *Annals of the Association of American Geographers*, 88, no. 2 ( 1998), pp. 209–26, for an intriguing account of the way in which women used 'polite politics' and subtle tactics in their negotiations of public space in New York.
7  Wilson, *The Sphinx in the City*.
8  *Ibid.*, p. 52.
9  See Judith Walkowitz, *Prostitution and Victorian Society: Women, Class and the State*

(Cambridge, 1980), and Wilson, *The Sphinx in the City*.

10  Alain Corbin, *Women for Hire: Prostitution and Sexuality in France after 1850* (Cambridge, MA, 1990).

11  Christine Stansell quoted in Peter Jackson, *Maps of Meaning* (London, 1989), p. 99.

12  Wilson, 'The Invisible Flâneur', p. 61. A discussion of the prostitute as the real and metaphorical 'public woman' in nineteenth-century Paris is also given in Buck-Morss, 'The Flâneur, the Sandwichman and the Whore'.

13  The term 'Victorian Lady Traveller' is commonly used but tends to overly generalize the various positions of a number of women who actually had quite different experiences of movement. For a critique of this term see Sara Mills, *Discourses of Difference* (London, 1991). I use it here in quote marks to denote a literature about women travelling from Imperial centres into the Empire during the nineteenth century. Karen Morin, 'A "Female Columbus" in 1887 America: Marking New Social Territory', *Gender, Place and Culture*, 2, no. 2 ( 1995), pp. 191–208, divides such accounts into celebratory modernist travel adventure accounts and critical post-structuralist accounts.

14  See Morin, 'Female Columbus'; Alison Blunt, *Travel, Gender and Imperialism: Mary Kingsley and West Africa* (New York, 1994); Birgitta Maria Ingemanson, 'Under Cover: The Paradox of Victorian Women's Travel Costume', in *Women and the Journey: The Female Travel Experience*, ed. Bonnie Frederick and Susan McLeod (Pullman, WA, 1993), pp. 5–24; Jane Robinson, *Wayward Women: A Guide to Women Travellers* (Oxford, 1989); and Mary Russell, *The Blessings of a Good Thick Skirt: Women Travellers and their World* (London, 1986), for a diverse array of accounts of 'lady travellers'.

15  Quoted in Blunt, *Travel, Gender and Imperialism*, p. 77.

16  Ingemanson, 'Under Cover', p. 5.

17  Catherine Barnes Stevenson, *Victorian Women Travel Writers in Africa* (Boston, 1982).

18  Quoted in Ingemanson, 'Under Cover', p. 8.

19  Orlando Lewis, *Vagrancy in the United States* (New York, 1907), p. 14.

20  *Ibid.*, p. 20.

21  See Tim Cresswell, 'Mobility as Resistance: A Geographical Reading of Kerouac's "On the Road"', *Transactions of the Institute of British Geographers*, 18, no. 2 ( 1993), pp. 249–62, and Linda McDowell, 'Off the Road: Alternative Views of Rebellion, Resistance and the "Beats"', *Transactions of the Institute of British Geographers*, 21, no. 2 (1996), pp. 412–19, for a discussion of this theme surrounding the activities of the Beat Generation.

22  See Gillian Rose, *Feminism and Geography: The Limits of Geographical Knowledge* (Cambridge, 1993) for the classic investigation of geography as a masculinist discipline.

23  Quoted in Orlando Lewis, 'The American Tramp', *Atlantic Monthly*, 101 ( June 1908), pp. 744–53 (p. 746).

24  Francis Weyland, 'The Tramp Question' (a paper presented at the National Conference on Charities and Corrections, St Paul, 1877), pp. 111–33 (p. 112).

25  *Ibid.*, p. 112.

26  *Ibid.*

27  Quoted in Michael Katz, *Poverty and Policy in American History* (New York, 1983), p. 159.

28  H. Rood, 'The Tramp Problem: A Remedy', *Forum*, 25 ( 1898), pp. 90–94 (p. 92).

29  See G. Weaver, *Our Home or Influences Emanating from the Hearthstone* (Springfield, MA, 1899), for an example of the contemporary discussion of home and hearth.

30  The literature on female tramps is not vast, reflecting the common perception that

tramps are men. See, however, Stephanie Golden, *The Woman Outside: Myths and Meanings of Homelessness* (Berkeley, CA, 1992), and Lynn Weiner, 'Sisters of the Road: Women Transients and Tramps', in *Walking to Work: Tramps in America, 1790–1935*, ed. Eric H. Monkkonen (Lincoln, NE, 1984), pp. 189–211.

31 Thomas Minehan, *Boy and Girl Tramps of America* (New York, 1934), p. 133.

32 Theodore Caplow, 'Transiency as a Cultural Pattern', *American Sociological Review*, 5, no. 5 (1940), pp. 731–9 (p. 733).

33 James Forbes, 'The Tramp; or, Caste in the Jungle', *Outlook*, 98/19 (August 1911), pp. 869–75 (p. 870).

34 *Sister of the Road* was actually written by Chicago reformer Ben Reitman, despite its claim to being an autobiography. The cover reads *Sister of the Road: The Autobiography of Boxcar Bertha. As told by Ben L. Reitman. Boxcar Bertha* later became the title of a bad Hollywood movie.

35 This material is in the Reitman archives, Circle Library, University of Illinois, Chicago.

36 Ben Reitman, *Sister of the Road: The Autobiography of Boxcar Bertha* (New York, 1937), p. 52.

37 *Ibid.*, p. 38.

38 *Ibid.*, p. 68.

39 Forbes, 'The Tramp; or, Caste in the Jungle', p. 875.

40 'Tramps', *Railroad Gazette* (23 April 1880), p. 127.

41 'Tramps' leader found to be a woman', *The New York Times* (7 August 1901), p. 1.

42 Quoted in Golden, *The Woman Outside*, p. 137.

43 *Ibid.*, p. 138.

44 The reactions to Miss Shelly and other female tramps dressed as men also seems to have created a kind of 'cultural anxiety' often seen in relation to cross-dressing. For a detailed history of such reactions see Marjorie Garber, *Vested Interests: Cross-Dressing and Cultural Anxiety* (London, 1992).

45 Frank Charles Laubach, 'Why There are Vagrants', PhD thesis, Columbia University, 1916. Interestingly Laubach also makes the claim that 'most women do not have the same roving disposition as men. It has been men who have done most of the exploring in history, who have manifested most of the spirit of adventure and love of taking chances, and who have constituted the radical wing of society, while women have been domestic and conservative. It may be that wanderlust is an allurement to which the male sex is most susceptible' (p. 71).

46 C. W. Noble, 'The Border Land of Trampdom', *Popular Science Monthly*, 50 (December 1896), pp. 252–8 (p. 255).

47 *Ibid.*, p. 256.

48 Wilson, *The Sphinx in the City*; Buck-Morss, 'The Flâneur, the Sandwichman and the Whore'.

49 Walter C. Reckless, 'Why Women Become Hoboes', *American Mercury*, 31, no. 122 (1934), pp. 175–80 (p. 176).

50 *Ibid.*, p. 178.

51 *Ibid.*, p. 179.

52 This account is to be found in the Reitman archives at the Circle Library in the University of Illinois, Chicago, Supplement I, box 96, Outcast Narrative no. 61.

53 Reitman, *Sister of the Road*, p. 283.

54 *Ibid.*, p. 66.

55 *Ibid.*, p. 69.

56 As with most accounts of subordinated social groups it is very difficult to establish their own views of themselves through the historical archive. These women were most often poor and illiterate and unlikely to have the time or inclination to tell their own stories in written form. What we have then are a series of female tramp autobiographical accounts which are heavily refracted through a number of lenses. *Sister of the Road* is actually told by Ben Reitman and is probably as much about him as it is about Boxcar Bertha. Other accounts are actually by middle-class women who take to the road as a picturesque adventure. See E. Lynn, *The Adventures of a Woman Hobo* (New York, 1917); B. Starke, *Touch and Go: The Story of a Girl's Escape* (London, 1931).

57 Golden, *The Woman Outside*, p. 136.

58 Cliff Maxwell, 'Lady Vagabonds', *Scribner's* (March 1929), pp. 288–92 (p. 289).

59 *Ibid.*, p. 292.

60 Garber, *Vested Interests*, p. 10.

61 For a good account, see Elizabeth Grosz, 'Bodies and Knowledges: Feminism and the Crisis of Reason', in *Feminist Epistemologies*, ed. Linda Alcoff and Elizabeth Potter (London, 1993), pp. 187–215.

62 Grosz, 'Bodies and Knowledges', p. 199.

63 Iris M. Young, *Throwing Like a Girl and other Essays in Feminist Philosophy and Social Theory* (Bloomington, IN, 1990), gives a good account of female bodily movement.

64 Reitman, *Sister of the Road*, p. 281.

65 *Ibid.*, pp. 282–3.

66 *Ibid.*, p. 283.

67 Young, *Throwing Like a Girl*, p. 123.

68 Sander L. Gilman, *Picturing Health and Illness: Images of Identity and Difference* (Baltimore, 1995), pp. 51–66. Gilman writes: 'The dichotomy is clear: The healthy is the beautiful, is the erotic, is the good, for it leads to the preservation and continuation of the collective. This is the norm against which the deviant is to be measured. The deviant is ill and therefore ugly and evil. (Being ill, the degenerate is excluded because of danger to the collective)' (p. 66). Once again the body of the tramp and the social body are linked.

69 Jennifer Terry and Jacqueline Urla, eds, *Deviant Bodies: Critical Perspectives on Difference in Science and Popular Culture* (Bloomington, IN, 1995), p. 1. This book includes a series of wonderful essays on just this process.

70 *Ibid.*, p. 2.

71 Judith Butler, *Gender Trouble: Feminism and the Subversion of Identity* (London, 1990), p. VIII.

72 *Ibid.*, p. ix.


5 PATHOLOGIZING THE TRAMP

1 Charles B. Davenport, *The Feebly Inhibited: Nomadism, or the Wandering Impulse, With Special Reference to Heredity* (Washington, DC, 1915).

2 *Ibid.*, pp. 28–9 (original italics).

3 *Ibid.*, p. 31 (original italics).

4 Ian Hacking, *The Taming of Chance* (Cambridge, 1990), p. 163.

5 Georges Canguilhem, *The Normal and the Pathological* (Cambridge, MA, 1989) also discusses the work of Broussais.

6 Hacking suggests that Comte was particularly fond of this idea because it helped

explain his own nervous breakdown as just a variation from the normal state rather than anything that could be labelled his fault: *The Taming of Chance*, pp. 167–8.

7 This Positivist use of the term normal is of course the one that has been reified in statistical methodology. Comte's task was to establish the normal and its limits of variation before looking at those cases (pathological) that were beyond the bounds of the normal.

8 Hacking, *The Taming of Chance*, p. 168.

9 *Ibid.*, p. 169.

10 Canguilhem, *The Normal and the Pathological*.

11 *Ibid.*, p. 329.

12 R. Dugdale, 'Hereditary Pauperism as Illustrated by the Juke Family', Conference of Charities, Saratoga, 1877. See M. Haller, *Eugenics: Hereditarian Attitudes in American Thought* (New Brunswick, 1963), for a thorough account of American eugenics.

13 Charles Loring Brace, 'Pauperism in the City of New York', National Conference of Charities and Corrections, 1874. According to Haller, Brace had read *The Origin of Species* thirteen times.

14 Davenport, *The Feebly Inhibited*; Haller, *Eugenics*.

15 Davenport, *The Feebly Inhibited*, p. 7.

16 *Ibid.*, p. 7.

17 Ian Hacking 'Les Alienes Voyageurs: How Fugue Became a Medical Entity', *History of Psychiatry*, 7, (1996), pp. 425–49; Ian Hacking, *Mad Travelers: Reflections on the Reality of Transient Mental Illnesses* (Charlottesville, VA, 1998).

18 Hacking, 'Les Alienes Voyageurs', p. 429.

19 *Ibid.*, p. 426.

20 Davenport, *The Feebly Inhibited*, p. 25.

21 Alexander Speek, 'The Psychology of the Floating Worker', *Annals of the American Academy of Political and Social Sciences*, 69 (1917), pp. 72–8 (p. 78).

22 Harvey M. Beardsley, 'Along the Main Stem with Red', *Chicago News* (29 March 1917), p. 13.

23 Allan Pinkerton, *Strikers, Communists, Tramps and Detectives* (New York, 1878), p. 26.

24 W. L. Bull, 'Trampery: Its Causes, Present Aspects, and Some Suggested Remedies' (a paper presented at the National Conference on Charities and Corrections, St Paul, 1886), pp. 188–206.

25 Frank Charles Laubach, 'Why There are Vagrants', PhD thesis, Columbia University, 1916, p. 42.

26 See David Horn, 'The Norm Which is Not One: Reading the Female Body in Lombroso's Anthropology', in *Deviant Bodies: Critical Perspectives on Difference in Science and Popular Culture*, ed. Jennifer Terry and Jacqueline Urla (Bloomington, IN, 1995), pp. 109–28, for an excellent discussion of Lombroso.

27 Haller, *Eugenics*, p. 42.

28 *Ibid.*, p. 42.

29 *Ibid.*, p. 49.

30 W. H. Brewer, 'What Shall we do with the Tramps?', *New Englander*, 37 ( 1878), pp. 521–32 (p. 522).

31 *Proceedings of the National Conference on Charities and Corrections* (St Paul, 1877).

32 Francis Weyland, 'The Tramp Question' (a paper presented at the National Conference on Charities and Corrections, St Paul, 1877), pp. 111–33 (p. 114).

33 Claude Quetel, *History of Syphilis* (Cambridge, 1990), p. 10.
34 Quoted in Laura Engelstein, 'Morality and the Wooden Spoon: Russian Doctors View Syphilis, Social Class, and Sexual Behaviour, 1890–1905', in *The Making of the Modern Body*, ed. Catherine Gallagher and Thomas Walter Laqueur (Berkeley, CA, 1987), p. 171.
35 Reitman Papers, Supplement II, VD reports #104, 21/8/38.
36 Reitman Papers, Supplement II, VD report #17, 21/8/38.
37 James McCook, 'Some New Phases of the Tramp Problem', *Charities Review*, I, no. 8 (1892), pp. 355–64.
38 *Ibid.*, pp. 355–6.
39 *Ibid.*, pp. 357–8.
40 *Ibid.*, p. 361.
41 Reitman Papers, 'Vote Selling and the Criminal Hobo', Supplement II.
42 Suzanne Poirer, *Chicago's War on Syphilis, 1937–1940: The Times, The Trib, and the Clap Doctor* (Urbana, IL, 1995), is a thorough account of the campaign and includes extensive information on Reitman's involvement in and around the campaign.
43 Allan Brandt, *No Magic Bullet* (Oxford, 1985).
44 Poirier, *Chicago's War on Syphilis*, p. 47.
45 Clearly Reitman's activities here were implicating him in the ever-extending reach of the medical gaze. Nevertheless, there was definitely something subversive about his part. He submitted 300 reports on syphilis in two years, all of which are available in the Reitman archive at the University of Illinois, Chicago.
46 Roger Bruns, *The Damndest Radical: The Life and World of Ben Reitman* (Urbana, IL, 1987), p. 277.
47 Poirier, *Chicago's War on Syphilis*, p. 157.
48 This belief supported the infamous Tuskagee Syphilis Experiment, which involved the deliberate non treatment of 400 poor black men in Alabama based on the premise that black men did not take the disease seriously and could not follow the course of treatment appropriately. President Clinton formally apologized to the families of the men in 1997. See J. Jones, *Bad Blood: The Tuskagee Syphilis Experiment* (New York, 1993).
49 Poirier, *Chicago's War on Syphilis*, pp. 141 2.
50 *Ibid.*, p. 142.
51 Weyland. 'The Tramp Question', p. 120.
52 Susan Sontag, *Aids and its Metaphors* (New York, 1988).


6 LAUGHTER AND THE TRAMP

1 Charles Chaplin, *My Life in Pictures* (New York, 1975), p. 76.
2 Charles Chaplin, *My Autobiography* (London, 1964), p. 150.
3 Robert Payne, *The Great God Pan: A Biography of the Tramp Played by Charles Chaplin* (New York, 1952), p. 121.
4 Chaplin, *My Autobiography*, p. 144.
5 When in the Eight Lancashire Lads, Chaplin did a duet comedy tramp routine as 'Bristol and Chaplin, the Millionaire Tramps'.
6 Nicole Vigouroux-Frey, 'Charlie Chaplin or the "Vaudeville Dispossessed"', in *Charlie Chaplin: His Reflection in Modern Times*, ed. Adolphe Nysenholc (Berlin, 1991), pp. 69–75 (pp. 69–70).

7 Rauol Sobel and David Francis, *Chaplin: Genesis of a Clown* (London, 1977), p. 97.
8 See Vigouroux-Frey, 'Charlie Chaplin', and Sobel and Francis, *Chaplin: Genesis of a Clown*, for accounts of the connections between pantomime, vaudeville, music-hall and slapstick humour.
9 Payne, *The Great God Pan*, pp. 87–8.
10 Vigouroux-Frey, 'Charlie Chaplin', p. 70.
11 Charles Ulrich, *The Tramp and the Actress: A Vaudeville Sketch* (Chicago, 1909).
12 *Ibid.*, p. 10.
13 Jessie Kelly, *The Tramps' Convention: An Entertainment in One Scene* (Boston, 1912).
14 *Ibid.*, p. 3.
15 *Ibid.*
16 *Ibid.*, p. 7.
17 *Ibid.*, pp. 8–9.
18 See John D. Seelye, 'The American Tramp: A Version of the Picaresque', *American Quarterly*, 15, no. 4 (1963), pp. 535–53, for more on this point.
19 See Lawrence Mintz, 'Humor and Ethnic Stereotypes in Vaudeville and Burlesque', *Melus*, 24, no. 4 (1996), pp. 19–28, for a discussion of this point.
20 Mark Winokur, *American Laughter: Immigrants, Ethnicity, and 1930s Film Comedy* (New York, 1996). See also James Dormon, 'American Popular Culture and the New Immigration Ethics', *Amerikastudien/America Studies*, 36, no. 2 (1991), pp. 179–93.
21 Sobel and Francis, *Chaplin: Genesis of a Clown*, pp. 108–20.
22 See M. Thomas Inge, 'Charlie Chaplin and the Comic Strips', in *Charlie Chaplin: His Reflection in Modern Times*, ed. Adolphe Nysenholc (Berlin, 1991), pp. 161–70.
23 Frederick Opper, *Happy Hooligan: A Complete Compilation, 1904–1905* (Westport, CT, 1977), pp. 10–11.
24 See John J. McCook, 'A Tramp Census and its Revelations', *Forum*, 15 ( 1893), pp. 753–61, for instance.
25 See Maurice Horn, ed., *The World Encyclopedia of Cartoons* (New York, 1981), vol. IV for notes on cartoon figures, including Nervy Nat.
26 Henri Bergson, *Laughter: An Essay on the Meaning of the Comic* (London, 1911).
27 Dormon, 'American Popular Culture and the New Immigration Ethics', pp. 181–2.
28 Joseph Bostin, *Humor and Social Change in 20th Century America* (Boston, 1979), p. 28.
29 Robert Sklar, *Movie-Made America: A Cultural History of American Movies* (London, 1978), p. 105.
30 Much of the information here is from Sklar, *Movie-Made America*, ch. 7.
31 *Ibid.*, p. 107.
32 Sobel and Francis, *Chaplin: Genesis of a Clown*, pp. 105–8.
33 Sklar, *Movie-Made America*, p. 109.
34 Sobel and Francis, *Chaplin: Genesis of a Clown*, p. 140.
35 *Ibid.*, p. 146.
36 Sklar, *Movie-Made America*, p. 113.
37 Sobel and Francis, *Chaplin: Genesis of a Clown*, p. 218.
38 See Dan Kamin, 'A Cure for Chaplinitis and the Geometry of Comedy: Preludes to a Movement Analysis of Charlie Chaplin', *Flashback*, 1, no. 1 (1990), pp. 12–19, for reflections on this theme.
39 William Paul, 'The Gold Rush', *Film Comment* (Sept–Oct 1972), p. 17.
40 Sobel and Francis, *Chaplin: Genesis of a Clown*, p. 134.

41 Bergson, *Laughter*, p. 29.

42 *Ibid.*, p. 38.

43 Kamin, 'A Cure for Chaplinitis', p. 18.

44 See Kamin's essay for an extended analysis of this process.

45 Umberto Eco, 'The Comic and the Rule', in *Travels in Hyperreality* (New York, 1980), pp. 269–78 (p. 273).

46 *Ibid.*, p. 273.

47 Chaplin, *My Autobiography*, p. 415.

48 Lenin in James Scott, *Seeing Like a State: How Certain Schemes to Improve the Human Condition have Failed* (New Haven, CT, 1998), p. 101.

49 See Sam Girgus, 'The Moral and Psychological Dilemma of Modern Times: Love, Play, and Civilization in Chaplin's Last Silent Classic', *Thalia: Studies in Literary Humour*, 16, no. 1 ( 1996), pp. 3–15; Winokur, '*Modern Times* and the Comedy of Transformation', for some intriguing insights into *Modern Times*.

50 Winokur, '*Modern Times* and the Comedy of Transformation', pp. 222–3.

51 Girgus, 'The Moral and Psychological Dilemma of *Modern Times*'.

52 Sobel and Francis, *Chaplin: Genesis of a Clown*, p. 159–60.

53 John Mackay, 'Walter Benjamin and Rudolf Arnheim on Charlie Chaplin', *The Yale Journal of Criticism: Interpretation in the Humanities*, 9, no. 2 ( 1996), pp. 309–14 (p. 312).

54 *Ibid.*, p. 313.

55 For an excellent thesis on this process of making the socially marginal symbolically central, see Peter Stallybrass and Allon White, *The Politics and Poetics of Transgression* (Ithaca, NY, 1986).

56 See Michel de Certeau, *The Practice of Everyday Life*, trans. Steven Kendall (Berkeley, CA, 1984) for a discussion of the way 'the weak' make use of the spaces of 'the strong'.

57 Kristin Ross, *The Emergence of Social Space: Rimbaud and the Paris Commune* (Minneapolis, 1988), p. 36. See also Dick Hebdige, *Subculture: The Meaning of Style* (London, 1988), for a discussion of bricolage in youth subculture.

58 See Alistair Bonnett, 'Art, Ideology and Everyday Space: Subversive Tendencies from Dada to Postmodernism', *Environment and Planning D: Society and Space*, 10 (1990), pp. 69–86.

59 De Certeau, *The Practice of Everyday Life*, p. 37.

60 Jonathan Raban, *Soft City* (London, 1974).

61 *Ibid.*, pp. 69–70.

62 *Ibid.*, p. 160.

63 Kamin, 'A Cure for Chaplinitis', p. 19.

64 Payne, *The Great God Pan*, p. viii, quoting Capp.

65 Eco, 'The Comic and the Rule', pp. 270–71.

66 Sklar, *Movie-Made America*, p. 105.

67 Morris Dickstein, 'Urban Comedy and Modernity: From Chaplin to Woody Allen', *Partisan Review*, 52, no. 3 (1985), pp. 271–81 (p. 278).

68 Mackay, 'Walter Benjamin and Rudolf Arnheim', p. 311.

69 M. Bakhtin, *Rabelais and his World* (Bloomington, IN, 1984).

70 *Ibid.*, p. 73. It should be noted here that Bakhtin's thesis was a highy coded critique of Stalinism in the Soviet Union, with its own form of icy, petrified seriousness.

71 *Ibid.*, p. 82.

72 *Ibid.*

73  See Ira Jaffe, 'Fighting Words: *City Lights* (1931), *Modern Times* (1936) and *The Great Dictator* (1940)', in *Hollywood as Historian: American Film in Cultural Context*, ed. Peter Rollins (Lexington, 1983), pp. 49–67.

74  Allon White, *Carnival, Hysteria and Writing* (Oxford, 1993), p. 134.

75  Barry Sanders, *Sudden Glory: Laughter as Subversive History* (Boston, 1995), p. 8.

76  *Ibid.*, p. 26.

7  PICTURING THE TRAMP

1  Alan Trachtenberg, 'From Image to Story: Reading the File', in *Documenting America, 1935–1943*, ed. Carl Fleischhauer and Beverly Brannan (Berkeley, CA, 1988), pp. 43–75 (p. 63).

2  See, for instance, Henry Mayhew, *Mayhew's London (Selections from London Labour and the London Poor* (London, 1851); A. Mearns, *The Bitter Cry of Outcast London: An Inquiry into the Conditions of the Abject Poor* (London, 1883); and E. Chadwick, *Report . . . on an Inquiry into the Sanitary Conditions of the Labouring Population of Great Britain* (London, 1842).

3  Peter Stallybrass and Allon White, *The Politics and Poetics of Transgression* (Ithaca, NY, 1986), p. 126. Stallybrass and White have brilliantly shown how such publications revealed a simultaneous loathing and fascination on the part of their middle-class readers.

4  Mayhew, *Mayhew's London*, p. 42.

5  This is continued in the present day with references to the 'jungle' when talking about the modern inner city.

6  See Ian Jeffrey, *Photography: A Concise History* (London, 1981), pp. 81–5; Peter Jackson, 'Constructions of Culture, Representations of Race: Edward Curtis's "Way of Seeing"', in *Inventing Places: Studies in Cultural Geography*, ed. Kay Anderson and Fay Gale (Melbourne, 1992), pp. 89–106.

7  Jacob Riis, *How the Other Half Lives: Studies Among the Tenements of New York* was first published in New York in 1890.

8  See David Ward, *Poverty, Ethnicity and the American City, 1840–1925* (Cambridge, 1989), pp. 71–5 for a discussion of Riis's rôle in defining the slum in New York.

9  Maren Stange makes this point well through an examination of Riis and others in *Symbols of Ideal Life: Social Documentary Photography in America, 1890–1950* (New York, 1989).

10  *Ibid.*, pp. xiv–xv.

11  Miles Orvell, *The Real Thing: Imitation and Authenticity in American Culture, 1880–1940* (Chapel Hill, NC, 1989), pp. 229–30.

12  See Hillel Schwartz, *The Culture of the Copy: Striking Likenesses, Unreasonable Facsimiles* (New York, 1996), pp. 282–4, for an account of this.

13  Cited in Schwartz, *The Culture of the Copy*, p. 288.

14  Schwartz, *The Culture of the Copy*, p. 288.

15  Riis, *How the Other Half Lives*, pp. 57–8.

16  Orvell, *The Real Thing*, p. 97.

17  See Stange, *Symbols of Ideal Life*.

18  See Ward, *Poverty, Ethnicity and the American City*, for an account of the tenement reform movement and Riis's involvement in it.

19  Jacob Riis and Roy Lubove, *The Making of an American* (New York, 1966), p. 267.
20  John Rogers Puckett, *Five Photo-Textual Documentaries from the Great Depression: Studies in Photography, no. 6* (Ann Arbor, MI, 1984), p. 4.
21  See Stange, *Symbols of Ideal Life*, for an elaboration of this argument.
22  *Ibid.*, p. 18.
23  Riis cited in Stange, *Symbols of Ideal Life*, p. 16.
24  For a development of this argument see Alan Trachtenberg, *Reading American Photographs: Images as History, Matthew Brady to Walker Evans* (New York, 1989).
25  The only account of McCook's specific use of photography I found is David Courtwright and Miller Shelby, 'Progessivism and Drink: The Social and Photographic Investigations of John James McCook', *Journal of Drug Issues*, 15, no. 1 (1985), pp. 93–109.
26  These biographical details are taken from the excellent introduction to the McCook archive, *The Social Reform Papers of John James McCook*, available on microfilm from the Antiquarian and Landmarks Society, Inc., of Connecticut (1977). This quotation is from pp. 3–5. The final description here refers to McCook's part in raising a $500,000 endowment fund for the College. All subsequent references to this archive will be to the McCook Papers. One account of his work is given in Roger Bruns, *Knights of the Road: A Hobo History* (New York, 1980), ch. 3.
27  See, for instance, John J. McCook, 'Some New Phases of the Tramp Problem', *Charities Review*, 1, no. 8 ( 1892), pp. 355–64; John J. McCook, 'A Tramp Census and its Revelations', *Forum*, 15 (1893), pp. 753–61.
28  Many were taken by his brother Philip. Others were taken at the studio of Charles T. Stuart, a Hartford photographer.
29  For a brilliant discussion of this theme see Stallybrass and White, *The Politics and Poetics of Transgression*.
30  Photography was used in a similar way in British representations of the peoples who inhabited the Empire. See James Ryan, *Picturing Empire: Photography and the Visualization of the British Empire* (London, 1997) for a good discussion of this enterprise.
31  John J. McCook, 'Leaves from the Diary of a Tramp, IV', *The Independent*, LIV, no. 2770 (1902), pp. 23–8 (p. 26).
32  *Ibid.*, p. 26.
33  McCook Papers, *Guide*, p. 31.
34  John J. McCook, 'Leaves from the Diary of a Tramp, III', *The Independent*, LIII, no. 2768 (1901), pp. 3009–13 (p. 3010).
35  *Ibid.*, p. 3010.
36  John J. McCook, 'Leaves from the Diary of a Tramp, V', *The Independent*, LIV, no. 2772 (1902), pp. 154–60 (p. 159).
37  Roving Bill Aspinwall, cited in John J. McCook, 'Leaves from the Diary of a Tramp, VI', *The Independent*, LIV, no. 2775 (1902), pp. 332–7 (p. 337).
38  McCook, 'Leaves from the Diary of a Tramp, III', pp. 3010–11.
39  McCook Papers, *Guide*, p. 31.
40  McCook, cited in Bruns, *Knights of the Road*, p. 74.
41  Paul F. Brissenden, *The I.W.W.: A Study in American Syndicalism* (New York, 1919), p. 448.
42  James Scott, *Seeing Like a State: How Certain Schemes to Improve the Human Condition Have Failed* (New Haven, CT, 1998).
43  See Trachtenberg, 'From Image to Story'; Lawrence Levine, 'The Historian and the

Icon', in *Documenting America, 1935–1943*, ed. Carl Fleischhauer and Beverly Brannan (Berkeley, CA, 1988), pp. 15–42; and Stange, *Symbols of Ideal Life*, for accounts of Tugwell, Stryker and the FSA.

44 Levine, 'The Historian and the Icon'.

45 F. Jack Hurley, *Portrait of a Decade: Roy Stryker and the Development of Documentary Photography in the Thirties* (Baton Rouge, LA, 1972).

46 This was the source of much friction between Dorothea Lange and Stryker. She wanted to control her own negatives and was eventually dismissed as a result of her insistence.

47 Roy Stryker, 'Documentary Photography', in *The Complete Photographer*, ed. William Morgon (Chicago, 1942), pp. 1364–6 (p. 1364).

48 The Roy Stryker archives are available in microfilm form at the New York Public Library. This extract from Reel 6, Series II, part B, is from 'A Project for the Publication of a Pictorial History of American Agriculture', a paper written with Harry Carman in 1936.

49 Stryker, cited in Orvell, *The Real Thing*, p. 229.

50 Roy Stryker archives, Reel 6, Section B, 'Documentary Photography', p. 1 (undated).

51 *Ibid.*, p. 2 (undated).

52 Trachtenberg, 'From Image to Story', p. 61.

53 Stryker archives, Reel 6, Part B, Section 3a.

54 Stryker archives, Reel 6, Part C, Section 3a.

55 Trachtenberg, 'From Image to Story', p. 70.

56 Sandra Phillips, 'Dorothea Lange: An American Photographer', in *Dorothea Lange: American Photographs*, ed. T. Heyman, S. Phillips and J. Szarkowski (San Francisco, 1994), pp. 10–41 (p. 10).

57 See F. Ward, 'Foreign and Familiar Bodies', in *Dirt and Domesticity: Constructions of the Feminine*, ed. J. Fuenmayor, K. Haug and F. Ward (New York, 1992), pp. 9–37, for an engaging discussion of the rôle of dirt and gender in documentary photography, including Lange's *Migrant Mother*.

58 Mary Douglas, *Purity and Danger: An Analysis of Concepts of Pollution and Taboo* (London, 1966), p. 35.

59 See Tim Cresswell, *In Place/Out of Place: Geography, Ideology and Transgression* (Minneapolis, 1996), and Tim Cresswell, 'Weeds, Plagues and Bodily Secretions: A Geographical Interpretation of Metaphors of Displacement', *Annals of the Association of American Geographers*, 87, no. 2 (1997), pp. 330–45, for discussions of this theme.

60 Ward, 'Foreign and Familiar Bodies', p. 10.

61 Cited in Phillips, 'Dorothea Lange: An American Photographer', p. 24.

62 Lange produced the book *An American Exodus: A Record of Human Erosion in the Thirties* (New York, 1939) with Taylor. The metaphorical connections between migrants and soil are made clear by the authors: 'By a curiously symbolic coincidence, Oklahoma is the most wind-blown state in the country, its newly-broken red plains are among the worst eroded, and its farm people are among the least rooted to the soil' (p. 67).

63 William Stott, *Documentary Expression and Thirties America* (New York, 1973), pp. 58–9.

64 Levine, 'The Historian and the Icon', pp. 22–3.

65 In 1978 the journal *American Photographer* located the actual person photographed by Lange in *Migrant Mother*. That is how we know her name to be Florence Thompson. In 1978 Thompson was 75 years old and living in a trailer park in Modesto, California.

When asked about the photo she asked what good it had done her. She was living off social security and medical support.

66  Ansel Adams, cited in Levine, 'The Historian and the Icon', p. 25.
67  See Charles Shindo, *Dust Bowl Migrants in the American Imagination* (Lawrence, KS, 1997).
68  Trachtenberg, 'From Image to Story', p. 53.
69  *Ibid.*, p. 54.
70  *Ibid.*, p. 55, citing Vanderbilt.
71  Martha Rosler, 'In, Around and Afterthoughts (on Documentary Photography)', in *3 Works*, ed. M. Rosler (Halifax, Nova Scotia, 1981), pp. 59–88 (p. 71).

AFTERWORD: THE SUBJECT STRIKES BACK

1  Jack London, *The Road* (Santa Barbara, 1970); Jack Kerouac, *On the Road* (London, 1957); *Lonesome Traveller* (New York, 1960).
2  Examples include Josiah Flynt, *Tramping with Tramps* (Montclaire NJ, 1972 [1899]); C. Fox, *Tales of an American Hobo* (Iowa City, 1989); Harry Kemp, *Tramping on Life* (New York, 1922); A–No 1 Livingstone, *The Curse of Tramp Life* (Cambridge Springs, PA, 1912).
3  See George Milburn, *The Hobo's Hornbook* (New York, 1930).
4  Practical knowledge refers to the embodied *savoir-faire*, which is often not conscious or deliberate, which we all employ in our daily lives. The idea is most finely developed in the work of Pierre Bourdieu; see Bourdieu's *The Logic of Practice* (Stanford, CA, 1990).
5  The notion of tactics whereby the weak are able to use and manipulate the spaces of the strong through mobile cunning is developed by Michel de Certeau in *The Practice of Everyday Life* (Berkeley, CA, 1984).
6  Jacob Riis, *How The Other Half Lives* (New York, 1971), pp. 66–7.
7  This is what Ian Hacking calls the 'looping effect' of social types; see Ian Hacking, *The Social Construction of What?* (Cambridge, MA, 1999).

# SELECT BIBLIOGRAPHY

Adler, Jeffrey S., 'A Historical Analysis of the Law of Vagrancy', *Criminology*, 27/2 (1989), pp. 209–29

Agnew, John, *The United States in the World Economy* (Cambridge, 1987)

Allsop, Kenneth, *Hard Travellin': The Story of the Migrant Worker* (London, 1993)

Anderson, Nels, *The Hobo* (Chicago, 1925)

Archard, Peter, 'Vagrancy – A Literature Review', in *Vagrancy: Some New Perspectives*, ed. Tim Cook (London, 1979), pp. 11–28

Bakhtin, Mikhail, *Rabelais and his World* (Bloomington, IN, 1984)

Bauman, Zygmunt, *Legislators and Interpreters* (Oxford, 1987)

—, *Life in Fragments: Essays in Postmodern Morality* (Oxford, 1995)

Beier, A. L., *Masterless Men: The Vagrancy Problem in England, 1560–1640* (London, 1985)

Berger, Peter and Thomas Luckmann, *The Social Construction of Reality: A Treatise in the Sociology of Knowledge* (New York, 1966)

Bergson, Henri, *Laughter: An Essay on the Meaning of the Comic* (London, 1911)

Berman, Marshall, *All That is Solid Melts into Air: The Experience of Modernity* (Harmondsworth, 1988)

Blomley, Nick, *Law, Space and the Geographies of Power* (New York, 1994)

Blunt, Alison, *Travel, Gender and Imperialism: Mary Kingsley and West Africa* (New York, 1994)

Bonnett, Alistair, 'Art, Ideology and Everyday Space: Subversive Tendencies from Dada to Postmodernism', *Environment and Planning D: Society and Space*, 10 (1990), pp. 69–86

Boorstin, Daniel, *The Americans: The National Experience* (London, 1966)

Bostin, Joseph, *Humor and Social Change in 20th Century America* (Boston, 1979)

Bourdieu, Pierre, *The Logic of Practice* (Stanford, CA, 1990)

—, 'The Practice of Reflexive Sociology', in *An Invitation to Reflexive Sociology*, ed. Pierre Bourdieu and L. Wacquant (Chicago, 1992), pp. 218–60

Brewer, W. H., 'What Shall we do with the Tramps?', *New Englander*, 37 (1878), pp. 521–32

Brissenden, Paul F., *The I.W.W.: A Study in American Syndicalism* (New York, 1919)

Bruns, Roger, *The Damndest Radical: The Life and World of Ben Reitman, Chicago's Celebrated Social Reformer, Hobo King, and Whorehouse Physician* (Urbana, IL, 1987)

—, *Knights of the Road: A Hobo History* (New York, 1980)

Buck-Morss, Susan, 'The Flâneur, the Sandwichman and the Whore: The Politics of Loitering', *New German Critique*, 39 (1986), pp. 99–141

Burgess, Ernest, 'The Growth of the City: An Introduction to a Research Project', in *The City: Suggestions for Investigation of Human Behavior in the Urban Environment*, ed. Robert

Park and Ernest Burgess (Chicago, 1925), pp. 47–62

Butler, Judith, *Bodies that Matter* (London, 1998)

—, *Gender Trouble: Feminism and the Subversion of Identity* (London, 1990)

Canguilhem, Georges, *The Normal and the Pathological* (Cambridge, MA, 1989)

Caplow, Theodore, 'Transiency as a Cultural Pattern', *American Sociological Review*, 5/5 (1940), pp. 731–9

Cappetti, Carla, *Writing Chicago: Modernism, Ethnography and the Novel* (New York, 1993)

Casey, Edward, 'The Ghost of Embodiment: On Bodily Habitudes and Schemata', in *Body and Flesh: A Philosophical Reader*, ed. Donn Welton (Oxford, 1998), pp. 207–26

Chaplin, Charles, *My Autobiography* (London, 1964)

—, *My Life in Pictures* (New York, 1975)

Clark, Gordon, *Judges and the Cities: Interpreting Local Autonomy* (Chicago, 1985)

Clifford, J., *Routes: Travel and Translation in the Later Twentieth Century* (Cambridge, MA, 1997)

Corbin, Alain, *Women for Hire: Prostitution and Sexuality in France after 1850* (Cambridge, MA, 1990)

Courtwright, David and Shelby Miller, 'Progressivism and Drink: The Social and Photographic Investigations of John James McCook', *Journal of Drug Issues*, 15/1 (1985), pp. 93–109

Cresswell, Tim, *In Place/Out of Place: Geography, Ideology and Transgression* (Minneapolis, 1996)

—, 'Mobility as Resistance: A Geographical Reading of Kerouac's "On the Road"', *Transactions of the Institute of British Geographers*, 18/2 (1993), pp. 249–62

—, 'Weeds, Plagues and Bodily Secretions: A Geographical Interpretation of Metaphors of Displacement', *Annals of the Association of American Geographers*, 87/2 (1997), pp. 330–45

Cronon, William, *Nature's Metropolis : Chicago and the Great West* (New York, 1991)

D'Andrade, C., 'Cultural Meaning Systems', in *Cultural Theory: Essays on Mind, Self and Emotion*, ed. R. Shweder and R. Levine (Cambridge, 1987)

Daniels, Stephen, *Fields of Vision: Landscape Imagery and National Identity in England and the United States* (Cambridge, 1993)

Davenport, Charles B., *The Feebly Inhibited: Nomadism, or the Wandering Impulse, With Special Reference to Heredity* (Washington, DC, 1915)

Davis, Kathy, ed., *Embodied Practices: Feminist Perspectives on the Body* (London, 1997)

Davis, Mike, *City of Quartz: Excavating the Future in Los Angeles* (New York, 1992)

De Certeau, Michel, *The Practice of Everyday Life* (Berkeley, CA, 1984)

Delaney, David, 'Geographies of Judgment: The Doctrine of Changed Conditions and the Geopolitics of Race', *Annals of the Association of American Geographers*, 83/1 (1993), pp. 48–65

—, *Race, Place and the Law* (Austin, TX, 1998)

Domosh, Mona, 'Those "Gorgeous Incongruities": Polite Politics and Public Space on the Streets of Nineteenth-Century New York City', *Annals of the Association of American Geographers*, 88/2 (1998), pp. 209–26

Dormon, James, 'American Popular Culture and the New Immigration Ethics', *Amerikastudien/ American Studies*, 36/2 (1991), pp. 179–93

Douglas, George H., *All Aboard! The Railroad in American Life* (New York, 1992)

Douglas, Mary, *Purity and Danger: An Analysis of Concepts of Pollution and Taboo* (London, 1966)

Duncan, Nancy, ed., *Bodyspace: Destabilizing Geographies of Gender and Sexuality* (London and New York, 1996)

Eco, Umberto, 'The Comic and the Rule', in *Travels in Hyperreality* (New York, 1980), pp. 269–78

Engelstein, Laura, 'Morality and the Wooden Spoon: Russian Doctors' View Syphilis, Social Class, and Sexual Behaviour, 1890–1905', in *The Making of the Modern Body*, ed. Catherine Gallagher and Thomas Walter Laqueur (Berkeley, CA, 1987)

Ferguson-Clement, Priscilla, 'The Transformation of the Wandering Poor in Nineteenth Century Philadephia', in *Walking to Work: Tramps in America 1790–1935*, ed. Eric Monkkonen (Lincoln, 1984), pp. 56–84

Flynt, Josiah, *Tramping With Tramps* (Montclaire, NJ, 1972 [1899])

—, 'The Tramp and the Railroad', *Century Magazine*, 58 (1899), pp. 258–66

Forbes, James, 'The Tramp; or, Caste in the Jungle', *Outlook*, 98, no. 19 (1911), pp. 869–75

Foucault, Michel, *Power/Knowledge* (New York, 1980)

—, *Discipline and Punish: The Birth of the Prison* (New York, 1979)

Garber, Marjorie, *Vested Interests: Cross-Dressing and Cultural Anxiety* (London, 1992)

Gilman, Sander L., *Picturing Health and Illness: Images of Identity and Difference* (London, 1995)

Golden, Stephanie, *The Woman Outside: Myths and Meanings of Homelessness* (Berkeley, CA, 1992)

Grossberg, Lawrence, 'Cultural Studies and/in New Worlds', *Critical Studies in Mass Communication*, 10 (1993), pp. 1–22

Grosz, Elizabeth, 'Bodies and Knowledges: Feminism and the Crisis of Reason', in *Feminist Epistemologies*, ed. Linda Alcoff and Elizabeth Potter (London, 1993), pp. 187–215

—, *Volatile Bodies: Toward a Corporeal Feminism* (St Leonards, NSW, 1990)

Gupta, Akhil and James Ferguson, 'Beyond Culture: Space, Identity and the Politics of Difference', *Cultural Anthropology*, 7/1 (1992), pp. 6–22

Hacking, Ian, 'Les Alienes Voyageurs: How Fugue Became a Medical Entity', *History of Psychiatry*, 7 (1996), pp. 425–49

—, *Mad Travelers: Reflections on the Reality of Transient Mental Illnesses* (Charlottesville, VA, 1998)

—, 'Making Up People', in *Reconstructing Individualism: Autonomy, Individuality, and the Self in Western Thought*, ed. T. Heller, M. Sosna, and D. Wellbery (Stanford, CA, 1986)

—, *Rewriting the Soul: Multiple Personality and the Sciences of Memory* (Princeton, NJ, 1995)

—, *The Social Construction of What?* (Cambridge, MA, 1999)

Haller, M., *Eugenics: Hereditarian Attitudes in American Thought* (New Brunswick, 1963)

Hannerz, Ulf, *Exploring the City: Inquiries Toward an Urban Anthropology* (New York, 1980)

Harring, Sidney, 'Class Conflict and the Suppression of Tramps in Buffalo, 1892–1894', *Law and Society Review*, 11 (Summer 1977), pp. 873–911

Harvey, David, *The Condition of Postmodernity* (Oxford, 1989)

—, 'From Space to Place and Back Again: Reflections on the Condition of Postmodernity', in *Mapping the Futures: Local Cultures, Global Change*, ed. Jon Bird *et al.* (London, 1993), pp. 3–29

Hebdige, Dick, *Subculture: The Meaning of Style* (London, 1988)

Hills, Patricia, 'Picturing Progress in the Era of Westward Expansion', in *The West as America: Reinterpreting Images of the Frontier, 1820–1920*, ed. William H. Truettner (Washington, DC, 1991), pp. 97–148

Hoffman, Victor, 'The American Tramp, 1870–1900', MA thesis, University of Chicago, 1953

Holbrook, Stewart, *The Story of the American Railroads* (New York, 1947)

Hubbard, Elbert, 'The Rights of Tramps', *Arena*, 9 (April 1894), pp. 593–600

Hurley, F. Jack, *Portrait of a Decade; Roy Stryker and the Development of Documentary Photography in the Thirties* (Baton Rouge, LA, 1972)

Inge, M. Thomas, 'Charlie Chaplin and the Comic Strips', in *Charlie Chaplin: His Reflection in Modern Times*, ed. Adolphe Nysenholc (Berlin, 1991), pp. 161–70

Ingemanson, Birgitta Maria, 'Under Cover: The Paradox of Victorian Women's Travel Costume', in *Women and the Journey: The Female Travel Experience*, ed. Bonnie Frederick and Susan McLeod (Pullman, WA, 1993), pp. 5–24

Jackson, Peter, 'Constructions of Culture, Representations of Race: Edward Curtis's "Way of Seeing"', in *Inventing Places: Studies in Cultural Geography*, ed. Kay Anderson and Fay Gale (Melbourne, 1992), pp. 89–106

—, *Maps of Meaning* (London, 1989)

— and Susan Smith, *Exploring Social Geography* (London, 1984)

Jaffe, Ira, 'Fighting Words: City Lights (1931), Modern Times (1936) and The Great Dictator (1940)', in *Hollywood as Historian: American Film in Cultural Context*, ed. Peter Rollins (Lexington, 1983), pp. 49–67

Jeffrey, Ian, *Photography: A Concise History* (London, 1981)

Katz, Michael, *Poverty and Policy in American History* (New York, 1983)

Kelly, Edmond, *The Elimination of the Tramp, Questions of the Day* (New York, 1908)

Kemp, Harry, *Tramping on Life* (New York, 1922)

Kolchin, Peter, *First Freedom: the Responses of Alabama's Blacks to Emancipation and Reconstruction* (Westport, CT, 1972)

Kouwenhoven, John, *The Beer-Can by the Highway: Essays on What's American About America* (Baltimore, 1961)

Kusmer, Kenneth Leslie, 'The Underclass: Tramps and Vagrants in American Society, 1865–1930', PhD thesis, University of Chicago, 1980

Lange, Dorothea and Paul Taylor, *An American Exodus: A Record of Human Erosion in the Thirties* (New York, 1939)

Laubach, Frank Charles, 'Why There are Vagrants', PhD thesis, Columbia University, 1916

Lavie, Smadar and Ted Swedenburg, 'Between and Among the Boundaries of Culture: Bridging Text and Lived Experience in the Third Timespace', *Cultural Studies*, 10, no. 1 (1996), pp. 154–79

Leigh, Leonard, 'Vagrancy and the Criminal Law', in *Vagrancy: Some New Perspectives*, ed. Tim Cook (London, 1979), pp. 95–117

Levine, Lawrence, 'The Histrorian and the Icon', in *Documenting America 1935–1943*, ed. Carl Fleischhauer and Beverly Brannan (Berkeley, CA, 1988), pp. 15–42

Lewis, Orlando, 'The American Tramp', *Atlantic Monthly*, 101 (June 1908), pp. 744–53

—, *Vagrancy in the United States* (New York, 1907)

Limerick, Patricia Nelson, *The Legacy of Conquest: The Unbroken Past of the American West* (New York, 1987)

Linder, Rolf, *The Reportage of Urban Culture: Robert Park and the Chicago School*, trans. Adrian Morris (Cambridge, 1996)

London, Jack, *The Road* (Santa Barbara, CA, 1970)

Lynn, E., *The Adventures of a Woman Hobo* (New York, 1917)

Mackay, John, 'Walter Benjamin and Rudolf Arnheim on Charlie Chaplin', *The Yale Journal of Criticism: Interpretation in the Humanities*, 9/2 (1996), pp. 309–14

Malkki, Liisa, 'National Geographic: The Rooting of Peoples and the Territorialization of National Identity Among Scholars and Refugees', *Cultural Anthropology*, 7/1 (1992), pp. 24–44

Massey, Doreen, 'Power-Geometry and Progressive Sense of Place', in *Mapping the Futures: Local Cultures, Global Change*, ed. Jon Bird *et al.* (London, 1993)

Maxwell, Cliff, 'Lady Vagabonds', *Scribner's* (March 1929), pp. 288–92

Mayhew, Henry, *Mayhew's London (selections from London Labour and the London Poor)* (London, 1851)

McCook, John J., 'Some New Phases of the Tramp Problem', *Charities Review*, 1/8 (1892), pp. 355–64

—, 'A Tramp Census and its Revelations', *Forum*, 15 (1893), pp. 753–61

McDowell, Linda, 'Bodywork: Heterosexual Gender Performances in City Workplaces', in *Mapping Desire: Geographies of Sexualities*, ed. D. Bell and G. Valentine (London, 1995), pp. 75–95

—, 'Off the Road: Alternative Views of Rebellion, Resistance, and the 'Beats'', *Transactions of the Institute of British Geographers*, 21, no. 2 (1996), pp. 412–19

Mearns, A, *The Bitter Cry of Outcast London: An Inquiry into the Conditions of the Abject Poor* (London, 1883)

Michigan State Library, *Laws of the Various States Relating to Vagrancy* (Lansing, MI, 1916)

Milburn, George, *The Hobo's Hornbook: A Repertory for a Gutter Jongleur* (New York, 1930)

Mills, Sara, *Discourses of Difference* (London, 1991)

Minehan, Thomas, *Boy and Girl Tramps of America* (New York, 1934)

Mintz, Lawrence, 'Humor and Ethnic Stereotypes in Vaudeville and Burlesque', *Melus*, 21, no. 4 (1996), pp. 19–28

Mitchell, Don, 'The Annihilation of Space by Law: The Roots and Implications of Anti–Homeless Laws in the United States', *Antipode*, 29, no. 3 (1997), pp. 303–35

—, *The Lie of the Land: Migrant Workers and the California Landscape* (Minneapolis, 1996)

Monkkonen, Eric H., ed., *Walking to Work: Tramps in America 1790–1935* (Lincoln, NE, 1984)

Morin, Karen, 'A 'Female Columbus' in 1887 America: Marking New Social Territory', *Gender, Place and Culture*, 2, no. 2 (1995), pp. 191–208

Nast, Heidi J. and Steve Pile, eds., *Places Through the Body* (London, 1998)

Opper, Frederick, *Happy Hooligan: A Complete Compilation: 1904–1905* (Westport, CT, 1977)

Orvell, Miles, *The Real Thing: Imitation and Authenticity in American Culture, 1880–1940* (Chapel Hill, NC, 1989)

Park, Robert, 'The Mind of the Hobo: Reflections upon the Relation Between Mentality and Locomotion', in *The City: Suggestions for Investigation of Human Behavior in the Urban Environment*, ed. Robert Park and Ernest Burgess (Chicago, 1925), pp. 156–60

— and Ernest Burgess, *The City: Suggestions for Investigation of Human Behavior in the Urban Environment* (Chicago, 1925)

Payne, Robert, *The Great God Pan: A Biography of the Tramp Played by Charles Chaplin* (New York, 1952)

Phillips, Sandra, 'Dorothea Lange: An American Photographer', in *Dorothea Lange: American Photographs*, ed. T. Heyman, S. Phillips, and J. Szarkowski (San Francisco, 1994), pp. 10–41

Philo, Chris, 'Introduction, Acknowledgements and Brief Thoughts on Older Words and Older Worlds', in *New Words, New Worlds: Reconceptualising Social and Cultural Geography*, ed. Chris Philo (Aberystwyth, 1991), pp. 1–13

Pierson, G. W., 'The M–Factor in American History', *American Quarterly*, 14 (1962), pp. 275–89

Pile, Steve, *The Body and the City : Psychoanalysis, Space, and Subjectivity* (London and New York, 1996)

Pinkerton, Allan, *Strikers, Communists, Tramps and Detectives* (New York, 1878)

Puckett, John Rogers, *Five Photo-Textual Documentaries From the Great Depression* (Ann Arbor, MI, 1984)

Raban, John, *Soft City* (London, 1974)

Reitman, Ben, *Sister of the Road: The Autobiography of Boxcar Bertha* (New York, 1937)

Relph, Edward, *Place and Placelessness* (London, 1976)

Riis, Jacob, *How the Other Half Lives: Studies Among the Tenements of New York* (New York, 1890)

Ringenbach, Paul, *Tramps and Reformers 1873–1916* (Westport, CT, 1973)

Robbins, William G., *Colony and Empire: The Capitalist Transformation of the American West* (Lawrence, KA, 1994)

Rose, Gillian, *Feminism and Geography: The Limits of Geographical Knowledge* (Cambridge, 1993)

Rosler, Martha, 'In, Around and Afterthoughts (on Documentary Photography)', in *3 Works*, ed. Martha Rosler (Halifax, Nova Scotia, 1981), pp. 59–88

Ross, Kristin, *The Emergence of Social Space: Rimbaud and the Paris Commune* (Minneapolis, 1988)

Russell, Mary, *The Blessings of a Good Thick Skirt: Women Travellers and Their World* (London, 1986)

Ryan, James, *Picturing Empire: Photography and the Visualization of the British Empire*, (London, 1997)

Sack, R., *Homo Geographicus* (Baltimore, 1997)

Said, Edward W., *Orientalism* (New York, 1979)

Sanders, Barry, *Sudden Glory: Laughter as Subversive History* (Boston, 1995)

Schneider, John C., 'Tramping Workers 1890–1920: A Subcultural View', in *Walking to Work: Tramps in America 1790–1935*, ed. Eric H. Monkkonen (Lincoln, NE, 1984), pp. 212–34

Schwartz, Hillel, *The Culture of the Copy: Striking Likenesses, Unreasonable Facsimiles* (New York, 1996)

Scott, James, *Seeing Like a State: How Certain Schemes to Improve the Human Condition Have Failed* (New Haven, CT, 1998)

Searle, John, *The Construction of Social Reality* (London, 1995)

Seelye, John D., 'The American Tramp: A Version of the Picaresque', *American Quarterly*, 15, no. 4 (1963), pp. 535–53

Shindo, Charles, *Dust Bowl Migrants in the American Imagination* (Lawrence, KS, 1997)

Sibley, David, *Geographies of Exclusion: Society and Difference in the West* (London, 1995)

Sklar, Robert, *Movie-Made America: A Cultural History of American Movies* (London, 1978)

Sobel, Rauol and David Francis, *Chaplin: Genesis of a Clown* (London, 1977)

Solenberger, Alice Willard, *One Thousand Homeless Men: A Study of Original Records* (New York, 1911)

Sontag, Susan, *Aids and its Metaphors* (New York, 1988)

Speek, Alexander, 'The Psychology of the Floating Worker', *Annals of the American Academy of Polical and Social Sciences*, 69 (1917), pp. 72–8

Stallybrass, Peter and Allon White, *The Politics and Poetics of Transgression* (Ithaca, NY, 1986)

Stange, Maren, *Symbols of Ideal life : Social Documentary Photography in America, 1890–1950* (New York, 1989)

Starke, B., *Touch and Go: The Story of a Girl's Escape* (London, 1931)

Stein, Walter J., *California and the Dust Bowl Migration* (Westport, CT, 1973)

Stott, William, *Documentary Expression and Thirties America* (New York, 1973)

Stryker, Roy, 'Documentary Photography', in *The Complete Photographer*, ed. William Morgon (Chicago, 1942), pp. 1364–66

Terry, Jennifer and Jacqueline Urla, eds, *Deviant Bodies: Critical Perspectives on Difference in Science and Popular Culture* (Bloomington, IN, 1995)

Tester, Keith, ed., *The Flâneur* (London, 1994)

Trachtenberg, Alan, 'From Image to Story: Reading the File', in *Documenting America 1935–1943*, ed. Carl Fleischhauer and Beverly Brannan (Berkeley, CA, 1988), pp. 43–75

—, *Reading American Photographs: Images as History, Mathew Brady to Walker Evans*, (New York, 1989)

Tuan, Yi-Fu, *Morality and Imagination: Paradoxes of Progress* (Madison, WI, 1989)

—, *Space and Place: The Perspective of Experience* (Minneapolis, 1977)

—, 'A View of Geography', *Geographical Review*, 81, no. 1 (1991), pp. 99–107

Valentine, Gill, 'The Geography of Women's Fear', *Area*, 21, no. 4 (1989), pp. 385–90

Velody, Irving and Robin Williams, eds, *The Politics of Constructionism* (London, 1998)

Vigouroux-Frey, Nicole, 'Charlie Chaplin or the "Vaudeville Dispossessed"', in *Charlie Chaplin: His Reflection in Modern Times*, ed. Adolphe Nysenholc (Berlin, 1991), pp. 69–75

Walkowitz, Judith, *Prostitution and Victorian Society: Women, Class and the State* (Cambridge, 1980)

Ward, David, *Poverty, Ethnicity and the American City, 1840–1925* (Cambridge, 1989)

Ward, F., 'Foreign and Familiar Bodies', in *Dirt and Domesticity: Constructions of the Feminine*, ed. J. Fuenmayor, K. Haug, and F. Ward (New York, 1992), pp. 9–37

Weiner, Lynn, 'Sisters of the Road: Women Transients and Tramps', in *Walking to Work: Tramps in America 1790–1935*, ed. Eric H. Monkkonen (Lincoln, NE, 1984), pp. 189–211

Weyland, Francis, 'The Tramp Question' (a paper presented at the National Conference on Charities and Corrections, St Paul, 1877)

White, Allon, *Carnival, Hysteria and Writing* (Oxford, 1993)

Wilson, Elizabeth, 'The Invisible Flâneur', in *Postmodern Cities and Spaces*, ed. Sophie Watson and Katherine Gibson (Oxford, 1995), pp. 59–79

—, *The Sphinx in the City* (Berkeley, CA, 1991)

Winokur, Mark, *American Laughter: Immigrants, Ethnicity, and 1930s Film Comedy* (New York, 1996)

—, 'Modern Times and the Comedy of Transformation', *Literature/Film Quarterly*, 15, no. 4 (1987), pp. 219–26

Wolff, Janet, 'The Invisible Flâneuse: Women and the Literature of Modernity', in *Feminine Sentences: Essays on Women and Culture*, ed. Janet Wolff (Oxford, 1990), pp. 34–50

Worster, Donald, *Rivers of Empire: Water, Aridity, and the Growth of the American West* (Oxford, 1985)

Wreford-Watson, John, 'The Sociological Aspects of Geography', in *Geography in the Twentieth Century*, ed. Griffith Taylor (London, 1951), pp. 463–99

Wright, J. K., 'Terrae incognitae: The place of the imagination in geography', *Annals of the Association of American Geographers*, 37 (1947), pp. 1–15

Young, Iris Marion, *Intersecting Voices: Dilemmas of Gender, Political Philosophy and Policy* (Princeton, NJ, 1997)

—, *Throwing Like a Girl and other Essays in Feminist Philosophy and Social Theory* (Bloomington, IN, 1990)

# LIST OF ILLUSTRATIONS

18  Ernest Burgess's Concentric Ring Model of 'Urban Areas', from Robert E. Park, 'The Growth of the City' (1925).

19  Ben Reitman in 1912. International Institute of Social History, Amsterdam (C3 P23).

20  Sketch by the author after Ben Reitman, *Outcast Islands, c.* 1910. Original in the Ben L. Reitman Papers, Special Collections, University Library, University of Illinois at Chicago.

21  The Historical Society of Pennsylvania (HSP), 'The Man Who Came to Your Door Last Night', from an Exhibition of the Philadelphia Society for Organizing Charity, Philadelphia [Family Services Papers, Mss #1961, box 19].

22  Illustration from *Harper's* magazine (1876).

23  Promotional material for Ben L. Reitman, *Sister of the Road* (New York, 1937). Ben L. Reitman Papers, Special Collections, University Library, University of Illinois at Chicago.

24  Charlie Chaplin as the 'Little Tramp'. © 2000 Roy Export Company Establishment.

25  W. C. Fields.

26  Harlequin.

27  Cartoon from *Puck*, XLV (1 March 1899), p. 1147.

28  Cartoon from *Puck*, XLV (16 July 1899), p. 1167.

29  Tom Browne's 'Weary Willie and Tired Tim', from *Illustrated Chips*.

30  Frederick Burr Opper, Happy Hooligan, 1904.

31  Detail from F. B. Opper, 'Did Happy Hooligan Get Another Job? Sure He Did!'

32  James Montgomery Flagg, Nervy Nat, from *The Judge*.

33  Chaplin eating his shoelaces in *The Gold Rush* (1925). © 2000 Roy Export Company Establishment.

34  Chaplin practising with the Feeding Machine while rehearsing for *Modern Times* (1936). © 2000 Roy Export Company Establishment.

35  Chaplin tightens bolts superfluously in *Modern Times* (1936). © 2000 Roy Export Company Establishment.

36  Chaplin caught in the cogs of modernity in *Modern Times* (1936). © 2000 Roy Export Company Establishment.

37  Chaplin on the road in *The Tramp* (1915). © 2000 Roy Export Company Establishment.

38–40  Three pictures taken during the filming of *City Lights*, 1931. Chaplin awakes in the arms of a statue, sits on the face of another and uses the third to thumb his nose at the audience. © 2000 Roy Export Company Establishment.

41  Jacob A. Riis, *Tramp in Mulberry Street Yard*, 1887. Museum of the City of New York, Jacob A. Riis Collection. Photo © Museum of the City of New York.

42  John McCook in his classroom. Butler–McCook Archives, Antiquarian and Landmarks Society, Hartford, CT.

43  Questionnaire sent by McCook to police chiefs in 1891. Butler–McCook Archives, Antiquarian and Landmarks Society, Hartford, CT.

44  *A Common Shovel Bum. Property man in Buffalo Bill's show . . . 'Lost my place . . . by getting in a boose'. May 1, 1893.* Butler–McCook Archives, Antiquarian and Landmarks Society, Hartford, CT.

45  *Dan the Dodger (left) and other fellow. They are a little unsteady, but by bracing against one another get through and are paid. April 25, 1893.* Butler–McCook Archives, Antiquarian and Landmarks Society, Hartford, CT.

46  *Michael Keefe. Ain't never going to vote again; the politicians think that a poor laboring man is always for sale. He isn't. May 6, 1893.* Butler–McCook Archives, Antiquarian and Landmarks Society, Hartford, CT.

# INDEX

Page numbers in *italics* indicate illustrations.